BECOMING MODERN

BECOMING MODERN

Young Women and the Reconstruction
of Womanhood in the 1920s

Birgitte Søland

PRINCETON UNIVERSITY PRESS

PRINCETON AND OXFORD

Copyright © 2000 by Princeton University Press
Published by Princeton University Press, 41 William Street,
Princeton, New Jersey 08540
In the United Kingdom: Princeton University Press,
3 Market Place, Woodstock, Oxfordshire OX20 1SY

Library of Congress Cataloging-in-Publication Data

Søland, Birgitte, 1959–
Becoming modern : young women and the reconstruction
of womanhood in the 1920s / Birgitte Søland
p. cm.
Includes bibliographical references and index.
ISBN 0-691-04927-0 (cloth : alk. paper)
1. Women—Denmark—History—20th century. 2. Sex role—
Denmark—History—20th century. 3. Feminism—Denmark—
History—20th century. I. Title.
HQ1672.S65 2000
305.4'09489—dc21   00-021053

This book has been composed in Sabon
and Benguiat display

The paper used in this publication meets the minimum requirements
of ANSI/NISO Z39.48-1992 (R1997) (*Permanence of Paper*)

Printed in the United States of America

www.pup.princeton.edu

10 9 8 7 6 5 4 3 2 1

For all the people on both sides of the Atlantic whom
I feel fortunate to call my family

Contents

Acknowledgments

As a European teenager in the late 1970s, I spent a good part of my life in cheap apartments and damp basement rooms, smoking cigarettes and discussing Karl Marx's *Das Kapital* with comrades who were as committed to the Revolution as I was. Off and on, when our discussions ran dry, I would visit my grandmother, who always offered coffee, pastries, and delightful company. Besides, she had impeccable working-class credentials, having worked as a cleaning lady her entire adult life while raising three kids on her own. It was therefore with incredulity that I heard her question my political activities. "I just don't know," she suddenly said one day. "Your generation, you seem so clever, so accomplished, but I don't think you know how to have fun like we did." At the time, I was too young and too self-absorbed to ask what she meant, but by now I realize that she may have been right. My grandmother, a "modern" young woman in the 1920s, certainly danced more than I ever did. And she dressed better. My first thanks therefore goes to my grandmother, Rosalie Christensen, who indirectly brought me to this topic.

In the years since then, I have incurred numerous other debts of gratitude. At the University of Minnesota, where I wrote the dissertation that preceded this book, I received crucial financial support for my research from the Graduate School and the History Department. A University of Minnesota dissertation fellowship, an Institute of International Education research grant, and a William Stearns Davis Memorial Fellowship all proved extremely helpful. I also benefited from the generous comments and constructive criticisms of many excellent teachers and scholars, including Sara Evans, Michael Metcalf, Gianna Pomata, and Ann Waltner. Barbara Laslett, in particular, asked challenging questions and has continued to push me to clarify my thinking. Nan Enstad, Sharon Dohorty, Tim Coates, Louise Edwards, Winston McDowell, John Wrathall, and other fellow graduate students read conference papers and chapter drafts, gave helpful suggestions, and offered their camaraderie. Special thanks to Susan Cahn, whose companionship contributed to making those years a rich chapter in my life.

But among the many Minnesota folks, I owe the greatest debt to Mary Jo Maynes. It was her brilliant teaching that first led me to stray from my commitment to return to Denmark after a brief stint as an intellectual tourist in the United States. As my adviser, she allowed me to pursue my intellectual interests, never questioning the validity of my topic or my approach, but providing ample advice and incisive criticisms. And long after her official duties came to an end, she has remained a generous mentor and a good friend.

In the years since leaving Minnesota, a Seed Grant from the College of Humanities at the Ohio State University and generous leave time from teaching obligations in the History Department made it possible to complete this project. I have also benefited enormously from the help of friends and colleagues who read drafts of this book, encouraged and supported me, offered their criticisms in the true spirit of intellectual exchange, and laughed at the right times. For that and for many other acts of random kindness, I would like to thank Susan Hartmann, David Hoffmann, John Rothney, Steven Conn, Michelle Mouton, Ken Andrien, Pippa Holloway, Katja David-Fox, and Sonya Michel. I am especially grateful to Leila Rupp, who has been an extraordinary colleague, mentor, and friend. Her enthusiasm and confidence in my work never failed, and without her help, advice, and tireless promotional efforts this book might never have seen the light of day.

I am also indebted to a host of people on the other side of the Atlantic. My thanks goes to the many Danish archivists and librarians who often went far beyond the call of duty in their efforts to help and to the many women who agreed to be interviewed for this project. I am deeply grateful for their willingness to share their time and their memories and for trusting me with their words.

Numerous Danish friends offered encouragement, companionship, and generous hospitality. I owe thanks—and many meals—to Dorthe Spåbæk, Aage Kirk, Lone Smetana, Peter A. Petersen, Susan Møller Jensen, Bahman Safanyia, Stig Winther Petersen, Hanne Nielsen, Hanne Møller Andersen, Jan Haverslev, Ole Christiansen, Ruth Grønborg, Søren F. Nielsen, Allan Andersen, and Aase Bak.

I would also like to thank my family, Aase Søland, Peter Søland, Lone Terp Søland, Jens Søland, Tine Mangart Søland, Henrik Skov Andersen, and Michael Ballegaard, for all their encouragement and support. I am particularly grateful to my sister, Anne Marie Søland, whose humor, wisdom, and companionship, in good times and hard ones, means the world to me, and to my father, Harald Søland, who taught me the love of learning and never wavered in his entirely unrealistic estimation of my abilities. Finally, my thanks goes to Nancy Guzowski for her support, her love, and her laughter—and for reminding me that there are days when it doesn't matter at all whether you can spell Thursday.

BECOMING MODERN

INTRODUCTION

IN AUGUST 1919, when Johanne Blom turned fifteen, her aunt gave her a diary. At first she thought it an odd gift, but in the years that followed she would fill its delicate cream-colored pages with detailed, and often humorous, descriptions of her family and friends, her work and leisure in a working-class neighborhood in Copenhagen. Occasionally, she would venture from these topics and use her diary as so many other young girls have done—as a place to record her dreams and desires, her hopes and longings. In one such entry, written on January 21, 1923, she noted that "I so look forward to getting married and having my own home. I would like to have children. Three I think. That seems a good number." A few years later, after she had met the man whom she would later marry, she repeated this vision of the good life. "I can think of nothing better," she enthused, "than becoming Ejnar's wife."

But despite her rather conventional dreams, Johanne thought of herself as anything but traditional. Already as a sixteen-year-old, she was adamant that her life was going to be different from her mother's. "All mother ever does is work. I don't know how she can stand it. . . . I will never live like that," she wrote on October 20, 1920. Obviously, Johanne was hoping for a more pleasurable existence, a life filled with more excitement, fun, and romance. "I am a modern young girl," she insisted the following year, after a furious fight with her parents over her right to go to a dance hosted by the Social Democratic Youth Club. "I want to go out. Mother and father are so old-fashioned. They always want me to sit at home, never do anything else, but I'm not like that."[1] Many decades later, as a woman in her late eighties, Johanne Blom still remembered her youthful ambitions. "I grew up at a time when everything was changing," she explained. "Young girls like us, we wanted things to be different. We wanted to be modern."[2]

This book is about women such as Johanne—Danish women who came of age in the 1910s and 1920s, self-consciously seeking to take advantage of the social and sexual upheavals that characterized those years, to reshape female identities and gender relations, and to establish what they perceived to be "modern" lives for themselves. This book follows them from adolescence through early adulthood and into the marriages that almost all of them would eventually enter, arguing that these women's ideas of what constituted female modernity and their efforts to translate these ideals into practical reality in their daily lives played a central role in the shaping of twentieth-century styles of femininity and womanhood.

But this study is not just about Denmark. It offers a broader analysis of the reorganization of gender relations that characterized most of Western Europe in the decade following World War I. At the end of the war, it was certainly not only Danes who believed that they were witnessing the collapse of "the world as we knew it," that "nothing is the same anymore, women are not the same anymore."[3] Across the continent, European observers were struck by the immense changes they seemed to be witnessing in women's lives. In the course of just a few short decades, virtually every aspect of nineteenth-century womanhood seemed to have come under attack, and by the late 1910s, the time when the housebound Victorian lady reigned as the uncontested feminine ideal seemed nothing but a faint memory.

In part, this perception stemmed from the legal and political gains women had made since the late nineteenth century. Not only had new educational opportunities allowed a small but growing number of university-educated women to make their way into the professions, but the burgeoning feminist and suffrage movements had brought women out of the home and into the public eye. By the end of the 1910s, feminists had even succeeded in many countries in securing women's suffrage and in pushing through other kinds of reform legislation that gradually improved their legal status. Collectively, these changes all seemed to liberate women from conventional ties and obligations, and even before the war, many contemporaries worried about the emergence of a "new" type of woman, who rejected Victorian concepts of domesticity and instead threw herself into a broad range of public activities previously deemed incompatible with proper womanhood.[4]

On a more immediate level, the sense of sexual upheaval grew from women's activities during World War I. As millions of European men departed for the front, middle-class women took up white-collar jobs, working-class women moved into better-paid industrial jobs, country girls swarmed into factories, and older rural women took charge of farms. As engineers and administrators, bricklayers and carpenters, railroad conductors and bus drivers, farm hands and munitions workers, women of all classes moved into positions they had never held before, and in the process they proved themselves perfectly capable of handling what had in the past been men's jobs. As if this was not troubling enough, many women seemed to enjoy their new activities, and young women in particular seemed disturbingly reluctant after the war to relinquish the freedoms and privileges that wartime salaries had afforded them.[5]

Given all this, it is perhaps not surprising that many Europeans concluded that they were witnessing the rapid dismantling of traditional forms of womanhood. But if just about everybody agreed that a profound breach with the past had taken place and that the old order could not be restored, they differed greatly in their assessments of what would replace the familiar patterns. Had World War I produced a "civilization without sexes," as French writer Pierre Drieu la Rochelle argued?[6] Would European societies become a new form of "Amazon republics," as others predicted?[7] Would the postwar world be one in which "wives rule their husbands, women leave women's work, and young girls do their best to ape men?"[8] Were women really "gaining the upper hand," as the Danish journalist Søren Pedersen-Tarp concluded after a trip through England and France in 1921?[9] Or were the postwar years likely to see "the birth of a new world in which man and woman stand side by side as equals," as many feminists hoped?[10] Would the 1920s mark "the dawn of a new era," where gender took a back seat to "character and accomplishments?"[11] Only one thing seemed certain: Social stability would not be restored before gender issues had been settled.

The 1920s, therefore, witnessed an enormous preoccupation with issues of female identity and women's proper role. Across Western Europe, politicians and labor leaders debated how best to regulate female employment and restore the sexual division of labor, and practically every national parliament spent considerable time devising legislation that would protect the family as a social institution. Outside the world of politics, teachers and physicians sought to define new standards for female education and health, while psychologists and social workers pontificated on the complexities of the "modern" female psyche. Sociologists threw their energy into surveying women's behavior, and journalists regularly polled readers on just about every topic, from girls' education and appropriate child-rearing practices to women's suffrage and the best use of leisure time. At the same time, a veritable outpouring of prescriptive literature sought to define women's new duties and responsibilities, and advice columnists and etiquette experts eagerly dispensed their counsel on proper female behavior in books, newspapers, and magazines. Not surprisingly, gender issues also permeated contemporary fiction, and both popular and elite writers offered troubling, and often scandalous, accounts of the consequences of the much-feared blurring of gender distinctions that supposedly was taking place.[12]

Only toward the end of the 1920s did this obsession with women begin to fade. In part, it was the onset of the Great Depression that shifted public attention toward different matters, but the dwindling concern about gender had other causes as well. Even though women's roles, behavior, and position in society would continue to change, the foundations of a new social and sexual order had by then been sufficiently established for most contemporaries to abandon the issue. While some conservatives never stopped longing for an idealized past when women supposedly had no ambitions other than marriage and motherhood, and many feminists continued to criticize sexual inequalities, at least the outlines of modern female identities and gender relations had been determined.

The decade following World War I therefore constitutes a pivotal transitional moment in the history of European gender relations during which Victorian gender arrangements met their final demise and a re-formed gender order gradually was established. Focusing less on what was destroyed than on what was put in its place, this study offers a historical analysis of the social, cultural, rhetorical, and political processes through which the creation of new and recognizably "modern" gender arrangements was accomplished in one of these European countries—Denmark.

THE 1920s—A DECADE OF LIBERATION FOR WOMEN?

Until feminist scholars began reexamining history, the 1920s were often described as the decade in which women became "liberated." The evidence for such an optimistic interpretation seemed plentiful. In most European countries, women's suffrage was granted by the end of World War I, and reform legislation continued to improve women's civil and legal status. Many remaining barriers to women's entry into the professions were dismantled, and employment opportunities expanded. Although still far below those of men, women's wages were increasing, allowing more women than ever before the pleasures of independent consumer spending. In addition, the granting of legitimacy to female sexual desire allowed women to discard a prudish and repressive sexual morality and engage in various forms of cultural and sexual experimentation.[13]

More recent studies of women's experiences in Germany, France, and England have forcefully punctured this myth of the Golden Twenties.[14] Historians such as Renate Bridenthal, Karin Hausen, James McMillan, Jane Lewis, and Miriam Glucksmann have all documented striking continuities in women's subordination in the home as well as in the workplace, their marginal impact on political decision making, and their limited access to resources.[15] Some scholars have even argued that the postwar decade witnessed a direct backlash against the gains women had achieved before and during the war, placing feminists and single, professional women especially on the defensive.[16] Still others have questioned the impact of new sexual ideologies, arguing that they largely functioned to limit women's control over their own sexuality and discredit any erotic choices other than heterosexual marriage.[17]

In light of this research, optimistic assertions about social change in the postwar decade lose much of their credibility. Clearly, women did not achieve sexual equality in any simple sense in the course of the 1920s, and the strides they made toward "liberation" may well have been so small as not to warrant much feminist attention. But by framing their arguments solely in terms of the long-term impact on women's lives, these historians have tended to overlook contemporary reports that described, with enthusiasm or anxiety, what many observers believed to be the rapid dismantling of traditional forms of womanhood and the emergence of new social and sexual patterns. While such reports may well, as French historian Mary Louise Roberts has noted, have been "wrong from a purely structural standpoint," postwar Europeans were nevertheless convinced that they were witnessing a profound upheaval; thus, rather than being dismissed, this cultural reality deserves our attention.[18]

As many cultural historians have pointed out, debates about gender such as those that characterized the decade following World War I always mask concerns both about gender and about "something else again".[19] In the case of the 1920s, the obsession with women's roles and behavior clearly reflected more general anxieties over social disorder, socioeconomic change, and the collapse of long-standing moral and ideological doctrines. Consequently, the impression that women were discarding all notions of proper female behavior was both fed by and feeding into already existing fears that the world was in disarray. Through analyses of a society's discourse on gender, we may therefore uncover central aspects of its values and fears, its hopes and conflicts, and its power relations and social dynamics. Adopting this approach, Mary Louise Roberts, Susan Kingsley Kent, and Billie Melman have provided acute insights into the ways in which French and British men and women made sense of and came to terms with a web of social, political, and cultural changes in the wake of World War I.[20]

Like these studies, this book takes seriously the sense of upheaval that characterized the 1920s, but its analytical focus is somewhat different. As many critics have noted, discourse analysis, no matter how careful and sophisticated, tends to leave us with little knowledge about men's and women's actual lives. Surely, the "Modern Woman"—the scantily clad, sexually liberated, economically independent, self-reliant female—was a rhetorical construction, the quintessential symbol of a world in disarray. But "modern women"—women who cut their hair, wore short skirts, worked for wages, and enjoyed themselves outside the home—were not just figments of anxious imaginations, and to read the postwar debates about women as solely, or predominantly, debates about the changes wrought by the war ignores both the social and sexual struggles that characterized the 1920s and the very real changes in women's behavior that this decade witnessed. The construction of a new gender order was therefore not only the product of elite discourses and male-made policies, but also the outcome of a highly contested process of social change, in which the beliefs and practices of a much broader array of actors played a crucial role. And although this process may not ultimately have overturned fundamental power relations between men and women, it transformed many patterns of daily life.

In addition to an analysis of the cultural discourses that developed to make sense of and regulate the emerging styles of modern femininity and womanhood, this book therefore focuses on the agency of "ordinary" working-class and middle-class people in the construction of a new order, and it argues that the young women who figured so prominently in the postwar discourse were not only the object of discourse but also central agents in the charting of new female identities.[21] When contemporaries struggled to determine how "modern" the "modern woman" would be, which characteristics would define attractive femininity and proper womanhood in the twentieth century, where the boundaries for women's new freedoms were to be drawn, and which features would characterize male–female relationships, the answers to those questions certainly grew not only from cultural discourses but also from the social practices of the women in question. An examination of social practices and lived experiences therefore promises to add yet another dimension to our understanding of the interrelationship between gender and change in the 1920s.

THE CAUSES OF UPHEAVAL

In the 1920s, virtually all cultural critics were convinced that, while other factors contributed to the destruction of long-standing gender arrangements, World War I played the greatest role in that process. Whether they blamed the absence of men from the home front, the killing of millions of male heads of households, or the return of thousands of crippled war veterans or believed that women's labor market participation, their experiences of financial independence, and the self-confidence they seemed to have gained were the main culprits, critics generally agreed that the war was a turning point, a transformative event that profoundly and irrevocably changed its survivors.

In the years since then, most studies of European women, men, and gender relations in the 1920s have focused on nations that were directly involved in the war, and they have, by and large, reinforced contemporary beliefs that it was the war that caused the upheavals. According to British historians Gail Braybon and Penny Summerfield, for example, once women had been let "out of the cage" and permitted to demonstrate their talents and capabilities in the labor market during wartime, the spell of female domesticity was broken, and it took a powerful mixture of ideological campaigns and coercive political measures to restore the sexual division of labor after 1918.[22] Close readings of British and German men's postwar writings have convinced other scholars that the horrors of trench warfare functioned to undercut the heroic image of the male warrior, destabilize masculine identities, and produce both a gulf between men's and women's wartime experiences and a misogyny among returning war veterans so intense as to short-circuit any return to prewar patterns.[23] Still others have argued that the atrocities led to a more general cultural crisis, triggering the re-thinking of all social relationships.[24]

Among those historians who take a broader look at social and sexual change in early twentieth-century Europe, the importance of World War I as a causal factor for postwar developments is often compounded by more long-term trends. As they point out, lower birthrates, smaller households, and industrially produced household goods had paved the way from the turn of the century for a restructuring of family life and marital relations; also, even before the war, rising wages had lifted many working-class families out of the direst poverty.[25] Mass production, rationalization, and a dramatic growth in the service sector—all developments that functioned to draw more women than ever before out of the home, away from agricultural and domestic work, and into shops, factories, and offices—also preceded the war. In their view, World War I thus only accelerated trends that had already begun to alter social and economic life before 1914, and even though women's contributions to the war effort brought them into the public eye, they did not significantly alter social and economic patterns that were already well under way before the war.

Whether historians grant World War I or more long-term social and economic developments the greater significance in their explanations, they generally agree that those two phenomena constitute the *sine qua non*, the foundations without which cultural upheaval in the 1920s would not have occurred. In Germany, England, and France, the countries that have attracted most scholarly attention, this may well be the case, but such explanations do not account for similar turmoil in nations that were neither involved in World War I nor as industrially advanced as the major European powers. Surely, Brazil in the 1920s did not belong in this category, yet concerns about women and gender definitions akin to those of Western Europe reverberated through Brazilian public discourse.[26] During those same years, Japan, another country that hardly belonged among the most industrialized nations in the 1920s, was embroiled in similar debates about the controversial appearances and behavior of the *moga*, the Japanese version of the modern girl.[27] Even China, among the least industrialized societies in the world, was not exempt from such concerns.[28]

Obviously, factors other than international warfare and industrial development were contributing to gender upheaval in the early decades of the twentieth century, and analyses of gender change in countries that were less economically developed and not directly involved in the war may therefore shed new light on the causes and dynamics of gender upheaval in the 1910s and 1920s. By focusing on Denmark—a small, non-belligerent and in the early decades of the twentieth century still largely agrarian country—this study offers one such analysis, seeking to explain how and why similar forms of social and sexual change took place in a context quite different from those that historians have typically explored.

GENDER UPHEAVAL AND THE DANISH CASE

In the early years of the twentieth century, Denmark was hardly among the Western nations spearheading social and economic change. With a population of merely three million people, an economy based on agriculture, few natural resources, very little heavy industry, and no colonial possessions to speak of, it belonged among the less powerful, prosperous, and advanced European countries. And despite improvements in farming techniques, the emergence of agricultural cooperatives, and strong commercial ties with other European countries, there were few indications that this was about to change in any significant way.[29]

Nevertheless, Denmark was still impacted by some of the same social and economic trends that characterized other parts of Western Europe in the early twentieth century. As elsewhere in the Western world, migration from rural to urban areas was beginning to alter demographic patterns.[30] Between 1900 and 1920, the proportion of the Danish population living in urban areas increased from 38 percent to 46 percent.[31] During those same twenty years, the percentage of Danes living in Copenhagen—the nation's capital and largest city—grew from 16 percent to 23 percent.[32] Simultaneously, the share of the population that secured its livelihood from farming decreased, dropping from 40 percent in 1901 to 30 percent in 1930.[33] Although the majority of the population would continue to live in the countryside throughout the 1920s, urban life was therefore becoming a more common Danish experience, and as elsewhere, city lights beckoned many country youths.

During these years industrialization was also making its mark on Danish society, although much slower and in a less substantial way than in many other countries. In the early decades of the twentieth century, handicrafts and nonmechanized production for local markets persisted, small workshops remained the norm rather than the exception, and most industrial enterprises were limited in size and not particularly advanced in terms of technology. By 1920, after thirty years of steady growth both in the number of industrial enterprises and the number of people employed in industry, this sector of the economy still employed only a small minority of the Danish work force.[34] Indicative of the Danish economic structure, most export goods, such as butter, cheese, bacon, canned goods, and other food stuffs, came from agriculture, and throughout the interwar years economic growth would continue to spring from agriculture and commerce rather than industry.[35]

During World War I this economic structure would prove an unexpected advantage. Needing to feed not only expansive armies but also their population on the home front, warring countries purchased great quantities of Danish food products. As a result, small companies exploded into booming businesses, and new enterprises mushroomed across the country, transforming modest merchants and small-scale businesspeople into a new class of nouveau riches, or "goulash barons" as they were known at the time.[36] In a more limited sense, wartime commerce also affected the lives of working people. In the course of the war, employment rates were high and wages rose. For skilled male workers, hourly wages increased 71 percent between 1914 and 1918, and the income of women workers rose at an a similar rate.[37] While shortages of goods, rationing, and inflation certainly limited the rise in living standards that such wage increases might suggest, the purchasing power of workers' incomes still grew by 60 percent between 1914 and 1920, allowing most Danish working-class families for the first time ever to position themselves, however tenuously, on the safe side of the poverty line.[38]

In the postwar decade, these very real economic advances were undercut by inflation, bankruptcies, and wildly fluctuating unemployment rates, leaving most Danish families less than financially secure. As elsewhere in Europe, the 1920s were generally years of crisis and instability, not years of economic boom, as was the case in the United States. Nonetheless, the Danish controversies over women and gender, while set in a context of economic insecurity, did not emerge in a situation of rapid industrialization or other fundamental changes in the social or economic structure.

Nor did they spring from experiences of wartime upheavals in the sexual division of labor or from the fear that women were taking over men's jobs. Because men did not have to leave for the front, Denmark never experienced an influx of women into the labor market as in those countries directly involved in the war. In fact, the percentage of the female population that worked for wages remained virtually unchanged between 1900 and 1930, consistently hovering around 25 percent.[39] However, the early decades of the twentieth century did witness a shift in the kind of jobs women held. From the turn of the century, more and more women began to desert agricultural and domestic labor.[40] During the war, many of these female workers were recruited into food, beverage, textile, and clothing industries, where they, by 1925, constituted up to 80 percent of the entire labor force.[41] Still, the total number of women employed in industry and manufacturing did not increase in the course of the 1910s and 1920s.[42] The only area in which any growth in female employment occurred during those years was the expanding service sector, where women were finding jobs mostly as low-level sales and clerical personnel, statistically off-setting the declining number of female agricultural workers and domestic servants .[43]

In general, then, World War I did not challenge, even temporarily, the sexual division of labor in Denmark, and it did not bring more women into the labor force. Neither did the 1920s. Even though Danish women had access to higher education on an equal footing with men, only very few women pursued professional careers, and throughout the postwar decade, the vast majority of working women remained confined to the kind of unskilled, low-paying jobs deemed appropriate for the female labor force. Since rising wages enabled a growing number of working-class families to realize the ideal of the male bread-winner and the female homemaker, one might even argue that the 1910s and 1920s strengthened the position of working-class husbands vis-à-vis their wives and children, who tended to become more financially dependent on male heads of household than they had been in the nineteenth century.[44]

Women's political enfranchisement also seemed to impact Danish gender relations relatively little, and it certainly does not explain the widespread sense of upheaval in the postwar decade. Even though many people had warned before the passage of women's suffrage in 1915 that granting women the right to vote would encourage them to abandon marriage and domestic responsibilities, such fears soon proved unfounded. The assumption that an expansion of the electorate to include women would significantly alter the political balance of power, and that female legislators would change parliamentary politics, proved equally mistaken. At the ballot box, women behaved much like men, and throughout the 1920s, female politicians were simply too few to make much of a difference. Besides, not all of the women elected saw themselves as advocates of women's rights, and in most cases it was party affiliation, not gender interests, that determined their political stands.[45] Presumably, a powerful, vocal, and highly organized feminist movement could still have triggered postwar concerns, but that was not the case, either. As was the case in so many other countries, the Danish women's movement, which had never been particularly strong even at its height during the early years of the twentieth century, was floundering in the postwar years, unable to attract new members to a cause whose purpose and goals seemed increasingly unclear to many women.[46]

In the absence of rapid industrial development, significant wartime upheavals, women's acquisition of substantial political power, or a strong feminist movement, it was obviously other kinds of changes that convinced postwar Danes that they were witnessing the rapid dismantling of established gender arrangements. As this book argues, the Danish sense of upheaval grew from a much more specific and easily identifiable phenomenon—namely, the emergence of a new generation of women who seemed to be waging an all-out attack on conventional notions of femininity and womanhood. Discarding all notions of order, propriety, and respect for their elders—or so it seemed to many contemporaries—they shortened their skirts, wore makeup, played sports, went out at night, danced, and flirted, insisting—like Johanne Blom—with frightening determination on being "modern" and leading "modern" lives. More than anything else, it was, according to one observer who seemed to speak for many of his contemporaries, such young women who were causing "so much of our current trouble."[47]

DANISH FEMALE YOUTH IN THE 1920s: A GENERATION OF REBELS?

Had contemporaries been able to pin unconventional behavior on a small, or at least a limited, number of young women, they may well have been less concerned. Unfortunately, they were offered no such comfort. On the contrary, young women's rebelliousness seemed to them a widespread, even generational, phenomenon. Young women who refused to follow conventions were not confined to urban areas, and they were not just the spoiled daughters of the elite. Instead, they seemed to come from all class backgrounds. Some were highly educated, others had left school with the most minimal of educations. They held all different kinds of jobs. Some lived in rural areas, others in towns and cities. But across all these divides, women who came of age in the postwar decade seemed to most contemporaries united by their styles, their manners, and their aspirations. As one critic insisted, "They all look the same, behave the same, want the same things."[48]

Surely, such sweeping generalizations do not accurately reflect reality. Even the most anxious observers had to admit that "young ladies who first and foremost see themselves as future wives and mothers still exist, even though they are becoming a rare species."[49] Nonetheless, across class lines, postwar female youths did in fact seem to understand and define themselves as a generation, a separate and distinct cohort with characteristics that set them apart from older women, suggesting that contemporaries may have been more accurate in their assessment than most historians trained to think about class differences would assume.

The strong generational identification among women who came of age in the postwar decade is particularly evident in their contributions to public discourse. In interviews with journalists, for example, and in letters to newspaper and magazine editors and responses to surveys and opinion polls, individuals frequently chose to speak as representatives of a cohesive group, peppering their language with phrases such as "young girls like us," "we young girls" and "our generation." While such collective language may well have been adopted for the occasion to give personal claims more weight and significance, other evidence also suggests a remarkably strong generational awareness and identification. When asked many years later to recall their youth in the 1920s, women still tended to answer questions about their own lives using "we" rather than "I." Significantly, fully fifty-three of the fifty-nine women interviewed for this project used the plural pronoun when describing their youth. The fact that a mixture of farm girls and city girls, working-class and middle-class daughters, unskilled workers and university graduates described themselves—both at the time and in retrospect—in virtually identical terms only reinforces the notion of generational identification.

But what was it that inspired this strong generational identification? Here contemporary observers also seem to have been at least partially right. In many ways, women who came of age in the 1910s seemed to share a set of fundamental hopes and aspirations. Both at the time and in retrospect, they spoke of themselves as being "modern," and they expressed their desire to have a "modern life." Even without having experienced the upheavals of war firsthand, and despite the fact that Denmark did not suffer social disruptions caused by rapid industrial development, these women clearly had a sense of the 1920s as a cultural watershed, a historical moment when long-standing gender arrangements were losing their validity and gender relations could be renegotiated; as their comments would suggest, they eagerly jumped at the chance, hoping to create a life for themselves that would be less restrictive and ultimately more gratifying.

But for all their determination to be "modern" and to have "modern" lives, it remained rather unclear throughout much of the 1920s—even to the young women themselves—what that meant, and without a blueprint to work from they had to find answers to a number of complicated questions. What exactly did it take to be "modern"? How "modern" were they going to be? What did a "modern life" look like? What were its key components? What would replace the normative models that had guided older generations?

Other contemporaries had to grapple with equally perplexing questions. If self-identified "modern girls" were no longer willing to play by the old rules, did that mean they would play by no rules at all? Might there still be ways of maintaining some semblance of gender order, or would young women's rebelliousness lead to chaos and disorder? Did their insistence on female modernity mean that adolescent girls and young women would avoid marriage and motherhood? And how might their desires be contained or at least channeled in appropriate directions?

To understand the complicated social, cultural, and political negotiations that would eventually produce the answers to those and other questions, this study is based on a broad array of archival and published primary sources, ranging from parliamentary transcripts, statistical evidence, and legal records to local and national newspapers, women's magazines, advice manuals, popular fiction, and personal advertisements.

However, in constructing a history of gender changes and gendered experiences in the 1920s, I also rely on personal narratives by women who were young in the decade following World War I. In addition to hundreds of unpublished autobiographical accounts collected by state and local archives, I conducted fifty-nine oral history interviews with women born between 1895 and 1911.[50] Of these, thirty-six were born in rural areas and small villages, twenty-three in towns and cities across the country. Some grew up in prosperous middle-class and upper-middle-class households and others in comfortable farm families, but most came from lower-middle, working-class, and poor families.[51] Despite these social and cultural differences in their background, they all worked for wages for a number of years during their youth. During these years, the vast majority lived in urban areas, residing either with parents or relatives, in other households as live-in domestic servants, or, in a few cases, in rented rooms and boarding houses. With three exceptions they all went on to marry later in life. And with only two exceptions they described themselves as having been "modern girls" in their youth.[52]

Exploration of these sources reveal that Danish postwar negotiations over the forms and content of modern womanhood centered on three main issues, which are explored in the following chapters. The first was female fashions and young women's personal styles. In the 1920s, adolescent girls and young women clearly tied female modernity to style and to the body. Modern girls dressed in particular fashions, sported particular haircuts, and looked in particular ways. These styles, and the controversies that surrounded them, are examined in chapter 1. But modern girls did not just favor a distinct look. They also used their bodies in special ways. They walked in particular ways. They sat in particular ways. They even shook hands in particular ways. Chapter 2 explores these aspects of modern young women's self-presentation, focusing not only on the ways in which they defined and sought to acquire "modern" bodies but also on the ways in which they thought to shape their personalities around their perceptions of modernity.

The second issue was female leisure and autonomy. In addition to fashions and the body, young women also tied female modernity to a particular lifestyle that disassociated them from the family. "Modern" girls were independent; they did not sit at home, and they did not confine their lives to family and domesticity. "Modern" girls went out to work, and they went out to play. While their jobs may have been drudgery, their free time was fun-filled and exciting, touched by the glamour of commercial entertainment and consumption. As chapter 3 demonstrates, this locked young women into intense battles with their parents and other older contemporaries over the boundaries of new female freedoms. These conflicts were only heightened by the fact that young women also associated modernity with particular kinds of interactions and relationships with men. "Modern" girls did not live in or appreciate a gender-segregated world. "Modern" girls lived alongside men, and they enjoyed their companionship. Nevertheless, as chapter 4 documents, relations between young women and young men were often fraught with conflict and as difficult to negotiate as cross-generational relationships.

Chapters 5 and 6 shift the attention toward the third major issue that dominated postwar debates on gender—namely, the nature of marriage and domestic labor. Because young women never challenged marriage or the financial dependence it typically entailed, these discussions were often less contentious, but because young women were determined to reconcile marriage and domesticity with their identities as "modern" women, these issues still proved difficult to negotiate. Chapter 5 examines the ways in which they sought to do so in relationships with their husbands, while chapter 6 focuses on their efforts to transform housewifery into a "modern" enterprise suitable for "modern" women.

Collectively, these six chapters present the key issues that permeated Danish debates about women and gender in the postwar decade. They also provide insight into young women's definitions of what it meant to be "modern." As we shall see, those understandings derived much of their substance from commercialized mass culture in general and from new mass-produced representations of women in particular. It was from sources such as films, fashion magazines, and advertisements that young women culled many of their ideas of female modernity, cross-gender camaraderie, and romantic love. The fact that young women in the 1920s did not "step outside of culture" to construct new styles of womanhood and gender relations does not diminish their role as agents of social and sexual change in the decade following World War I.[53] In the face of considerable opposition, these women experimented with new gendered styles, and they pioneered new manners and mores that permitted women more personal freedom, more pleasure, and more self-expression.

But acknowledging the significance of consumer culture and new cultural representations in the creation of a decidedly twentieth-century style of womanhood permits new understandings of the upheaval in gender relations that swept through the Western world, and many other countries around the world, in the 1920s. It allows us, for example, to explain why this upheaval was not confined to highly industrialized countries directly involved in World War I. Recognition of the role played by such cultural forces and acknowledgment of young women's agency in this process of change throw into question the political and economic explanations on which most historians have rested their analyses of change in the 1920s. If it were, to a large extent, new cultural representations that triggered Danish women's desire for change, might that not also be the case among women in other countries, irrespective of those countries' political and economic situation? In this light, it certainly becomes easier to explain why so many young women in the 1920s, living around the globe under very different circumstances, began to imagine female modernity in very similar ways across all national, political, and economic divides.

PART I

From Victorian Ladies to Modern Girls:
The Construction of a New Style
of Femininity

BY THE MID-1920s, it was clear to most contemporaries that the delicate, refined Victorian lady had had her day. As one elderly newspaper editor nostalgically noted, the world would "probably never again" enjoy the sight of a "lady who let her long skirt trail behind her." Much to his regret, the "innocently blushing young girl" also seemed a character of the past. "Modern young girls," he concluded, "are so very different from the ladies we courted."[1]

It was the crowning in 1926 of the first Miss Denmark that prompted these editorial musings. In the spring of that year, *Vore Damer*, a popular magazine for women, announced that it would be sponsoring the first national Danish beauty contest. Such contests had already been held in several other nations—including neighboring Sweden—and it was time, the editors contended, that Denmark caught up with rest of the world.[2]

In the following days and weeks, hundreds of young women from across the country responded to the magazine's call for contestants by submitting photographs that gave the requested "clear impression" of their "face and figure."[3] From among these entries a panel of judges selected a number of young women who were invited to participate in the actual contest, and on August 1, 1926, the fortunate few assembled at the upscale Marienlyst seaside resort just north of Copenhagen for what the magazine promised to be a "lovely and stylish" event.[4]

Unfortunately, the weather was less than cooperative that day, but despite cold winds and grey skies the outdoor contest went ahead. In the course of the afternoon, thousands of curious spectators were treated to musical entertainment and "the impressive sight" of "young slender women in

Fig. 1. Edith Jørgensen after having been elected the first Miss Denmark in 1926. (Reproduced from *Vore Damer*, 1926)

their becoming bathing suits."[5] After a few hours, the judges announced their decision, and seventeen-year-old Edith Jørgensen was crowned the first Miss Denmark.

In the weeks before the contest, *Vore Damer* had assured its readers that the judges would not have a particular feminine ideal in mind. They were simply given the task of identifying the woman who seemed to them "the most beautiful."[6] Nonetheless, on the day of the contest, the judges apparently felt compelled to justify their choice. From among dozens of contestants, they explained, they had selected the slender young girl as the first-prize winner because of her "childish, sweet smile," her "natural grace," "large, beaming eyes," and "completely flawless and lovely figure." Besides, they added, the new beauty queen combined in her personality an appealing mixture of girlish spunk, boldness, and charm, enhanced by an unassuming demeanor and an air of wholesome naiveté.[7]

With these qualities, Edith Jørgensen embodied a new ideal of attractive femininity that had been gaining cultural currency not only in Denmark but also throughout much of the rest of the world for more than a decade. In marked contrast to the elegant, refined, ladylike ideals of the nineteenth century, feminine beauty had by the mid-1920s become identified with simple, unadorned youthfulness. Adolescent innocence had clearly replaced more mature ideals, and a slight, childlike physique had triumphed over more womanly curves. In addition, attractive femininity had by the mid-1920s become associated with a particular style of spunky, girlish personality. Vivaciousness, exuberance, and cheerfulness had gradually replaced innocence, modesty, and reserve as the most attractive qualities in a woman. No wonder that the elderly newspaper editor was struck by "the enormous changes we have witnessed within the last generation."[8] The following two chapters trace the emergence of this new style of femininity, the conflicts this style engendered, and the processes through which it gradually became the dominant cultural ideal.

CHAPTER 1

The Emergence of the Modern Look

IN 1926, when Edith Jørgensen became the first Miss Denmark, nobody commented on the fact that following her victory the new beauty queen chose to meet the press wearing a short, sleeveless dress, silk stockings, and high-heeled ankle-strap shoes. By the mid-1920s such fashions had already become acceptable apparel for young women. Yet only one decade earlier, when short-skirted women first appeared in public, they had elicited considerable attention. As Emilie Spang-Bak recalled, "One year when I was a little girl—it must have been in 1913 or 1914—my parents went to a new year's party. At that party some young lady was wearing a short dress. Nothing like that had ever been seen in [the town of] Aarhus before, and my mother talked about it for days."[1]

In the mid-1910s, Emilie Spang-Bak's mother was certainly not the only person to take notice of the changing styles in women's clothing. Already in the spring of 1914, one newspaper editor noticed that women's appearance seemed to be undergoing a "remarkable change."[2] Instead of sensible or attractive clothes, young women had allegedly begun to wear "the strangest and most impractical form of dress."[3] The following year, one fashion commentator was astonished to find that "the entire female silhouette has been altered."[4] Other journalists marveled at the growing numbers of women in "these strange, narrow, tight-fitting dresses" and urged their readers to avoid such "awkward and bizarre" apparel.[5]

Surely, the observer who insisted in 1916 that "all young girls" had fallen for this "latest folly of fashion" was wrong.[6] Most adolescent girls and young women stuck with more conventional styles at least until the end of the decade. Even in the 1920s a few never adopted the new female fashions. Nonetheless, the second half of the 1910s did witness striking changes in the appearances of many young women. During those years, young women from prosperous families discarded the elaborate, cumbersome gowns that women of their class had previously worn, and large numbers of working-class and middle-class daughters abandoned the shirtwaist blouses and long skirts that had been their daily wear. Instead, these young women began to favor dresses that were simpler, shorter, less fitted, and more colorful than the ones their mothers had worn.

When young women adopted the new styles, they were clearly following the fashion of the day. Since the late nineteenth century the trend in women's clothing had been changing toward simpler, slimmer, less ornate styles that allowed for increased freedom of movement.[7] In the early years of the twentieth century, celebrated French fashion designer Paul Poiret had promoted this new look, and in the years preceding World War I many other designers had followed his lead. Departing from an older ideal dominated by the S-shaped corset, frou-frou skirts, and pastel colors, they had turned the world of haute couture into a place where tall, slender women increasingly wore straight, simple, loosely fitted gowns.[8]

From the early 1910s, this new look quickly transcended the elitist confines of Parisian fashion circles. International fashion journals such as *La Vie Parisienne*, *La Mode de Paris*, *Chic Parisien*, *Vogue*, *Weldons*, and *Vanity Fair* introduced their readers to the new trends. In urban areas across Europe, including Copenhagen, the latest fashions were displayed in the windows of clothing shops and department stores, and by the mid-1910s carefully staged fashion shows were becoming an increasingly common merchandising technique, providing at least some women with yet another opportunity to become acquainted with the new styles.[9] Illustrated fashion columns in newspapers and popular magazines served to familiarize much broader audiences with the new look, and popular films in which actresses sported the new styles helped disseminate the latest fashion information to even larger groups of girls and young women.[10] Popular theater also proved a source of fashion authority, and throughout the 1910s and 1920s, women's magazines regularly carried feature articles on the hair and clothing styles of celebrated stage actresses. Crucial to the dissemination of the new look in Denmark were also the drawings of Gerda Wegener, a young Danish painter, graphic designer, and fashion illustrator living in Paris. In the 1910s and 1920s, reproductions of her elegant, Art Deco–inspired sketches of fashionable women appeared everywhere from newspapers to book covers and greeting cards. As Stine Petersen recalled, "I grew up on a farm in Western Jutland, far from anywhere, but of course we knew what was in style. We saw it in pictures and magazines and movies. I don't think you could *not* know."[11]

For fashion-conscious young women, familiarity with the new styles often translated into a desire to model their appearances accordingly. Of course, their ability to do so depended in part on the money they had at their disposal. For daughters and young wives of the social elite the acquisition of a fashionable wardrobe was relatively easy. From their travels to Paris and other European fashion centers they brought home expensive designer dresses, and if unable to make purchases in person they ordered the latest styles from fashion houses and clothing stores that gladly shipped their commodities to anyone willing and able to pay the price.

For most young women, such extravagant spending was never a possibility, but as the production of ready-made clothing increased in the early twentieth century, modern fashions came within the financial reach of more and more people. Middle-class women were certainly able to afford most ready-made dresses, and while department stores carried the largest selection, smaller clothing stores began to offer a range of models and styles at a reasonable price. Even women of very modest means were not precluded from acquiring a new fashionable appearance. In working-class neighborhoods and small towns, local shopkeepers offered products that their customers could afford, and like their counterparts in wealthier areas, they introduced new forms of credit purchases, layaway plans, and installment systems of payment that eased the way to a stylish appearance for many young women.[12] Poorly paid seamstresses, working in small shops or out of their own homes, offered dozens of modestly priced models to local customers. And if women could afford neither ready-made garments nor the work of a seamstress, dress patterns for home sewing were readily available through fashion journals, popular magazines, and special pattern books.[13] In the second half of the 1910s, not only were fashions becoming familiar to most people, but acquiring a fashionable wardrobe was also becoming a practical and financial possibility even for women of very modest means.

DRESSED IN INDECENCY: PUBLIC CRITIQUES OF WOMEN'S FASHIONS

In the mid-1910s, when the modern fashions were first introduced on the Danish scene, they provoked relatively little controversy. Even though the vast majority of fashion commentators found the new styles unfortunate, and fashion pioneers—such as the woman at the new year's party—met with gossip and disapproval within their own social circles, short dresses did not trigger much public opposition. After all, wealthy women were known to be given to extravagances, making them the easy victims of any designer whim. That a few working-class daughters adopted similar styles was not surprising either, given their notoriously "poor" taste and unfortunate propensity for flashy outfits. It was only when broader groups of young women began to adopt the new styles that public concern grew.

Certainly, there were contemporaries who found any debate over this matter superfluous. As they saw it, the new styles were merely a temporary folly, doomed to vanish as quickly as it seemed to have appeared. But this was the view of a minority. Most people took the styles much more seriously, believing them to be a sign of more profound changes. In their eyes, young women who adopted shorter skirts, lower necklines, simpler cuts, and higher heels were doing more than simply altering the specific details of fashionable female apparel. In a more fundamental way, they seemed to be departing from older styles of proper and attractive femininity. Although some observers welcomed the new fashions as charming diversions from the older, more formal styles of dress, most older adults therefore watched the emergence of the "modern look" with considerable unease. At a time when the values and virtues associated with nineteenth-century womanhood were already under attack and long-standing gender arrangements seemed to be crumbling, these changes in women's dress were interpreted as yet another sign of rebellion against the status quo.

Still, it remained rather unclear to most observers what these new styles might mean and what consequences they might have; as more and more women adopted the new styles, their efforts to determine the answers to these questions intensified. As a result, debates over women's fashions soared in the second half of the 1910s, and while some voices were risen in their defense, the vast majority of those who expressed their views publicly were deeply troubled and critical of the new styles.

Although critics disagreed about which particular aspect of the new styles was more objectionable, they were unanimous in the complaint that modern fashions seemed to violate both gender norms and class hierarchies. The latter was not the least of their concerns. According to one observer, the new fashions obliterated "all differences among people. You can no longer tell who is the daughter of a common laborer and who belongs to the better circles."[14] Some observers blamed this on upper-class women's surprising preference for simplicity over adornment. Others faulted young working-class women and their inappropriate enthusiasm for "new fashionable finery."[15] Less judgmentally, others argued that the erasure of visible class distinction was the inevitable outcome of ready-made clothes. But no matter where they placed the blame, contemporary observers generally agreed that visual class differences were becoming increasingly blurred. The dangers of this were clear enough: Without the obvious visual clues of class status, an unsuspecting soul might inadvertently mistake a working-class girl for a young lady, or—worse yet—a young lady for a working-class girl.[16]

In general, though, observers were more concerned about the new styles because they seemed to refute older codes of female virtue and modesty. What particularly troubled many critics of the new styles was the increased display of the female body. Even though hemlines would remain below the knee throughout the 1910s and 1920s, shorter dresses still revealed significant parts of women's legs, and sheer silk stockings displayed ankles and calves in more suggestive ways than did traditional wool stockings. Simultaneously, lower necklines and sleeveless tops also made women's upper bodies more visible, leading one Copenhagen city council member to conclude that the new styles of dress "obviously" did not "have the purpose of warming and protecting the body, but rather the opposite: to reveal as much as possible."[17] Besides, the fashions also seemed to call attention to the body beneath the clothing in new and disturbing ways. Even those parts of women's bodies that were in fact clothed seemed more exposed and accessible than ever before.[18] As the amount of fashionable female underwear was reduced to brassieres, underpants, and light corsets, the fact that merely a few layers of delicate fabric shrouded the female body only furthered this sense.[19]

For other critics, the increased display of the female body seemed less disturbing than the sexually provocative nature of the new styles. While admitting that modern dresses carried the advantage of allowing a woman to dress herself without assistance, the fact that they also made it possible for her to undress "in the twinkling of an eye" was not lost on contemporaries.[20] According to some alarmists, this might well lead to unchecked promiscuity and even prostitution among young women.

Other social conservatives expressed concern that the new styles eliminated the visible differences between respectable and disreputable women, or—in the parlance of the early twentieth century—between "ladies" and "women of the streets." In a public lecture, Copenhagen mayor Ernst Kaper, for example, decried that "the ideals that define the appearance of almost all women have completely blurred the distinction between professional prostitutes and respectable citizens."[21] "The look," he explained on another occasion, "short hair, lipstick, powder and make-up, the few pieces of clothing, is often the same."[22] Adding to this argument, one newspaper editor noted that it would be most difficult for men to respect a woman when "she faces us in the attire of a whore."[23]

These criticisms notwithstanding, the more frequently voiced objections to women's new fashionable styles were of a quite different nature. While some (female) fashion columnists complained that they new styles were plain and unattractive, most men reacted quite differently. Although historians, cultural studies scholars, and fashion specialists have often focused on the fact that the new fashions deemphasized womanly curves and removed visual attention from breasts, waists, and hips, arguing that this gave women an androgynous or even boyish look, it was certainly not an impression of juvenile asexuality that struck most Danish men at the time.[24] In their eyes, the modern fashions seemed to endow young women with a new sexual attractiveness, which they flaunted in public and private. As one newspaper reporter noted, "They are everywhere—in the street, at the cafe, on the beach—presenting themselves in their new attire, unabashedly showing off their feminine charms."[25]

Under other circumstances such displays of female beauty and style might have prompted appreciation, but in the second half of the 1910s it was the cause of much male resentment. The new styles, they complained, made women too attractive and too sexy, giving them an unfair edge in the ongoing battle between the sexes. As one journalist grudgingly noted,

"Women are becoming more and more beautiful, and still more seductive under the devilish rule of his majesty King Fashion, and the rest of us are undeniably—only men."[26]

The underlying concern about the sexual balance of power helps explain the visceral response to female fashions that dominated much of the popular press in the late 1910s. Because many men perceived the modern fashions as posing a more fundamental threat to a sexual order based on male control and initiative and female modesty and passivity, they responded with vehement anger. Some commentators warned that scantily clad women created a dangerously erotic atmosphere, where men aroused by the sight of female bodies would not be able to control themselves. Others claimed that they "did not mind that the ladies are dressed like that, but in return all sections of criminal law pertaining to rape ought to be abolished."[27] Surely, they argued, women's "undressed [appearances] entail a diminution of male responsibility—they appeal so openly and aggressively to the baser elements in man's nature that it becomes a directly extenuating circumstance if temptation becomes too strong for him."[28]

As more and more young women began to adopt the new styles, such criticisms became more and more intense. By the end of the 1910s, a host of journalists and literati, academics and politicians, and ministers and moral reformers publicly denounced the new styles and the women who wore them. Yet, exactly at this moment when public opposition was reaching its crescendo, a counterdiscourse in defense of women's fashions began to emerge. After years of relative silence, fashion advocates threw themselves into the battle over women's dress, and surprisingly quickly they managed to quell much of the opposition.

Ironically, it was the efforts of a group of older, reform-minded women to have the infamous garments removed from department store windows that first began to sway many critics from their otherwise adamant stance against the new styles. These efforts first came to the attention of the public on November 25, 1919, when Carla Meyer, the charismatic and controversial president of the newly formed Housewives' Organization, published on open letter to department store owners in which she urged them to "halt the window display of half-naked women's costumes."[29] Behind this initiative stood not only Carla Meyer but also members of moral reform groups and many feminists who feared that the new styles would throw into question young women's ability to make sound judgments and thereby potentially damage all women's claims to sexual equality. Jointly, these women had formed the Committee Against the Dissemination of Modern Apparel, which on November 27 published yet another official protest endorsed by twenty-six of its most prominent members. Given the "irresponsibility . . . of our big, respected firms," they wrote, they felt compelled to express their objection, since "we cannot tolerate that such harlot's garb be introduced into our country and thus help destroy the sense of decency shared by men and women from all strata of society."[30]

Whether the members of the committee had actually expected business owners to comply with their request remains unclear, but they had certainly not anticipated the kind of backlash they would encounter in the wake of their action. Rather than support their efforts, many of the very same reporters and newspaper editors who previously had railed against the new fashions used these older women's action as an opportunity to denigrate and ridicule them. Obviously preferring fashionable young girls as the embodiment of "liberated" twentieth-century womanhood over more serious-minded—and potentially more threatening—female reformers, *Folkets Avis*, for example, called their criticism a "comical act" and mockingly suggested that "some people may be entirely relieved to know that the leaders of the Housewives' Organization will not wear any of [the dresses]."[31] The Social Democratic daily, *Klokken 5*, characterized the incident as "a protest of the old and the ugly, the holy and much too prudish ladies."[32] Even the otherwise sober Copenhagen newspaper *Politiken* joined the chorus. Lashing out at the grammar, intelligence, and appearance of female activists, the paper felt compelled to "call to the attention of the 'cultivated' hyenas that a costume cannot be *half-naked*; a woman, rather, is capable of that, even without being stupid, as long as she is attractive. On the other hand, it does not require attractiveness to be a competent housewife. It was, however, unknown to us, until the publication [of the protest] that stupidity was a prerequisite."[33]

Such tirades placed women struggling to protect and defend older styles of femininity on the defensive. By reducing their concerns to issues of sexual jealousy and female competition over men, male journalists managed to challenge both their sincerity and the moral authority to which they, and other older women, laid claim. Faced with ridicule and accusations of dowdy unattractiveness, most of these women quite understandably preferred to withdraw from public controversy, and after their initial bold offensive, few of them ever commented publicly on the issue of fashion again.

The 1919 incident had other consequences as well. For supporters of the new fashions, the unprecedented attack on older, reform-minded women provided at least an indication of how they might construe an effective argument in favor of the modern styles. By latching on to the critique of female activists as frumpy, prudish, and self-righteous, they might be able to position fashionable young women as their positive contrast and thereby curb the harshest criticisms of their appearances.

Fig. 2. The media invariably portrayed the women who protested against the display of modern fashions, as dowdy and unattractive old maids. The caption for this 1919 cartoon has a fictional "Miss Adelajde Gommesen" decry the way in which "these department stores want us women dolled up." (Reproduced from *Vore Herrer*, 1919)

For that reason, fashion advocates quickly embraced the media's portrayal of older female activists as unattractive and unfeminine. In the following months and years, they eagerly promoted the increasingly popular stereotype that feminists, female reformers, and educated women in general failed to take interest in their appearances and actually prided themselves in this negligence. "I was once honored with an invitation to spend an evening in the company of . . . brilliant and influential women," one young female journalist thus wrote in the early 1920s. "It would have been an delightful affair," she continued, "if all the ladies had been represented through the radio and had not been present themselves, as they were all to an extreme degree lacking in beauty. And it quickly dawned on me that they were proud of their careless appearance."[34] In comparison, young women who embraced the new fashions were obviously more feminine in their pursuit of beauty and style, and unlike older female activists who dared to be in the public eye without necessarily striving to be pleasing to look at, they would offer no such challenge to social conventions.[35]

To bolster the credibility of this argument and further distance fashionable young women from an older generation bent on women's emancipation, proponents of the new styles supported sharp distinctions between men's and women's clothing. They assured critics that equality between the sexes, established with women's suffrage in 1915, rendered the masculine attire—such as jackets and neckties—worn by some older feminists both inappropriate and unnecessary. Sexual difference, they promised, would remain highly encoded in modern fashions. If young women wore clothes that could in any way be deemed inappropriate for their gender, fashion advocates continued, it was for reasons of comfort or practicality only. Thus, when an American fashion designer in 1920 introduced a combined housecoat/pajamas, *Vore Damer* ensured that "it is exceedingly feminine, not the least bit mannish, and it does not appeal to any kind of desire for independence in the young lady who wears it. Rather, the pants . . . are reminiscences from the delicate Oriental women's costumes."[36] From the end of the 1910s, fashion reporting thus concentrated on affirming the gender-appropriate nature of the modern styles. Over and over again, in a seemingly endless litany to femininity, every single item of women's clothing from summer hats to walking shoes was characterized as elegant, graceful, charming, delicate, or refined, and the overall fashionable style as womanly and ladylike.

Contrasting the appealing femininity of fashionable young women with the allegedly frumpy, unattractive, and occasionally mannish appearance of an older generation proved an effective strategy for advocates of the new styles. While placing female critics on the defensive, it simultaneously provided a platform from which fashion enthusiasts were able to respond to male critics who interpreted women's changing appearance as a sign of the erosion of proper womanhood and a challenge to the established gender and sexual order, and within a few years they managed to convince most skeptics that the new styles were not a sign of rebellion or women's efforts to gain control over men. On the contrary, the new styles were, according to fashion advocates, the sign of a renewed and reinforced femininity that admittedly incorporated heightened attractiveness and erotic appeal, but did not endanger female respectability or conventional gender arrangements.

As a result, the controversies over modern fashions all but disappeared within a couple of years of the 1919 incident. Most contemporaries either lost their determination to battle the new styles, or they became convinced that they posed no real threat. And those who remained concerned about the implications of the new fashions soon had their attention drawn to another change in women's appearance even more disturbing than the modern dresses. In the mid-1920s, growing numbers of women began to discard one of the most cherished icons of femininity—namely, their long hair. After a slight lull in the early 1920s, controversies over women's appearances therefore reached a new peak.

THE EMERGENCE OF SHORT HAIR FOR WOMEN

In February 1924, *Illustreret Fagblad for danske Damefrisører*, one of the leading trade journals for Danish women's hairdressers, reported that short haircuts for women were becoming increasingly common throughout most of Europe. Although the trend had not yet reached Denmark, it was likely to do so, the journal predicted, since "we have seen within the last couple of months the first signs of . . . shorn hair here in Copenhagen."[37]

The prediction proved correct. In July 1925, *Ugens Spejl*, another trade journal, reported that the new fashion was spreading "like fire in old houses."[38] That same year, the president of the Ladies' Hairdressers Association estimated that 25 percent of Copenhagen's female population had their hair cut short.[39] The following year, one Copenhagen barber claimed that no less than 75 percent of women under the age of 30 had adopted the new styles, leading the editor of yet another trade journal, *Danmarks Barber- og Frisørtidende* to conclude that "there is something almost epidemically contagious about the advancing shingling. Each and everyone who lets her locks fall for the scissors immediately draws four or five others with her."[40]

Although contemporaries may have exaggerated the numbers, contemporary street photography and surviving photo albums suggest that a significant number of young women did in fact dispose of their long hair in the second half of the 1920s. It is also telling that no fewer than 48 of the 59 women interviewed for this project recalled having their hair cut short before 1930. As Anne Bruun explained many years later, "That was just what you did. If you were young and wanted to be in style, that was definitely the look. Anybody who wanted to be up-to-date did that."[41] Helene Berg agreed. "Short hair made you look chic, made you look modern," she claimed.[42] Besides, as Louise Ege pointed out, short hair

Fig. 3. By 1926, when this photo of chorus girls at the prominent Scala Theater in Copenhagen was taken, short hair had obviously become the dominant style among fashionable young women. (Courtesy of the Royal Library, Copenhagen)

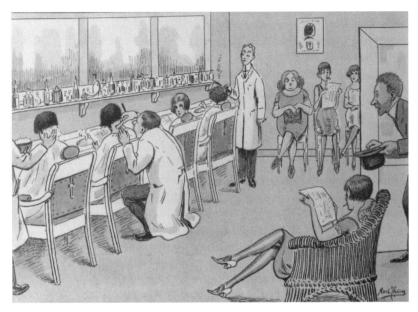

Fig. 4. Because ladies' hairdressers generally refused to cut women's hair, young women had to patronize barbershops in order to acquire the new stylish look. As suggested by this 1925 cartoon, many men found this a disturbing intrusion into traditionally male space. (Reproduced from *Blæksprutten*, 1925)

"kind of fit with the other things that were fashionable. Short dresses and all that."[43]

But despite their enthusiasm for the new hairstyles, actually acquiring one of the fashionable bobs was not always easy. While the number of beauty salons had been growing since the turn of the century, women's hairdressers generally shied away from providing their female customers with the short haircuts they desired.[44] For decades women's hairdressers had worked hard to create a respectable female profession by promoting themselves as specialists in hygiene and conventional feminine beauty, an accomplishment they were not willing to sacrifice by embracing the controversial new styles. Moreover, since most hairdressers were only used to working with combs, brushes, and curlers, few were actually competent to cut hair. As a result, many women had to enter male barbershops to have their hair cut, a step many took with considerable trepidation.

The difficulties of finding a stylist both willing and able to cut a woman's hair was not the only obstacle to a fashionable appearance. Many fathers and husbands explicitly prohibited the new styles. Others let their disapproval be known more indirectly.[45] As Magda Gammelgaard Jensen recalled, "I really wanted to get my hair [cut] short, but I didn't know how to go about it. It wasn't so easy when there was a man around."[46] According to Mr. H. M. Christensen, the president of the Danish Grooming, Toilet and Sanitary Workers' Union, many women therefore chose to "have their hair cut at a time when their husbands and fathers [were] not at home."[47]

Outside the private sphere, other forces also strove to contain "that unfortunate tendency among young ladies to shear their hair."[48] Some workplaces openly discriminated against women who adhered to the new fashion. Several prominent department stores did not hire women who sported the new hairstyles. Others fired employees after a visit to the hairdresser. In 1924, the personnel director at Crome & Goldschmidt, one of the leading clothing stores in Copenhagen, flatly declared that he "would absolutely not engage or employ any young woman with bobbed hair."[49] Other businesses had similar policies. The president of Salomon David Jr. Inc., Inger Diemer, explained that she had "banned bobbed hair." "I demand," she continued, "that the women who work with us, sign [a contract] that they will not wear short hair. In my mind, that is not proper in an old, highly esteemed firm."[50] The director of Bispebjerg Hospital, Charlotte Munck, also banned short hair for all nurses under her supervision.[51] Even women in less publicly visible occupations faced ostracism if they chose to adopt the modern styles. Inger Mangart, for example, who worked as a part-time cleaning assistant in a private home in the late 1920s, recalled being dismissed the first day she arrived with short hair.[52]

The press was equally adamant in its stance against the new styles. To discourage young women from following fashion, newspapers and popular magazines delighted in sensationalist stories about domestic turmoil caused by short hair. Divorces, physical abuse, family disintegration, and even murders were described as tragic, but predictable, outcomes of women's changed appearances.[53] Assuming, however, that young women were more likely to follow fashion prescription than sensible guidance, journalists and other commentators figured that the most efficient way to combat the modern styles was simply to declare them unfashionable. "Bobbed hair is no longer in style," one beauty advice columnist thus warned as early as 1922, several years before the new styles hit Denmark.[54] "We hardly have to repeat that bobbed hair has already received the death sentence abroad," another fashion expert claimed that same year.[55] "There is no doubt that this fad, the short hair, is coming to an end," *Ugebladet* asserted a couple of years later, and in 1925, *B.T.* was pleased to report that "all countries now agree that the fashion of short hair is finally on the retreat."[56]

Yet despite these elaborate efforts to suppress the new haircuts, women's enthusiasm did not wane. Many critics therefore felt compelled to explain the dangers of the new styles in the hope that young women would be swayed by their arguments. Some journalists and beauty advice columnists sought to discourage young women from having their hair cut through use of the kind of racist imagery that permeated early twentieth-century European culture. By labeling the new styles "Hottentot hair" or "Apache cuts," they strove to impress upon young women the incompatibility of short hair with refined Western womanhood. "Surely, no young lady wants to look like a monkey," one reporter thus argued, apparently hoping that young women would recognize the similarity between women's short hair and animal fur.[57]

Other observers claimed that short hair simply made women look ugly and unattractive. Cutting one's hair was therefore inevitably at the risk of losing "the man's admiration and desire."[58] Although some men admitted that a short-haired woman might serve "as a drinking buddy," those who participated in the public debate all insisted that the new styles did not mix with marriage and motherhood, implying that short-haired women could expect to live out their lives as spinsters and old maids—an argument that presumably would dissuade any young woman from such reckless behavior.[59]

While most female critics tended to focus on the aesthetic aspects of the new styles, it was quite different considerations that fueled much of the vehement male opposition. Like many other people in the early twentieth century, these commentators believed there was a direct correlation between external appearance and internal self.[60] When a woman cut her hair, she was not only defying conventional standards of femininity but was also prone to develop some of those mental traits that usually characterized people with short hair—namely, men. As Ludvig Brandt-Møller, a male hairdresser who opposed the new styles, explained, "Short hair tends to emancipate the woman. It is as if it affects her psychologically."[61] Others found that short-haired women became "like men in character and gestures," insisting that "that 99 out of 100 women with short hair have simultaneously acquired boyish or mannish manners."[62]

A few alarmists saw even greater dangers ahead. The very act of cutting a woman's hair, they argued, would eventually alter a woman's biological constitution and turn her into a man. Believing that the mass of hair on a human body was constant, some argued that short hair would necessarily cause women to grow beards.[63] Others predicted the advent of female baldness. "The evidence is right there, since 60 percent of all men over forty [who presumably had cut their hair since childhood] are bald, while less than 0.1 percent of all women [who had never previously cut their hair] suffer from this weakness," another critic of the new styles explained.[64]

While men had tended to object to short dresses because they rendered women *too* attractive, their reactions to short hair were therefore quite different. According to male critics, short hair "emancipated" women and made then unwomanly, even masculine, and *not attractive enough*, a violation of gender norms that seemed to them much graver and ultimately more unpleasant than women being overly sexy and seductive. Even those who did not necessarily believe that short hair would actually turn women into men found this quite disturbing because, as one correspondent wrote to the editor of the newspaper *B.T.* in 1925, "If there is something we men cannot stand, it is precisely women void of femininity."[65] Young women's seeming disregard of men's opinions about the new styles only made matters worse. Apparently, young women were no longer pursuing physical beauty and style for the purposes of male pleasure and admiration.[66] How, then, were men to understand women's enthusiasm for short hair as anything but a sign that women cared less about male approval than about their own "emancipation"? Some even feared that the popularity of the new styles might indicate an explicit sexual and emotional detachment from men.

In comparison with those who defended short dresses when they first appeared, supporters of the new hairstyles were therefore faced with a much more difficult task. The opposition to women's short hair was much fiercer than the opposition to short dresses had ever been, as short hair connoted emancipation, female defiance, and rebellion against men's judgment in a way that short skirts never had.

During this entire controversy, the voices of women who cut their hair were rarely heard in public. Under heavy fire, most young women seemingly preferred to avoid the discursive battles that raged around them.[67] On the few occasions that any of these women did speak up, they generally adopted a very cautious stance, seeking to diffuse the opposition by reassuring critics of their whole-hearted commitment to femininity and respectable womanhood. In 1925, one young woman who described herself as "old-fashioned" despite her short hair thus sought to counter criticisms of the new styles by denying that there was any link between appearance and identity. "Why in the world should a young girl not be equally feminine and good whether she has bobbed hair or long hair?," she wondered. "It does, after all, not change the nature of the young girl to have her hair cut off."[68] More often, young women simply tried to skirt criticisms by emphasizing the very pragmatic concerns that allegedly had led them to the barbershop. "Much can be said both for and against the bobbed hair, but the fact that it is a practical way of wearing one's hair, nobody can deny," one woman argued.[69]

Nonetheless, the relative silence on the part of the women who wore the new hairstyles did not mean that no voices were raised in their defense. Complicating the picture of vocal male opponents and a largely silent group of female supporters, the chief public advocates of short hair for women in the 1920s were in fact male barbers. Not that barbers were a particularly fashion-conscious bunch or especially committed to young women's right to determine their own appearance. These men simply saw the new styles as a means to propel their profession out of the crisis in which it had lingered for decades. The rise of the medical and dental professions had dealt the first blow to the former surgeon-barbers, eliminating what had been the most profitable areas of their occupation. Later, when men began to shave themselves rather than frequenting the barber twice or three times weekly, the financial base of most barbershops had been further undercut, and scattered attempts at cultivating new areas of business expertise such as facial massage and manicure had contributed only little to their economy. In this context, the fashionable new styles for women seemed a god-send for barbers eager to cultivate both a new clientele and new sources of income, and since women's hairdressers generally opposed the short hairstyles and most often refused to cut women's hair, barbers were left with the uncontested responsibility for providing young women with the look they desired.

Of course, barbers were not oblivious to the offense women's short hair provoked or the wrath they might incur by accommodating female customers. It was therefore in their own best interest to counter the opposition, and toward that end they adopted the same strategy that fashion advocates had successfully used a few years earlier, namely, to attempt to disassociate short hair from any kind of subversive intentions on the part of women. Short hair, they insisted, had nothing to do with defiance of feminine conventions or even modern fashions. It was a style adopted for reasons of comfort, ease, and practicality only. "It is not the senseless mimicking of fashion follies that has led women to allow their hair to be cut off," one barber thus insisted in 1926. "Rather, it is the natural development in all social strata that has forced the women to choose a practical hairstyle."[70]

To give credibility to this claim, barbers traced the origins of women's short hair not to feminist rebels or decadent fashions, but to that highly respectable, self-sacrificing female heroine, Florence Nightingale. "When a war begins," one writer explained, "masses of younger and older women who wish to be nurses in the army immediately sign up. The healthiest among them are selected, and the first step on the road to their new vocation is to cut their hair as short as men's, first, because the daily care takes too long time, and secondly, because a nurse cannot run around with a zoo of carnivores [sic!] in her long hair."[71] Upon their return, the reasoning continued, admirers adopted similar hair styles.

Although there was little historical evidence to support such an explanation—after all, Florence Nightingale's reputation had been established during the Crimean War almost three quarters of a century earlier, and few women had followed her example in the intervening years —this argument had several advantages. First, it disassociated short hair from any kind of female defiance. Second, it sought to ground the popularity of the new hairstyles in admirable, patriotic concerns. And third, it tied short hair to notions of health and hygiene. From the mid-1920s, particularly the latter, combined with arguments about the practical requirements of the labor market, formed the core in the defense of women's short hair.

In addition, barbers also sought to address anxieties over the seeming dissipation of gender differences by calling attention to the cultural and historical versatility of hair styles. In an article entitled "Masculine Girl Hair and Feminine Boy Hair," the author set out to prove that "women have not been 'the long-haired sex' for as long as we believe." A sampling of Greek, Roman, and Persian traditions led him to conclude that "long hair appears just as frequently on men as on women when one examines history, which is why hair has nothing whatsoever to do with sexual character."[72] Just as long hair did not make men less masculine, short hair would not eradicate women's femininity. In fact, some argued, it held the potential of actually heightening it by drawing attention to women's fine facial features. "The shape of the face, the beauty of the skin, as well as the soft lines of the neck" were accentuated by short hair, one barber wrote, poetically comparing a woman's face to a "painting [that] is also seen more clearly in a simple frame."[73]

In the case of modern dresses, fashion advocates had gradually managed to convince most critics of their compatibility with conventional womanhood. Short hair fared differently. Short, simple haircuts for women never gained acceptance in the 1920s, at least not among the men and women who publicly expressed their opinions. The controversy over women's hair only died down at the end of the decade, when a new, modified style of short hair became popular.

Ironically, this new short style, which eventually appeased critics, emerged from the beauty salon run by women's hairdressers. Having been entirely unsuccessful in their attempts to coax women into preserving their long hair and eager to regain some of the professional territory lost to barbers, women's hairdressers found themselves forced to dispense with their rejection of the short fashions. Still unwilling, however, to embrace the bobbed look, they devised a new strategy. Arguing that short hair unfortunately had been "carried to extremes . . . by the less cultivated segments of the female population" and was sported by "each and every factory and shop-girl," (middle-class) women were offered a chance to distinguish themselves as "finer ladies" through "feminine and graceful styles with curls and waves" while they were waiting for their hair to grow out again.[74]

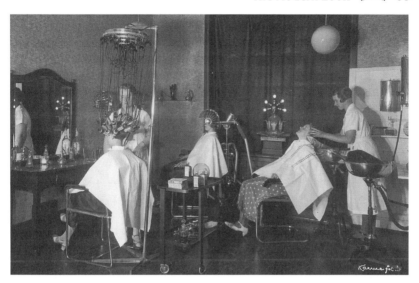

Fig. 5. With the introduction of permanent waves in the late 1920s, short hair for women acquired a more acceptably "feminine" form, but the process was time-consuming, uncomfortable, and expensive. (Courtesy of the Local Historical Archives for Aalborg Municipality, Aalborg, Denmark)

By fashioning themselves as aides to women concerned with the reestablishment of their femininity and by presenting their care for short hair as a form of damage control, hairdressers were able to legitimize their growing interest in women's new hairstyles. With relatively few ideological scruples they were therefore able to plunge into this profitable market during the last years of the 1920s, gradually recapturing the patronage of most women.

However, that women left the barbershop and (re)turned to the beauty salon did not indicate that long hair was regaining its popularity. Fashionable hairstyles for women remained short for the rest of the decade. What did change was the way short hair actually looked. Female hairdressers, one fashion columnist noted with applause, did "everything to give the short style a more feminine air than earlier."[75] Permanent waves and curls, artificial hair pieces, decorative combs, ribbons, and barrettes all contributed to this goal. This new, feminized version of short hair quickly gained popularity among women interested in variation and possibly weary of public hostility. Within just a few years the original simple, straight styles had virtually been abandoned.[76] Customers, one hairdresser noted with pleasure in 1927, now wanted "to become more feminine, not with completely long hair, but with longer short hair, enough to be curly in the back and around the face . . . so that the repulsive boyish head becomes beautified and more feminine."[77]

Thus, after a brief but troubling intermission where women's adoption of short hair seemed to be blurring gender differences, new curlier versions of bobbed hair marked the reestablishment of gender distinctions in fashionable self-presentation. Even though women continued to cut their hair, the clear stylistic differences between short hair for men and short hair for women soothed critics, and gradually their opposition faded. With their confidence in the stability of sexual difference restored, some of the harshest opponents were even able to admit a few years later that they actually found short hair quite charming and attractive—if not on their wives, then at least on their daughters.[78]

THE MODERN LOOK: EMANCIPATION FOR WOMEN?

In the 1910s and 1920s, some people took particular offense to short skirts. Others were more disturbed by the sleeveless tops, delicate fabrics, and sheer stockings that young women fancied. Still others judged short hair the most troubling of fashion innovations. Yet no matter which aspect of the new styles they found more provocative, critics shared one fundamental conviction: They believed modern fashions to be part of a broader rebellion against conventional gender arrangements and therefore inextricably linked to the issue of female emancipation. Whether they talked about short skirts or short hair, they generally agreed that the new styles made women "much freer" and "more independent," both physically and psychologically, and that the reason for their enthusiastic embrace of the modern fashions lay in this fact.[79]

In the years since then, both popular and professional historians have tended to reproduce this belief. With few exceptions, they have presented postwar fashions as a sign of young women's refusal to accept the constraints of nineteenth-century femininity and as evidence of their insistence on new physical freedoms. Like commentators at the time, they have emphasized the ease and practicality of the new styles, assuming that it was these qualities that held particular appeal to young women in general and working women in particular.[80]

Such claims are not without merit. When asked why they liked the new styles, many women who embraced modern fashions in the 1910s and 1920s pointed to their simplicity and convenience. In retrospect, Henny Nedergaard, for example, explained that "old-fashioned dresses were so complicated. I remember in my childhood, it took forever for my mother to get dressed. The modern dresses were much easier. You just slipped them on—that was it."[81] Charlotte Hansen also described the older styles of female dress as confining and appropriate only for a sedentary existence. "Our generation was different," she explained. "We were not content to just sit still and do nothing. Corsets and stays, that was not for us. We did not want to wear all those heavy clothes. They just did not fit us."[82] According to Edith Jensen, the new styles "made it easier for women to move."[83] "Short dresses were much more practical," added Lily Enevold, "especially if you had to work. You couldn't really work in those long dresses."[84] Some women endorsed short hair for the same reason. "Who in the world had time to comb and brush and put up long hair," Henriette Marie Markfeldt wanted to know, "when you had to be at work at seven o'clock in the morning? No, short hair was a lot easier."[85]

To deny that the new styles were in fact easier and more comfortable than the restrictive, corseted fashions and the elaborate coiffure of the nineteenth century would be pointless. But to argue that the new fashions freed women from physical restrictions and eliminated time-consuming grooming would be equally untrue. Short, narrow skirts did not exactly promote free and unrestricted mobility. Neither did the high heels that became so popular in the postwar era. Silk stockings may have felt more comfortable than the older wool stockings, but they were also more fragile and more frequently in need of mending. Similarly, short hair may have required less daily attention, but it demanded regular trimming, and when curls and waves became the new fashionable norm, most women had to spend considerable time, not to mention substantial sums of money, at the hairdresser.

In addition, the new fashions demanded a slenderness that had not been a requirement for older generations of women. As fashion historian Valerie Steele has pointed out, stylistic change applies to bodies as well as clothes, and with the new, slimmer lines in women's clothing went slimmer female bodies.[86] From the beginning of World War I, when the new fashionable styles first gained popularity, the "tyranny of slenderness" thus began its ascendancy over all women who wanted to be in style.[87]

In the postwar decade, this led to an unprecedented emphasis on dieting, a phenomenon still unfamiliar to most women in the early 1910s.[88] Yet already in the mid-1910s when the new styles were first introduced to broad audiences, advice on how to obtain a slender body became a regular feature in women's magazines. At first, such advice was rather infrequent and not particularly demanding. "The most efficient method is to eat minimally," one newspaper advised in 1915, acknowledging, however, that "this is of course not entirely convenient when one has a good cook."[89] As a solution to this dilemma, the journalist recommended standing up for twenty minutes after each main meal, an exercise that supposedly would counteract the unfortunate effects of (too much) good food. Gradually, dieting became more rigorous and sophisticated, and by the mid-1920s beauty experts were prescribing strict diets of grapefruit,

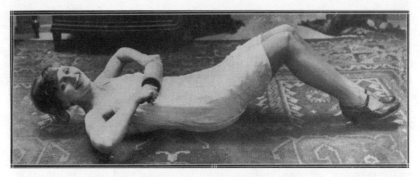

Fig. 6. In the course of the 1920s advice on dieting became more and more common in women's magazines, and the admonitions to be thin more and more stern. Among the more humorous suggestions for how to obtain the ideal slender body was this rolling-pin massage. (Reproduced from *Vore Damer*, 1926)

fish, and raw vegetables "not just for a few days at a time, but . . . day in and day out, year in and year out."[90]

Other recommended ways of acquiring the slender body were equally taxing. In addition to dieting, women were encouraged to engage in various forms of physical exercise, not for the pleasure this might entail but for the results it would produce.[91] If both of these strategies failed, a variety of commercial products promised shortcuts to a slender body. From the early 1920s, a multitude of remedies, including oils, drinks, salts, and tablets, promised female consumers instant health and gradual thinness.[92] Finally, women aiming for a sleek-looking body could—and very often did—turn to modernized versions of the traditional corset. Most famous for being discarded during the 1920s, corsets were in fact simply remodeled to suit the new styles. Replacing whalebone and canvas, tough elastic material flattened breasts and stomachs and eliminated the visible curves of hips and thighs. Obviously, then, the fashions that made women more mobile and less physically restrained also made them more self-conscious about measuring up to the new "look." And no matter which strategy women chose in order to obtain the desired shape and weight, they had to engage in the immensely demanding process of self-surveillance and self-disciplining that the American historian Joan Jacobs Brumberg has labeled the twentieth-century female "body project."[93]

But if the new styles were neither as easy, simple, nor carefree as they have often been described, why did young women so eagerly embrace these fashions? At the time, answers to this question were rarely articulated by the women who adopted the new styles, especially not in writing. After all, fashion is, as Mary Louise Roberts has pointed out, "something to wear, not [something] to write about," and even though journalists were fond of querying their readers about virtually any topic under the sun, they apparently never thought to ask young women to explain their enthusiasm for the new styles.[94] But when asked several decades later, most women had an answer at hand. "It was what was fashionable back then and of course you wanted to be fashionable," said Dora Ingvard-sen.[95] Lily Enevold gave a very similar explanation. "I guess it was just what was in style, and you know how young girls want to be stylish."[96] Others, including Stine Petersen, explained that "for me, it wasn't really a big deal. I just wanted to look good."[97]

Had contemporaries heard such explanations, they may well have been less perturbed than most of them were. For some women, the new styles clearly had no significance beyond being the prescribed fashion. Their reason for liking the new styles was not that they permitted women new physical freedoms, and they did not associate short dresses or short hair with any kind of rebelliousness against the status quo. As Marie Hede-gaard poignantly remarked, "I belonged to Conservative Youth, but being politically conservative had nothing to do with that. Of course, we wore short dresses, and most of the girls [who belonged to the organization] had short hair."[98]

Still, the women who recalled their stylish appearances as merely the result of fashion prescription constituted a minority. Far more frequently women gave another explanation. In general, they claimed to have liked the new styles neither for their practicality nor for their ease, but because they were a particularly effective way of displaying their difference from older generations of women and asserting a distinctively "modern" female identity. As Agnes Nyrop explained, "We were young and gay and full of life, and we wanted to look like that, look modern."[99] Voicing the same sentiment, Louise Ege explained, "Those dresses did not just make you look stylish, they made you look modern."[100] "Having short skirts and short dresses, that was part of being modern," added Gertrud Øst.[101] "It made you feel free and young and modern. Stylish, you know, glamor-ous, and that was what we wanted," according to Amanda Christensen.[102]

Whether or not the new styles were in fact easier, more practical, and more convenient, this was obviously not the only factor in determining these women's fashion choices. The fact that the new styles set young women visually apart from an older generations whose confining lives they did not care to emulate was at least as important. As Thora Smed recalled, "My mother, she never had a moment of ease in her life. It was always toil and moil for her. I think most of us dreamed of a life that would not be like that."[103] For her, and for many other women who were young in the 1920s, sporting the new fashionable styles was simultane-ously an expression of this desire and part of its fulfillment. In her words, "We wanted something more, something better, and I guess [wearing fashionable clothes] was in a way part of that."[104] Simply wearing the new fashions certainly seemed to provide many women with a sense of glamour and style that lifted their existence into a "modern" realm of luxury, pleasure, and indulgence unfamiliar to most of their mothers. As a result, even the stringent requirements for slenderness and the laborious aspects of other forms of beauty care seemed well worth the effort. In fact, engaging in such beauty care was in itself a privilege that many young women treasured. "I have to admit that [we] spent a lot of time on looking good," confided Vera Thorsen. "But it was fun. Trying different things, trying this and that. No, it was fun."[105]

But the new fashionable styles did not only play a role on the individual level. They also signaled young women's collective embrace of a new identity as "modern" women and their commitment to creating a life for themselves that would be "modern" in a much broader sense. Ingrid Kristensen's answer to the question of why she liked the new styles was therefore less a non sequitur than it first appeared. After a brief pause, she explained that "young girls had a lot in common back then. We wanted something different." After yet another pause, she added pensively, "I think that was why we liked [the new fashionable styles]. It was like— like that was what you let people know when you looked like that."[106]

Clearly, then, young women did not consider the new styles emancipatory in and of themselves. Still, to dismiss the women who wore them as merely clothes horses and fashion plates would be mistaken. Their pursuit of the modern look may have been informed by mass-produced images of female glamour and style, and the acquisition of a fashionable appearance unquestionable tied young women into elaborate patterns of consumption and individual beauty care. But to the extent that the new styles provided young women with an individual and collective identity as "modern" women, fashion and appearance were part of young women's rebellion against the past. While they did not define themselves as feminists in any way, they were certainly not willing to accept the restricted, joyless lives they believed their mothers and grandmothers to have lived, and in their own understanding, this was exactly what they signaled through their adoption of the new fashions.

⟨≡⟩

From the mid-1910s, young women's adoption of new fashionable styles, including short hair and short dresses, profoundly changed female appearances. To most older contemporaries these new styles seemed not only a troubling rejection of conventional notions of female beauty but also a provocative violation of feminine virtues such as modesty and reserve. Worse yet, the modern fashions seemed to eradicate visible differences between respectable and disreputable women, and short hair threatened to blur gender differences. But those who feared that "women no longer want to be women" worried unnecessarily.[107] While young women's fashion choices challenged older notions of attractive femininity, young women themselves never questioned a woman's duty to be feminine. On the contrary, they seemed delighted to embrace the argument of professional fashion advocates that the new styles made women *more* feminine, not less, and they willingly accepted the time-consuming and labor-intensive beauty and body care that the new look required. Nonetheless, young women did not adopt the new styles simply because of fashion prescription. In their imagination, wearing the new styles was both the expression and the confirmation of a commitment to female modernity that went far beyond being young, elegant, and fashionably dressed.

CHAPTER 2

Fit for Modernity

WHEN OLDER men and women looked at adolescent girls and young women in the postwar decade, it was not only their short skirts and bobbed hair that convinced them that female youths no longer were "like girls used to be."[1] Just as often, it was their seemingly endless supply of energy, vitality, and bounce that produced that impression. According to observers, young women were constantly "hurrying along," "always in motion, always rushing, dashing down the streets, coming and going, always part of some lively action."[2] In the morning, they would "fling themselves on their bicycles," and after a long day of work, they seemed to "delight in a brisk walk . . . completely irrespective of the weather."[3] Whenever they had time off, they would "swarm into the countryside," turning country roads into "one big bicycle stadium."[4] In the summer, there was "not one single Danish beach where you will not find a group of young women immersing themselves in the blue waves."[5] And after all these exertions, young women were supposedly always ready to go out and have fun at night.[6]

Young women's enthusiasm for organized sports and exercise only reinforced this perception of unprecedented female vigor. In the 1910s and 1920s, new sports clubs sprang up everywhere, and older ones attracted more female members than ever before.[7] Swimming clubs flourished, and from the early 1920s, the popularity of handball and other ball games created the basis for both local and regional tournaments. In urban areas, hockey clubs offered another opportunity for competitive team sport, and track and field began to attract its first female athletes.[8] Canoeing and kayaking also appealed to many adolescent girls and young women.[9] Less affordable but equally popular were tennis and fencing.[10] Some adventurous young women even explored more rugged sports, including hunting, sharpshooting, motorcycle and auto racing, wrestling, and soccer.[11]

That large numbers of young women took to dancing during these years also added to the impression of their seemingly unlimited physical energy. Across the country, young men and women spent days and evenings struggling to learn the complicated moves and steps of such new dances as the tango, the Charleston, the Turkey Trot, the Bear Dance, the Crayfish Dance, and the Apache Dance.[12] By 1918, more than 50,000 Copenhagen youths attended dance classes annually, and of these at least two-thirds were adolescent girls and young women.[13] A few years

Fig. 7. Field hockey was one of the team sports that appealed to many young women in the 1920s. (Courtesy of the Royal Library, Copenhagen)

later, observers found that young women completely dominated both public and private dance floors, supposedly "delirious with joy and excitement."[14]

Surely, not all young women were as lively, active, and exuberant as contemporaries claimed, and not all were athletically inclined. Nonetheless, as elsewhere across the Western world, physical activities did acquire an unprecedented popularity among young Danish women in the 1920s. Part of the explanation for this undoubtedly lies in the fact that sports and other forms of physical activity provided hours of inexpensive fun, excitement, and pleasure for young girls with a bit of time and money they could call their own. But the unprecedented popularity of all kinds of physical activity among female youths in the 1920s was also the result of the enormous significance the postwar generation of women placed on the body as a site of female modernity. According to Netta Nielsen, "You simply couldn't be modern if you wore old-fashioned clothes." But as she also pointed out, a fashionable appearance was "not enough" for a woman to be considered truly "modern" in the 1920s.[15] To be able to claim that label and identity, a woman needed a body and a personal style that were as "modern" as the outfits she wore. In the words of Ingeborg Rerup, "Clothes and how you carried yourself—it all had to go together."[16]

Of course, the definition of what constituted a "modern" female body varied. For some young women, it meant the kind of slender body prescribed by fashion. For others, it was a body not (yet) worn by pregnancies, childbirths, and physical labor. But across these differences, most young women seemed to agree that a "modern" body was a healthy body, a body untouched by the problems ranging from "anemia, tuberculosis, and indigestion" to "bloated stomachs, sway-backs, double chins, stooping shoulders, a waddling walk, and other infirmities" that supposedly plagued older generations of women.[17] To avoid such miseries and maintain a healthy body, sports and physical exercise were therefore seen as essential activities by young women keen on being "modern."

But physical health and well-being was more than just a means to an end. Having an active, energetic body—and a personality to match—was central to young women's definition of what it meant to be "modern", and it was one of the ways in which they distinguished themselves from earlier generations of women who supposedly had done little but "sit by the window with an embroidery."[18] "Girls like us," explained one young woman in 1925, "will not be restrained in such a manner. We want to move, go out, have fun. We are not frail old maids."[19] When asked to explain many years later what it meant to be "modern" in the 1920s, many women struck a similar chord. Edith Jensen, for example, explained, "Being modern—that was what you wore, of course. But it was much more than that. If was how you acted, how you walked, what you did."[20] Lily Enevold agreed, defining a "modern" woman as "someone who was physically active, lively. Someone who knew how to have fun."[21] "Being modern," added Emilie Spang-Bak, "that was not just how you looked. It was how you carried yourself."[22] "For us young women," summarized Marie Hedegaard, being "modern" "had to do with many different things—whether you were active or not, whether you were sporty or not, what attitude you had."[23]

The image of young women in the 1920s as lively and vibrant —an image that dominated the postwar years and still permeates many popular and scholarly accounts of the era—is therefore not entirely unfounded.[24] The generation of women who came of age in the 1910s and 1920s did in fact come across as remarkably light-hearted and exuberant, and they demonstrated an exceptional enthusiasm for physical activities. But the assumption that this physical and emotional exuberance simply derived from the fact that "the times [had] changed," as one young woman argued in 1924, or that it was the logical or natural response to new kinds of freedom for women, is less accurate.[25] On the contrary, the lively and enthusiastic personality and the physical energy that characterized so many young women in the postwar decade were, as this chapter demonstrates, parts of a carefully constructed style, a deliberate effort to reshape the female body and the female personality in accordance with young women's own definitions of female modernity.

OUT OF BOUNDS?

In the early decades of the twentieth century, physical activity and exercise for girls and young women were not a new or unknown phenomenon in Denmark. Already in the 1810s, lawmakers had considered making gymnastics part of the primary school curricula for all girls and boys, but after a brief trial period they decided to restrict such instruction to boys only.[26] Despite this setback, many physicians and physical educators continued to advocate physical education for girls throughout the nineteenth century, and from the 1850s, a number of private girls' schools began to incorporate physical education among its required subjects.[27] From the 1870s, the privately funded Danish folk high schools followed suit and introduced physical education for both male and female students.[28] After a government commission found in 1884 that 25 percent of all six-year-old and 51 percent of all thirteen-year-old schoolgirls were "sickly," public concern over women's health led to the creation of new exercise programs designed to strengthen the female body through fitness.[29] As a result, physical education became a curricular reality for all school-age girls from 1904.

Throughout the nineteenth century, physical educators, physicians, and health reformers were the key advocates of physical exercise for women, but interest in such activities was not confined to their circles. In the second half of the nineteenth century, upper-class women often enjoyed leisurely games of croquet and tennis, along with other sporting activities such as archery, fencing, and horseback riding.[30] Rowing and gymnastics also appealed to some young women from prosperous families, leading to the founding in 1886 of Copenhagen's Female Gymnastics Association and, in 1890, Copenhagen Women's Rowing Club. When bicycling became popular in the late 1880s, middle-class and elite women acquired yet another opportunity for athleticism.[31] Although many critics found bicycle riding unsuitable for women, the Women's Bicycle Club was founded in 1893, and as mass production lowered the price, more and more women were able to afford the immensely popular new vehicle.[32]

What struck contemporaries as so new and different in the 1910s and 1920s was therefore not women's participation in various forms of physical exercise per se but the large number of post-school-aged women who engaged in such activities and their seeming enthusiasm for virtually any kind of sport and physical fun. According to observers, there was by the early 1920s "hardly the type of sport in the world in which women [had] not taken an active interest" and "hardly a young girl who [did] not practice one or more forms of sport."[33] Given these new realities, concern about the appropriateness and desirability of women's physical activities moved from the margins to the center of cultural debate, and as young women threw themselves into one kind of sport after the other, controversies over their activities flared and public criticism grew.

The strongest opposition to women's newfound enthusiasm for physical activities came from older, conservative physicians trained within the framework of nineteenth-century science and medicine and their adherents. The female body, they insisted, was inherently fragile and easily damaged by external forces.[34] Consequently, physical activities threatened to endanger women's natural constitution. "Good health is often lost on the sports ground," one elderly male observer warned Danish women in 1919.[35] Another critic found strenuous physical activity entirely incompatible with "women's much more delicate build, which does not tolerate the required acrobatics and exertion."[36] Still other health experts cautioned women against the risks involved in "the shaking and shivering, and pushing and shoving" that supposedly took place on modern dance floors.[37]

But women's health was not the only issue at stake. By disrupting the delicate balances of the female body, physical exercise might, some physicians added, also jeopardize the femininity and attractiveness of young women. As a result of too much or too strenuous activity, the female body would inevitably be turned into a facsimile of the male body, and women would begin to look like men.[38] Rounded curves would be replaced by angular lines, softness by hardened muscles, and feminine refinement by bodily strength.[39] Worse yet, unbridled female physicality might also destroy some of the most salient psychological characteristics of true womanhood. Many forms of sport encouraged competitiveness, for example, a character trait otherwise ascribed to men. And like unchaperoned public dancing, athletic competition was thought to undermine female modesty. Some even found that women's new physical activities instilled in them "unwomanly arrogance and an unhealthy self-assurance" detrimental to marital happiness.[40]

To most contemporaries, however, this frenzy over women's physical activities sounded somewhat overwrought. Confronted with exuberant young women brimming with energy and health, medical predictions about the consequences of female physicality simply failed to be convincing, and already from the late 1910s they began to fade from public discourse. In their place, a new cultural consensus around the generally positive qualities of women's physical activities began to take shape.

Ironically, some of the strongest support for women's new physical activities would also come from within the medical profession. From the late 1910s, a younger generation of physicians sided with physical educators in an outspoken defense of female physicality. Driven by concerns over women's physical well-being in general and their reproductive health in particular and believing fitness an effective means of stamping out various physical disorders, these physicians strongly recommended that girls and women of all ages be physically active. "Make sure to walk, bike, stretch and do light exercises every day. In the summer, attempt to swim at least twice weekly," one physician lectured women in 1918.[41] Even dancing got the official stamp of approval as a legitimate form of exercise capable of improving women's health and general well-being. "Don't criticize your daughters so harshly for their fondness of music and dance," another doctor advised. "Enjoyed in moderation, dance and other forms of movement to music will only serve to correct her posture, make her breathe freer, and give her more energy."[42] In contrast to those who argued that exercise might undermine women's physique, more and more of these younger doctors concluded that it was likely to make women stronger and healthier, better fit for marriage and motherhood, and able to recover more easily from childbirth.

Appreciation of young women's physical enthusiasm was also shared by contemporaries with a specific interest in women's performance in the labor market. Seeing physical health and strength as prerequisites for acceptable performances in the workplace, many employers, economists, and labor leaders, as well as some feminists, applauded young women who engaged in physical activities in their spare time, provided of course that these activities were appropriate, "rational," and "reasonable."[43] This built stamina and staying power, they argued, countered physical exhaustion, and relieved tension and stress. Karla Nilson, president of the Female Clerical Workers' Union, for example, encouraged all members to take a brisk walk or bicycle ride after work. This would, she promised, chase away "low spirits and fatigue" and instead produce "fresh, cheerful and zesty young women."[44]

Nevertheless, the growing acceptance, even popularity, of female physicality from the late 1910s did not mean that public controversies over women's new activities came to an end. Rather, they merely shifted ground. In the early 1920s, both critics and defenders of female physical exercise began to leave behind the question of *whether* women ought to play sports, exercise, and dance. Instead they increasingly focused their attention on *which forms* of physical activity were suitable for women, agreeing that some guidance was called for. Because young women's energy and enthusiasm seemed to know no boundaries, they felt called upon to interfere, steering them away from the roughest, most unladylike forms of dance and sport and into physical activities deemed more appropriate. Simultaneously, then, with the gradual acceptance of a new, more physical style of womanhood, new cultural boundaries for women's activities were under construction.

CHANGING BOUNDARIES FOR WOMEN'S
PHYSICAL ACTIVITIES

By the early 1920s, the older generation of physicians who insisted that athletics would damage women's fragile bodies had largely been discredited. Nonetheless, concern that women's participation in vigorous exercise programs, competitive sports, and other forms of strenuous physical activity would undermine "natural" gender differences lingered through the rest of the decade. After all, sport had developed in the nineteenth century as a male preserve, a domain in which men expressed and cultivated masculinity through athletic competition.[45] Women's assumption of such "manly" activities therefore continued to unnerve many contemporaries who questioned the social consequences of their unprecedented exploits. How could a woman who "on the stroke of six [o'clock] . . . jumps out of bed, throws herself on her bicycle and races like a newspaper boy out to the tennis court or the gymnasium, and then arrives at the office at nine, completely out of breath" possibly retain her femininity, wondered some observers.[46] Could women who participated in "mannish" activities such as soccer and boxing be truly womanly outside the sports arena? And was it not possible that unrestrained physical activity might really, as some critics suggested, cause young women to "shake off a part of their sex and acquire a considerable part of the robust and rough assurance of a masculine being?"[47]

For those who harbored such concerns, the media's endless fascination with extraordinary female physical feats did little to alleviate their worries. Throughout the postwar decade, newspapers and magazines reveled in stories about women, both from Denmark and abroad, who broke gender conventions as soccer players, wrestlers, hammer throwers, long-distance runners, motorcycle drivers, sharpshooters, and parachute jumpers. Photographs of female firefighters, bus drivers, ditchdiggers, and construction workers only added to this carnivalesque display of female modernity that simultaneously announced the arrival of a new type of physically active woman and the collapse of distinct male and female preserves.[48]

Equally popular were stories of female accomplishments that seemed to throw into question men's physical supremacy. When, for example, the young Danish-American swimmer Harriet Mille Carson managed to cross the English Channel in record time in 1926, while "the first-class male swimmer" against whom she competed had to "give up due to wind and waves," she did so under intense media coverage.[49] And the following year, when the seventeen-year-old Edith Jensen became the first person ever to cross the Sound between Denmark and Sweden, only one day after

Fig. 8. Much to the dismay of contemporaries, a few women took up such "masculine" sports as motorcycle racing. Among them were Inga Francke, here photographed in front of her apartment building in 1929. (Courtesy of the Danish Women's Photo Archives, Copenhagen)

a male swimmer had failed to reach that goal, the press once again touted young women's stunning physical strength and endurance.[50]

While most ordinary Danes probably found such spectacular female feats more exciting and entertaining than threatening, those who participated in the public debate were generally troubled by such activities. In their minds, these were examples of the worst aspects of women's physical activities—vulgar in their competitiveness, excessive in their aim, unfeminine in their vigor, and immodest in their public display. Instead of promoting stronger, healthier female bodies, such activities, they feared, would ultimately undermine women's physical well-being and, rather than making them more beautiful, might make women mannish and muscular. It is therefore hardly surprising that many contemporaries felt that some guidance was called for lest young women slip entirely out of control and lose themselves in unhealthy competition and damaging excesses.

Even advocates of female exercise were often uncomfortable with young women's enthusiasm for strength, speed, and record-breaking. While interested in promoting physical freedom and athletic enjoyment for women, the vast majority of them were also committed to preserving gender difference, and they saw competitive strife as an unfortunate and eccentric American phenomenon that threatened to ruin not only "the sound Danish tradition of women's exercise" but also women's physical health and femininity.[51] In response to charges of masculinization and out of concern about women's health and well-being, they therefore began to

Fig. 9. The development of rhythmic movement, physical harmony, and feminine grace was the main goal of many female physical educators in the 1920s, including the influential Agnete Bertram whose students demonstrate the new style in this 1927 photo. (Courtesy of the Royal Library, Copenhagen)

articulate a philosophy of female athleticism that defined proper physical activities for women as fundamentally different from those of men.[52] Women, they argued, should carefully choose only those forms of activity that suited their constitution. Exercise should not exert, and it should never "develop a woman's body so that she becomes too muscular."[53] Besides, women should not engage in competitive sports. Not only might frenzied competition lead a woman to loose her composure and "aesthetic appearance," but it also brought out aggressiveness and other "most unfortunate character traits in a woman."[54] Rather than athletic prowess and bodily strength, the development of soft and harmonious feminine bodies ought to be the objective, and women should therefore confine themselves to the "feminine" category of pleasurable exercise and physical fitness, leaving "masculine" sports to men.[55]

Female physical educators, including exercise instructors, gymnastics teachers, and physical culture specialists, were particularly adamant in this stance. By the 1920s, these women had for decades been striving to develop specifically female exercise programs.[56] Criticizing nineteenth-century traditions of gymnastics and physical exercise for their masculine bias, their emphasis on disciplining and strengthening the body, and their stiff, militaristic bent, they insisted on the importance of acknowledging gender difference and cultivating exercise systems for women that were not a "blind imitation" of men's.[57] Instead of strenuous drills and apparatus-based gymnastics that developed muscular strength, they encouraged light floor exercises, rhythmic movement, and figure training that called forth physical expressions of women's feminine nature.[58]

According to its advocates, specifically feminine exercise programs had numerous advantages. First, they took place in gender-segregated spaces and made it possible for women to exercise under the guidance of female instructors without exposing themselves to the lewd gaze of male spectators. Second, in contrast to competitive sports and masculine styles of gymnastics, which were deemed "too brutal and therefore [threatened] to ruin the harmony of the female physique," the new styles of exercise offered physical activities that were designed to preserve and enhance women's "figure and feminine grace" and make them "supple, graceful and rounded in form and movements."[59] Typically described as relaxing yet invigorating, such exercises allowed women a measure of organized physical expression without violating their femininity. Third, and perhaps most importantly, these forms of physical activity did not seek to "turn women into athletes" or encourage them to become "unappealingly emancipated," but allowed each woman to develop her body to its fullest aesthetic potential.[60] A harmonious, fit female body, radiating health and "natural" feminine beauty, was the inevitable result of such proper exercise.

Considering their emphasis on style over strength, physical attractiveness over athletic accomplishment, and gender segregation over mixed-sex companionship, it is not surprising that advocates of the new exercise systems met with widespread support even among many former critics of women's physical activities.[61] By advocating new forms of moderate physical exercise that promoted health and fitness along with feminine beauty, female physical educators had clearly managed to stake out a culturally legitimate position. Edged between modern sports and conventional physical restraint, they proposed a compromise that merged athletic enjoyment with activities suitable for female bodies and psyches.

YOUNG WOMEN AND THE JOYS OF MODERN EXERCISE

While physicians, physical educators, and other interested parties debated these issues, young women continued to pursue a variety of physical activities. Some paid scant attention to the words of authorities, delighting in many of those exact activities that most horrified contemporaries. Amanda Christensen, for one, was never deterred from her love of competitive bicycle racing. "I knew, of course, that girls were not supposed to do that," she conceded, "but that never stopped me. Why should people tell me what I could do?"[62]

Most young women were much less assertive and self-confident. While they were enthusiastic about sport and physical exercise, they were also concerned about how their participation in different activities might be perceived. As one young woman wrote to an advice columnist, "I want to have fun, but I am not sure whether it is appropriate for young girls to play hockey."[63] Despite the desire to have fun and take part in what were perceived as "modern" activities, she and many other young women did not want to violate too many cultural norms, and they were unwilling to risk too much social ostracism. Besides, most young women were as concerned about their femininity as were other contemporaries, and despite their interest in physical exercise they did not want to risk appearing "mannish" and unattractive.[64]

Not surprisingly, many girls and young women therefore responded positively to the new forms of exercise advocated by female physical educators. From the early 1920s, both devoted sports enthusiasts and women who had never before participated in organized physical activities flocked to exercise classes. According to Jenny Okkels, "We all took exercise classes."[65] Regitze Nielsen agreed. "Any young girl took exercise classes back then," she recalled, adding with obvious delight that "it was so much fun, such camaraderie."[66]

Part of the appeal of exercise classes for young women lay in the very qualities stressed by advocates of physical exercise. Clearly, the cultural respectability of such activities enabled even cautious young women to engage in various forms of female physicality without exposing themselves to charges of improper behavior.[67] Within a wholesome atmosphere, apart from men and under the supervision of female instructors, they found welcome opportunities for pleasurable and fun-filled physical activity.

Moreover, the particular forms of exercise promoted by female physical educators in the postwar decade offered young women a chance to reshape their bodies in ways that simultaneously set them apart from older generations of women and fit their perception of what constituted a "modern" physical style. Key components of this coveted style included physical self-confidence, a graceful feminine body language, and a certain "natural" ease—all characteristics that female exercise instructors strove to teach their students. Aja Packness, who participated in exercise classes during her youth in the 1910s, recalled, for example, how she and her classmates learned to "swing and sway and twirl so we looked like butterflies. We learned rhythm, graceful poses, and arm movements, but first and foremost we learned to behave freely and unconstrained. I am to this very day grateful to Miss Schjellerup [the instructor] because she taught

Fig. 10. Exercise classes provided many young women with an appealing mixture of physical fun and easy camaraderie. (Reproduced from *Vore Damer*, 1926)

us to walk freely across a dance floor where many people were watching us. And we learned to sit properly on a chair—not shyly out on the edge."[68] Because many physical educators adhered to the philosophy that "each individual [is] endowed by nature with a personal rhythm," exercise classes also encouraged the pursuit of individuality and personal expression, both factors young women associated with female modernity.[69]

In addition to these appealing qualities, the enthusiasm that many young women displayed for the exercise classes sprang from the legitimacy they seemed to grant to sensual pleasure and the pursuit of physical beauty, an undertaking that nineteenth-century moralists had often criticized as evidence of female vanity and self-absorption. Physical educators idealized the healthy, harmonious, physically fit female body, and they were never sparing in their praise of "the beautiful sight of many young, slender female bodies engaged in rhythmic exercise."[70] Many of them actively encouraged women to pay attention to their appearances and to take pride in their efforts to attain "cheerful, agile and healthy" bodies.[71] Of course, the praise bestowed on those who strove to be physically fit entailed an implicit critique of those who failed to do so, but even as they enforced a new set of standards for what constituted an attractive appearance, advocates of women's exercise and physical culture nevertheless succeeded in claiming for women the right to take new kinds of pleasure and pride in their bodies.[72]

In the course of the 1920s, then, the tension between young women eager to explore new forms of physical activity and older contemporaries concerned about the consequences of unrestrained female physicality gradually faded as physical educators managed to develop new forms of female exercise that were sufficiently feminine to deflect charges of improper masculinization and, at the same time, sufficiently exciting and physically gratifying to attract large numbers of young women. Although some female athletes continued to excel in competitive sports and to upstage men in spectacular feats of performance, the fact that the majority of young women turned their energy toward feminine exercise seemed to quell much of the opposition that initially surrounded women's forays into the sporting world.

THE MODERN BODY AND THE MODERN PERSONALITY

That physical educators played an important role in the shaping of the "modern" female body is beyond question. Their arguments contributed to the cultural legitimacy of physical exercise and fitness for women, and their instruction taught many young women to carry themselves in a freer, more self-confident manner. Nonetheless, the particular image of "modern" female physicality that young women sought to cultivate through such exercise programs did not derive from within the circles of physical educators. Instead, that image typically came from popular entertainment and the mass media.

Films, in particular, played a crucial role in the shaping of their ideal. When young women went to the movies, they closely watched not only the clothes and hairstyles of female stars, but also their poses, gestures, and general physical demeanor.[73] Even decades later, Anne Bruun still remembered "that special way Mary Pickford would throw her curls."[74] Gertrud Øst had similar memories. "We were crazy about movies and movie stars," she declared. "We would go [to the movies] as often as we could, and we would read all about [the stars]. We had to see all their films. My favorite was Gloria Swanson. She had such an air about her."[75] Ernestine P. Poulsen was equally enamored with the movies, but her idol was Louise Brooks. "This is pretty embarrassing," she recalled with a giggle, "but sometimes I practiced walking like her. I don't know what it was but she had this special walk."[76]

Closer to home, Danish stage actresses played a similar role in the creation of new images of attractive physical styles. Even though only a minority of young women actually had a chance to witness their performances, media coverage kept fans abreast of the latest news from their

Fig. 11. Movie stars and stage actresses played a crucial role in the dissemination of information about modern styles. Among the most popular Danish stars was Liva Weel whose fashionable appearance and exuberant personality made her an ideal for many young women. (Courtesy of the Royal Library, Copenhagen)

shows, and illustrated newspaper and magazine articles allowed even country girls who never set foot in a theater to get a glimpse of their lively physical styles.[77]

What these movie stars and actresses had in common—and what partly captivated adolescent girls and young women in the postwar decade— was their energetic physicality. Both on the printed page and on the movie screen these icons of female modernity invariably came across as exceptionally dynamic and exuberant, beaming with health and energy. Of course, their beauty and glamour also mattered, but at least in retrospect it was as often their physical style that women who came of age in the 1910s and 1920s seemed to recall. According to Mary Ellen Madsen, Louise Brooks was "always so lively."[78] Lily Enevold remembered Gloria Swanson's "dynamic presence,"[79] and Agnes Sejr thought the Danish actress Liva Weel "wasn't actually very pretty, but there was something about the way she carried herself. You just couldn't help finding her attractive."[80]

But physical demeanor was not the only aspect of star behavior that caught the attention of adolescent girls and young women. The personal dynamism and vivacious, fun-loving attitude that these women seemed to exude was as striking to female fans as their physical exuberance.[81] Meta Hansen, for example, remembered that she admired the immensely popular Danish actress Marguerite Viby for her "liveliness" and Erica Voigt, another star of the Danish entertainment world, because she "always sparkled with her high spirits."[82] Others recalled their favorite actresses as "cheerful," "spunky," "spirited," "gleeful," and "joyful."[83]

For young women it was this combination of a healthy, active, and energetic body and an exuberant personality that constituted a "modern" female style. It is therefore not surprising that those who were eager to appear as "modern" and attractive as their female heroines tried to emulate their styles and to model not only their physical bodies but also their emotional disposition.

For many young women the new style of active and energetic physicality came rather easily. After all, physical activity was pleasurable and gratifying, and with relatively little effort healthy young women were able to be become fit. Besides, many adolescent girls and young women seemed to enjoy physical activities immensely. In photographs from the 1920s, they virtually beam with excitement, and many years later, women still recalled how much fun they had and how much physical pleasure they derived from sport and exercise.[84]

In comparison, a consistently exuberant personality involved more elaborate and self-conscious efforts, especially for those who were not inherently cheerful, easy-going, and optimistic. Such exuberance was certainly not in accordance with the natural inclination of Henny Nedergaard, who described herself as "rather quiet." However, she found that "in my youth, it seemed like you always had to be cheery and chatty. That was not really my cup of tea, but sometime you do things to conform a little, don't you?"[85]

With these last words, Henny Nedergaard pointed both to the constructedness of the emerging style of animated, cheerful femininity and to the popularity that this new style quickly acquired. Among those young women who saw themselves as "modern," it certainly became not just desirable but also practically required. As Esther Winther explained, "If you wanted to be modern, you had to be buoyant. That was just part of it."[86] "If you were sullen or pouty, nobody wanted to hang out with you," recalled Charlotte Hansen, another of the women interviewed for this project.[87]

In the postwar decade, such demands would be reinforced by the larger culture, in which the new female ebullience that had at first struck many contemporaries as silly or shallow soon began to receive widespread support. From the late 1910s, journalists, popular writers, employers, politicians, and other social observers began to lavish praise on young women for their sunny disposition.[88] Having overcome their initial reservations, they clearly found dazzlingly positive, optimistic, smiling, and cheerful young women a charming contrast to the austere Victorian matron and the fragile, delicate lady. When compared with these older models of womanhood, "modern" young women seemed delightfully uncomplicated and robust. As one newspaper joyfully announced in 1920, "Gone is the languid lady of yesteryear. Her time is forever past. In her place, we find the active, sporty, industrious, smiling young daughters of Copenhagen."[89]

But once this particular style had gained cultural currency, it quickly took on a strict normative character. It became, in other words, the expected behavior of all women, and as the 1920s wore on, many of its supporters and advocates turned into rigid enforcers of these norms. In the course of the 1920s, a host of beauty experts, advice columnists, and magazine editors thus took it upon themselves to guide young women toward that "appealing mixture of sweetness and charm" that increasingly became seen as the appropriate "modern temperament" for women.[90]

"AN APPEALING MIXTURE OF SWEETNESS AND CHARM"

From the time they first appeared, exuberant young women were hailed by beauty experts as "a wonderful sight."[91] "All of a sudden young women seem to grace our streets with their charming smiles," marveled one of these experts.[92] Another found them "an adornment" of the urban landscape.[93] Still others praised their "pretty smiles" and "sparkling eyes so full of life."[94] From the early 1920s, beauty experts therefore emerged as some of the most enthusiastic advocates of the new style of feminine exuberance.

Throughout the remainder of the decade, they eagerly promoted this style not only for young women but also for older women. After decades of counseling women on how to highlight their most attractive features and conceal the less fortunate elements of their appearance, they shifted their focus toward advising women on how to attain the proper attitude. Of course, advice on how to disguise a low brow and big ears or how to hide freckles and prevent noses from turning red in cold weather continued to fill part of their columns, but because they saw attitude as central to a woman's attractiveness, experts began to argue that women should scrutinize their emotions as carefully as their appearances. In the word of one beauty counselor, women always ought to make sure that "the mental face" was given "as much attention as the physical face."[95]

In practice, this meant that women should seek to bridle any negative emotions. Most importantly, they should eliminate low spirits, sullenness, anger, and weariness from their emotional repertoire. One way of ensuring this was for women to ask themselves every night whether they had succeeded that day in being, among other things, "simultaneously kind, cheerful, alert, sensitive, and yet firm." "Be sure at all times to watch your disposition," the expert proceeded. "Surround yourself with smiles, and strive to spread happiness."[96]

The promised results of such emotional house-cleaning were considerable. While ill humor would inevitably "reduce one's beauty," cultivating one's personality would automatically improve one's appearance.[97] Wrinkles, for instance, could be prevented or smoothed by a positive outlook on life. "First of all, do not grieve over them," one beauty advice columnist thus advised a distraught twenty-seven-year-old mother of three who had located the first creases around her mouth. "Altogether do not lose yourself in worries. . . . Pay attention to your face every time you fall into thoughts, close your mouth firmly or smile. . . . Seek to be happy, it is amazing what your willpower can accomplish in that respect."[98] Similarly, a magazine article warned that "adverse thoughts," "lies," and "envy" would always be revealed in a person's eyes. "Therefore," the beauty expert concluded, "everything hinges on remaining in control over one's inner emotions if one wants to have beautiful eyes."[99]

But curbing ill humor and anxieties was not enough. According to beauty specialists, women ought to undertake a much more comprehensive emotional reconstruction. "From the minute you wake up," one of these specialists reminded female readers in 1922, "you ought to be out of bed, since laying in bed, dozing, pondering yesterday's events and the tasks of the coming day, often . . . generates too much material for self-reflection and meditation which frequently settles into a certain bitter mood which in turn might pull down the facial lines. . . . If you do not have a sense of humor, be sure to acquire it not least because it flatters."[100] Others encouraged women to take nature walks, read humorous books, and generally "keep [your] eyes open to everything delightful around you" because that would encourage the right kind of positive, optimistic attitude.[101] Should such activities still fail to produce the desired results, beauty experts recommended courses at one of the new "charm schools" that specialized in teaching women the essentials of a appropriate, "modern" demeanor.[102]

For beauty experts, the pursuit of female exuberance was always in the interest of physical beauty, and even though an attractive appearance was increasingly seen as a woman's duty and responsibility, counsel to be cheerful was generally issued as a form of advice. The same cannot be said about similar admonitions from other supporters of the new styles of femininity. Instead, these supporters, most of whom were older and male, began to promote the kind of light-hearted optimism that young women had first introduced not as an option or a means to a beautiful appearance but as a moral obligation for all women.

The logic behind their thinking was simple. As women gained more and more legal rights and social privileges, it was, according to these commentators, their responsibility to modernize their attitude accordingly. "Since slavery has now been abolished, no one—not even the housewife in the privacy of her own home—has the right to pose as 'master,' demanding with egotistical despotism the slavish consideration of all others," one writer reminded women.[103] "A woman no longer has the right," another expert added, "to poison her environment with her bad mood. In our day and age, ignoring consideration and putting aside efforts to cooperate cannot be tolerated."[104] It was time, it seemed to these commentators, that women in general, and feminists in particular, repay their gains by "lightening up."

So-called mood hygienists, a category of self-help experts that emerged in the late 1910s, were particularly adamant in this stance. Over and over again, they attacked what they saw as the forbidding stiffness and self-righteous moralism of older generations of women, reminding them of their "absolute responsibilities not to infect others with their bad mood."[105] Instead they urged women "to practice seeing that life, despite the adversity one might face, has many more bright sides."[106] Admittedly, this was not always easy. As at least one expert conceded, "It can, I suppose, take some time before one has acquired a light and cheerful outlook and disposition, but through watchfulness and exertion of the utmost willpower it *can* be done."[107] And, the experts claimed, it *should* be done. Already by the mid-1920s, the austerity and moral superiority associated with nineteenth-century womanhood had become an inappropriate relic of the past, and the light-hearted style embodied by "modern" women was the new norm to which all women should adhere.

In the course of the 1910s and 1920s, young women successfully pioneered a new style of attractive femininity that incorporated elements of physical and personal expressiveness. Despite considerable opposition, they created a freer, less restrictive physical style than that of their mothers, and they succeeded in securing for themselves the right to new forms of physical activity.

Their success in this endeavor had its price, however. While physical activity granted women new pleasurable experiences and new forms of physical self-confidence, their activities remained severely circumscribed by a (new) set of cultural boundaries for what constituted appropriate feminine behavior. And when young women strove to imitate the carefully cultivated expressiveness and exuberance of popular movie stars and stage actresses, they ended up promoting a new set of stereotypical personality traits against which all women would be measured. Besides, the emergence of new cultural prescriptions suppressing female assertiveness and encouraging light-headed charm tied women into an immense project of psychological self-surveillance that unquestionably functioned to discipline their newfound energy.

Moreover, by committing themselves to an image of cheerful, girlish femininity, young women actively undercut older forms of female authority, and by rejecting the more confrontational tone of early twentieth-century feminists and embracing instead a decidedly pleasant, unantagonistic demeanor, they effectively curbed the potential threat presented by the independent, "modern" woman. In fact, the gradual acceptance of young women's new physical and emotional styles rested largely on contemporaries' emerging conviction that the "modern" woman would be entirely, delightfully feminine, neither frightening nor feminist.

PART II

The New Eve and the Old Adam? The Creation of Modern Gender Relations

In the early summer of 1919, while many contemporaries were still struggling to come to terms with slinky dresses and short skirts, public confidence in young women's morals suffered another blow. In May of that year, a number of foreign naval ships arrived in Copenhagen's harbor. The first few days of the international visit were peaceful enough. Curious locals stopped by the harbor on their way home from work or strolled by in the evening to look at the vessels. But soon crowds of adolescent girls and young women began to flock to the Langelinie wharf, where the ships were lying at anchor. Night after night, they paraded back and forth on the pier in their finest fashions, whistling and cheering, throwing flowers and letters to the sailors. When invited to join private parties on board they eagerly accepted, and opportunities to spend an evening out on the town in the company of the visitors did not go unheeded.

By the end of June, the unruly behavior of Copenhagen's female youth had become an issue of widespread concern. Newspapers railed against "the ill-mannered girls" who "unabashedly and totally openly [forced] themselves on the foreign sailors."[1] Christian groups petitioned authorities to put an end to the "indecency" that "threatens to ruin our society."[2] Prominent women's organizations earnestly appealed to parents to watch their young daughters.[3] And respectable citizens who ventured out at night to inspect the commotion were horrified to find neighboring parks turned into "sites of shameless conduct."[4] Worse yet, observers had to admit that not all of the young women on the harbor were "unemployed factory girls and former domestic servants," from whom such wanton behavior might be expected.[5] Among the culprits were also many "young ladies from very nice families," and to the dismay of observers, these supposedly well-bred daughters often seemed "the most aggressive.[6]

In early July, public concerns became infused with a sense of national embarrassment when British and French naval officers announced that they were considering requesting police protection against the young women's sexual advances. Never, one seasoned French officer explained, had he seen anything like it—"not even in China or on Malta"—and considering that his crew consisted of "largely inexperienced young men," he saw no other immediate solution to the problem.[7] Eager to circumvent such a request, the police took immediate action. On July 6, the entire Langelinie wharf was cordoned off, officially for traffic related reasons, and, the authorities declared, it would remain so "as long as there are foreign ships in the harbor."[8]

The Langelinie affair thus came to an end. The girls and young women disappeared from the wharf. Calm and order were restored. Eventually, toward the end of the summer, the last of the visiting ships departed and the entire episode faded from public memory. For historians, however, the affair is worth recalling because it provides a fascinating glimpse of postwar social and sexual struggles otherwise difficult to discern. For a brief but spectacular moment, large numbers of rowdy young women collectively insisted on their right to new kinds of fun and excitement in the public arena and on their right to engage in forms of cultural and sexual experimentation of which earlier generations of women would never have dreamed.

To most contemporaries, this was anything but a trivial matter. Already troubled by modern fashions, new forms of female independence, declining parental authority over children, and sexual promiscuity, they interpreted the raucous, carnivalesque atmosphere on the harbor as evidence of a problem larger than the "the poor manners of impertinent girls."[9] In their eyes, an entire generation of cocky, self-confident young women, corrupted by a dangerous mixture of independent earnings, unsupervised leisure time, and decadent Hollywood films, seemed to be slipping out of control. As a result, not only members of the older generation, but also young men leveled an all-out attack on the so-called Langelinie girls, eventually succeeding in eliminating their collective presence from public sight.

Fig. 12. Modern young girls on the Langelinie Harbor. (Courtesy of the Copenhagen Municipal Museum, Copenhagen)

If the dramatic, almost theatrical character of the Langelinie affair was unique, the cultural conflicts and anxieties it revealed were not. Throughout the postwar decade large numbers of young women from all social backgrounds continued to rebel against norms and expectations that restricted their pursuit of romance, fun, and excitement. Although rarely as openly and defiantly as that first summer, they continued to push at the boundaries for acceptable female behavior, demanding greater personal freedom and more individual liberties than had traditionally been granted women. Not surprisingly, such demands caused enormous controversy and concern, and particularly in the first half of the 1920s young women met with much opposition. At home they found themselves in constant conflict with parents worried about their daughters' virtue and safety, and in the public arena their behavior remained subject to intense scrutiny. Even the young men whose company they sought and whose backing they counted on often proved more critical than supportive of their longings.

Convincing parents of their right to free time beyond the home was therefore only one of the challenges young women faced. In addition, they had to negotiate very carefully their public presence and their interactions with young men. The ways in which they did this, and the outcomes of their struggles to create more "modern" lives for themselves, are the focus of the following two chapters.

CHAPTER 3

Good Girls and Bad Girls

DESPITE all the media coverage of the Langelinie affair, the voices of the young women who haunted the harbor were practically never heard in contemporary newspaper reporting. Apparently, journalists were more concerned with interpreting the events and assessing their potential consequences than with understanding what drove young women to the pier. But many years later Nikoline Sørensen confided that she had in fact been among the troublemakers. "The newspapers made this big deal out of it," she recalled. "I don't really know why. We were just young girls. It wasn't really anything. We just went there to look. All those sailors from foreign countries—of course it was exciting! So we would bike down and look, hang around for a bit. We were modern young girls, and we wanted a little fun. It was really quite innocent." But when asked what her parents thought of their sixteen-year-old daughter's nightly excursions, she had to admit that she "never told them. Perhaps I did, but I don't think so. They were rather old-fashioned, not very understanding."[1]

Among the many women interviewed for this project, Nikoline Sørensen was the only person to recall having been among the rowdy Langelinie girls, but the story she told echoed the stories of many other women who came of age in the late 1910s and 1920s. Like Nikoline Sørensen, most of these women described themselves as having been "modern" in their youth. And with few exceptions, their definition of what it meant to be "modern" in the 1920s included not just a fashionable body and appearance but also a certain life style that incorporated new forms of individual freedom, enjoyment, and self-expression. As Gerda Eriksen explained, "To be modern, that was how you looked, how you dressed and all that, [but] it was also what you did. We wanted to go out, to decide for ourselves."[2]

As their actions and words made abundantly clear, self-identified "modern" young women were not going to settle for a life centered around duties, obligations, and self-sacrifice, as their mothers and grandmothers presumably had. Domesticity, a main feature of nineteenth-century womanhood, seemed equally unappealing. "To sit at home—no, that was not for us. We wanted more out of life than that," according to Gudrun Skall-Sørensen.[3] Instead, she and many other young women insisted on their right to fun, pleasure, free time, and leisure activities beyond the confines of the home. Because these were claims no generation of young women had ever made before and because insisting on such privileges challenged conventional ideas about parental control, filial subordination, and proper womanhood, they were profoundly controversial. Like Nikoline Sørensen, many women who were young in the 1910s and 1920s therefore found themselves pitted against parents in intense battles over rights and restrictions in their lives.

CLAIMING NEW RIGHTS: YOUNG WOMEN AND LEISURE

As was the case in most other European countries in the early twentieth century, the vast majority of Danish girls left school at the age of thirteen or fourteen.[4] Subsequently, part-time or full-time work soon filled their daily lives, but for young girls being a wage earner did not translate into personal autonomy in any simple sense. In most cases, daughters continued to live with their parents until marriage.[5] Of course, many girls who entered domestic service ended up residing with their employers, and young women from the countryside often found employment that made living at home impossible or impractical, but most daughters who grew up in urban environments tended to stay in their parents' households, whether for financial or practical reasons, or, as Henriette Marie Markfeldt explained, because "that was simply what you did back then."[6]

Most frequently, such living arrangements meant the continuation of young women's obligations to their families. By the 1920s, only the very poorest Danish families had to depend on the economic contributions of adolescent children for survival, but in most households daughters were still expected to help supplement the household income by handing over their pay. Especially in their first years as wage earners, parental control over children's income was considerable. Mothers in charge of the family budget generally kept most of the wages, permitting adolescent wage earners only a limited weekly allowance for personal expenses.

Young women's family responsibilities continued in other ways as well. While sons were given much more leeway, daughters were generally expected to contribute their labor to the household after they arrived home from work. "In my family, all the children were sent out to work after their [Christian] confirmation [at the age of thirteen or fourteen], and we all had to give mother some of the money we earned for housekeeping," Gerda Eriksen recalled of her working class youth in the early 1920s. "But," she continued, "the girls also had their chores—running errands, peeling potatoes, setting and cleaning the table, doing the dishes, bringing up coal from the basement. My brothers never had to do any of that. That was women's work."[7]

But if contributing wages and labor to the household continued to be the unquestioned norm, young women's sense of their rights and obligations vis-à-vis the family was nevertheless changing in other ways in the early decades of the twentieth century.[8] When earnings were sufficient, some daughters decided to strike out on their own and live independently in rented rooms, small apartments, or boarding houses, but given their low wages this was a possibility for the very few. More frequently, young working women sought to use their earnings as leverage to negotiate a stronger position within the family. Especially after World War I, when most families were able to place themselves safely beyond the poverty line, the necessity of individual sacrifice for household survival began to fade.[9] This allowed even working-class daughters to assert their right to new privileges in exchange for their economic contributions, and in the 1920s they did so in increasing numbers.

Young women's sense of what they could legitimately demand from their families clearly sprang from their status and experiences as wage earners outside the home. In the labor market, and particularly in jobs other than domestic service, young women learned a rhythm of time and labor that divided daily life into paid work and one's "own" time. This was a rhythm already familiar to most men, whose lives had long been split into realms of work and leisure. Therefore, (male) wage earners were the obvious beneficiaries when Danish government regulations in 1919 limited the work day to eight hours, allowing working men more free time than ever before. Married women, on the other hand, did not experience a similar shortening of the workday. Whether they worked outside the home or not, housework, child-rearing, cooking, and cleaning were never-ending tasks, and unlike their husbands, they had to snatch their few leisured moments in between domestic responsibilities.[10]

As working women, daughters were precariously positioned between these different patterns of daily life. Even though they took on wage labor much like their fathers and brothers, young women were simultaneously expected to share the steady burdens of domestic work with their mothers and to devote their nonworking time to household labor. It was this discrepancy between expectations fostered by labor market participation in the context of increasing standards of living, and the realities of family life that became increasingly intolerable for many young women in the 1910s and 1920s. In their minds, earning a living and bringing home money positioned them on a par with male members of the family, entitling them to at least some of the same prerogatives. Consequently, while they did not resist having to hand over a substantial part of their earnings, they more and more openly resented that their financial contribution did not always earn them what they considered its reasonable counterpart, namely the right to free time. As a result, families with adolescent daughters were plunged into conflicts about the degree of personal autonomy that labor market participation and wages ought to bestow.[11]

Intrafamilial conflicts are often difficult for historians to document, but in this case tensions between parents and children are easily discernible. They surface, for instance, in the immensely popular advice columns of the 1910s and 1920s.[12] Convinced of their right as wage earners to at least some free time and exasperated by their parents' unwillingness to grant them this privilege, some young women turned to advice columnists, hoping for replies that would affirm the legitimacy of their demands. Among the correspondents was "Betty" who openly questioned her parents' authority. "I work from 8 A.M. to 6 P.M. every day," she explained. "When I come home, I am tired, but I still have to fix dinner and look after my younger sister. In the evenings my parents say I have to do needle-work, but I would rather read or go for a walk. Can they really demand that I stay at home? I am seventeen and a half years old, and I pay my mother Dkr. 8 every week."[13] Similarly, "a Copenhagen girl" found the relationship between rights and duties in her life unreasonable. "Before I leave in the morning," she complained, "I have to light the fire, make coffee and pack lunches. When I come home, the dishes are still sitting there, and there are errands to be run. Sometimes I want to meet my girlfriend at night, but my parents will almost never let me go. They say there is no reason to 'gad about,' but I don't understand what is wrong with having a little bit of fun at night when you work all day."[14]

Other evidence also suggests that many young women openly struggled to obtain the right to leisure and independent activities they thought they deserved. Personal narratives often reveal both the intensity of such conflicts and the ingenuity of young women bent on getting their way. Emilie Johansen, who grew up in a middle-class family in a suburb of Aarhus recalled, for example, how she and her sister enlisted the help of an older aunt in their conflicts with an authoritarian father. "He was so strict. He would never allow us to have any fun, never allow us to go anywhere. It was hopeless. But then my aunt—I guess she was feeling sorry for us— we talked to her, and she hired us to do some cleaning and stuff. And we would get there and she would say, 'Why don't you girls run off to see a movie?' I don't remember if we ever actually did any work."[15] Equally resourceful, Copenhagen native Anna Eriksen depended on the backing of an older brother, who, in exchange for small favors, would promise to act as her chaperon outside the home only to vanish as soon as the siblings were out of their parents' sight.[16]

In addition to such evidence, numerous magazine articles and newspaper columns from the 1910s and 1920s chronicle the anger and bewilderment of parents who found themselves in constant conflict with their daughters. For mothers, this seemed particularly difficult. Not only did their daughters' desire for a "modern" life seem a rejection of their own

Fig. 13. The styles, activities, and behaviors of "modern" young women often brought them into conflict with mothers concerned about their daughters' safety and reputations. Nonetheless, this mother and daughter appear to enjoy their afternoon stroll. (Courtesy of the Danish Women's Photo Archives, Copenhagen)

norms and values, which in itself was hard to bear, but on top of that, some girls directly flaunted their disrespect of maternal authority, especially if fathers were absent, indulgent, or merely lackadaisical.[17] "When my daughter is not at the office, she thinks life has to be lived in a café, or in other places where people are judged according to their dress and style," "Ninka's mother" wrote to a women's magazine in 1921. "If I tell her to stay home even a few nights a week, she acts as if I've just imposed a life sentence on her."[18] "She doesn't listen to me," another mother complained of her seventeen-year-old daughter. "When I tell her to stay home, she just laughs and says that you are only young once, that this is the twentieth century and not the Middle Ages, and that she is already wasting too much of her youth in a dirty factory. Besides that, she has her own money."[19] Even more desperate, the mother of one of the much maligned Langelinie girls told a newspaper journalist that she had "begged and pleaded with [her daughter] not to go there, but it doesn't help. I have to go to work, and my neighbor tells me that as soon as I am out the door, she takes off."[20]

Using whatever means it took, many young working women who came of age in the late 1910s and 1920s thus pushed for new personal freedoms and especially the right to free time. While some parents never gave in to their pressure, most young women seemed gradually to succeed in carving out of daily life at least some uninterrupted time devoted to relaxation and their own enjoyment. From the mid-1920s, the frequency of daughters' publicly voiced complaints declined dramatically, and coming-of-age stories no longer featured such conflicts. Apparently, Ernestine P. Poulsen, born in 1902, described a phenomenon that extended beyond her family when she explained that "I fought a lot of battles with my parents [over the right to leisure]. Perhaps I cleared the way because when my [younger] sisters came along, they did not have to do the same. My parents had kind of accepted that girls also needed time of their own."[21]

This did not mean, however, that conflicts between parents and daughters faded. Rather, the grounds of conflict merely shifted. Much resistance to giving young women free time derived from the material conditions of daily life—the practical assistance of grown daughters was still important for the well-being of many working-class households—and from a more general reluctance to give up control over children. But parents' reluctance also stemmed from their misgivings about young women's actual use of their leisure time. Had daughters simply demanded more time to pursue leisure activities within the home, had they insisted on participating in cooking classes and sewing circles, or had they wanted to attend lectures on hygiene and housewifery, they would probably have been met with more understanding. But these were not the kinds of activities young women longed to engage in, and therefore the question of female leisure remained a contentious issue throughout the postwar decade.

"GOING OUT": A NEW FORM OF FEMALE LEISURE

Working-class and middle-class daughters had of course not been entirely without time of their own prior to the 1920s. Nor had they been completely confined to the home. Girls from the countryside had always been allowed to participate in regional fairs, celebrations, and local get-togethers of young people. Urban working-class daughters had long socialized outside the home on staircase landings and front steps, in backyards, and on city streets or in neighborhood parks, and many middle-class daughters belonged to women's clubs and organizations. What constituted the major departure from convention in the 1910s and 1920s was young women's insistence on their right to "go out," an activity significantly different from the kind of casual socializing that took place outside their parents' windows or in clubs and organizations under adult supervision. "Going out," Regitze Nielsen recalled, "that was when we got dressed up and went somewhere."[22] More specifically, "going out" meant pursuing pleasures that took young women away from home and family, into the public, and, in particular, toward new forms of commercial recreation, including movie theaters, cafés, dance places, and amusement parks.

As a social practice, this form of "going out" challenged older norms for female behavior in several ways. First, it obviously entailed their deliberate desertion from the domestic world, if only momentarily. Second, "going out" meant young women venturing outside familiar neighborhoods and beyond the realm of adult control and surveillance, claiming for themselves the right to an independent, unsupervised social life distinct from familial traditions. Third, as opposed to more traditional forms of leisure for women, "going out" was a strictly peer-oriented activity in which kinship ties had much less significance than freely chosen and carefully cultivated friendships among girls and young women who usually met in school, at work, in clubs and organizations, or in the neighborhood where they lived. Finally, and perhaps most importantly, "going out" meant women's entrance into public spaces traditionally defined as male territory and often imagined as sites of immoral activity where men and women freely mingled, potentially transgressing social and sexual boundaries.

Because each of these four aspects seemed to pose a fundamental threat to the social and sexual status quo, intense controversies between parents and children over young women's new leisure activities reverberated throughout the postwar decade.[23] Years after families had conceded to daughters' demands for more time of their own, parents struggled to control or at least influence their use of that time. By dictating curfews, prohibiting particular activities and specific locations, insisting on being introduced to friends and companions, and demanding the chaperonage of brothers, parents sought not only to protect their daughters against potential dangers but also to maintain at least some authority. Consequently, when young women ventured out into the public sphere, they generally did so under the intense scrutiny of parents who continued to hold some power to revoke their newly won privileges. Thus, even as "going out" gradually became a regular part of young women's lives, treading carefully remained an often perplexing prerequisite.

"PARTNERS IN CRIME": FEMALE FRIENDSHIPS AND PUBLIC LEISURE

Young women who pioneered female participation in public leisure in the early years of the twentieth century found themselves in a difficult position. As feminist scholars have pointed out, women in public always run the risk of being taken for "public women."[24] The city, in particular, is an ambiguous territory for women. It is a zone of individual freedom where ties of family and kinship may be loosened and avenues of escape may open up. Yet exactly because of its promise of freedom and adventure beyond the constraints of family and community control, the city is also a hazardous place where women on their own become vulnerable to moral questioning, sexual advances, and even physical danger.

These were well-known realities to all women who ventured beyond the home. Whether out shopping, taking care of family business, running errands, going to and from work, or traveling independently, women always had to negotiate their public presence. Yet as the postwar generation of young women stepped out, they soon discovered that their insistence on being in public with no other purpose than personal pleasure made their behavior not just the focus of parental concern but also the object of public criticism. Because young women's intrusion into public arenas previously reserved for men disrupted, in the words of Judith Walkowitz, "the public/private division of space along gender lines," and because their unescorted public presence blurred the distinction between respectable and disreputable women, it provoked cultural controversy.[25] In the face of overt hostility, public condemnation of their collective morality, and disparaging remarks about their individual virtue, young women who were eager to explore new forms of fun and excitement, but also concerned about their reputations, therefore had to devise a series of strategies for their own protection.

In her study of young working-class women in turn-of-the-century New York, Kathy Peiss discovered that one prominent strategy to counteract vulnerability in public was to seek safety in numbers.[26] This was a strategy also adopted by young Danish women, who found that going out in pairs or groups made them less exposed to the physical and moral dangers associated with activities beyond familial and community control and protection. As a result, having a girlfriend or being part of circle of female friends was essential for young women eager to have fun. For new migrants to the city, establishing such friendships was therefore one of their first concerns. "I have lived here for two months, but I have no girlfriends yet. Would you please tell me about organizations and the like where a young girl can go alone and meet other young people," one woman thus asked the editor of a women's magazine.[27] "My biggest wish is to get a girlfriend," another wrote. "Could you please tell me how I get that?"[28]

Recollections of women who came of age in the 1910s and 1920s also suggest the importance of female friendships and the prominent role they played in young women's lives. Many years later, Margrethe Jensen recalled, "I had a best girlfriend. We first met in school where we were seated next to each other, but soon we were together all the time. We did everything together, and we had so much fun."[29] Anna Eriksen told an almost identical story. "My best friend was named Ella. We were always together, and we always talked about everything. For a while we even worked in the same place. We would walk there together in the morning, and walk home together after work . . . When we had free time, we usually went places together. . . . 'Partners in crime'—that was how we used to refer to ourselves."[30] Even more pointedly, Thora Smed declared that "things are difficult when you're young. They were for us, at least. You have to figure everything out—what to do, what is right and what is wrong. We were a group of young girls, and we always talked about everything—things you couldn't talk to anyone else about. Hardly a thing we didn't talk about."[31]

As suggested by these accounts, the importance of female friendships rested in part on the emotional intimacy and support they provided. "Being together all the time" and "talking about everything" were central elements in almost all stories about girlfriends. In their efforts to determine what constituted proper behavior and activities, female friends clearly counted on each other for guidance and advice. Yet the importance of female friends as companions in unknown territory and as sources of protection of both physical safety and sexual reputations is also evident. "Unless you were engaged, you couldn't go out with a young man. That didn't look good," Agnes Sejr explained, "and you couldn't go out alone—that didn't look good either—but if you were a group of girls, that was okay. Then you could go out and have fun."[32]

The frequency of letters to correspondence columns, in which young women vented their anger at female friends who had deserted them in public spaces or canceled plans for a night out, also speaks to the significance of this particular aspect of female companionship. In 1923, "Gerda," for example, complained that "for more than three weeks I had plans with my girlfriend to go to a dance in the sports club to which we both belong. The day before [the dance] she told me that she did not want to go. Because I would never consider going out alone at night, this meant that I had to stay at home too. . . . Should she not have been more considerate?"[33] Other young women were infuriated by girlfriends who disappeared with a male companion, leaving them to walk home alone after a dance. Still others threatened to break off friendships after having been stood up in a café or a restaurant. Having a "best friend" or a close-knit circle of "pals" thus seemed to constitute both a safety net and a kind of passport into the world of public sociability without which few young women in the 1910s and 1920s ventured far from home. Although surly, the remark of one male observer that young women "prefer to run in packs" was therefore not without its merit.[34]

Thus, while the importance of female kin for companionship and support clearly declined in the early decades of the twentieth century, the importance of female companionship did not. On the contrary, in a context of cultural uncertainty and social experimentation the significance of close female friends seemed to grow. Especially for "modern" young women interested in exploring new activities in public—including new forms of unsupervised interaction with men—female friendships were crucial.[35] Established on the basis of shared experiences and desires, nourished by the need for counsel and companionship, and carefully cultivated as a strategy to counteract sexual vulnerability and safeguard female respectability in public arenas, these friendships were prerequisites for any successful negotiation of new, difficult, and potentially dangerous territories.

YOUNG WOMEN AND THE PROBLEM OF FEMALE RESPECTABILITY

Where women actually went when they "went out" varied. Depending on where and with whom they lived, which forms of activities and amusements were available to them, how much money they had at their disposal, and how adventurous they felt, young women chose their leisure pursuits from a variety of possibilities ranging from the widely acceptable to the highly controversial. Interestingly, however, geographic location and individual assertiveness seemed more important than class background in their choice of leisure pursuits. Cautious young women came from all classes and backgrounds; so did those who proved most daring, experimenting, or free-spirited.

Because young women of all classes had limited spending money, their most popular forms of public entertainment consisted of a variety of free, outdoor activities. For young women who lived in towns and cities, walking up and down shopping streets, looking at the window displays, evaluating the goods, discussing prices and styles, and occasionally making minor purchases while keeping an eye on other strolling shoppers provided a particularly popular form of entertainment.

In many towns, local choirs, musical ensembles, and military bands gave free Sunday afternoon concerts in public squares and parks, attracting especially young men and women, but also many working-class and lower-middle-class families whose budgets did not afford them other, more expensive forms of leisure activities. Without provisions for seating, these concerts provided ample opportunity to parade one's Sunday best, mingle, meet old friends and new acquaintances, chat, and exchange flirtatious glances.[36] Similarly, ice skating, another conventional pastime that attracted both young people and their parents, remained firmly within the boundaries of respectable behavior.[37] Despite mixed-gender audiences, the participation of older adults in such activities contributed to their

Fig. 14. Bicycle trips were generally one of the more respectable ways for young women to enjoy leisure time outside the home. (Courtesy of the Danish Women's Photo Archives, Copenhagen, Denmark)

respectability, and even the most old-fashioned parents rarely objected to such outings. After all, shopping had long been a central component of middle-class women's leisure, and ice skating and military music hardly incited raucous behavior.[38]

Equally popular among young women were new forms of commercial leisure activities that catered particularly, if not exclusively, to a cross-class and mixed-gender clientele of adolescents and young adults. Movie theaters, for instance, attracted swarms of working-class and middle-class youths. Although many older contemporaries remained uncomfortable with the inappropriate mingling across gender and class lines and with the cheap thrills and seemingly loose moral standards of Hollywood films, young moviegoers found that the darkened auditorium offered hours of exciting, inexpensive, and easily accessible entertainment as well as a convenient place for meeting with friends and possibly engaging in courtship.[39]

Enclosed swimming areas and public beaches also became increasingly important sites for fun, relaxation, and mixed-gender sociability in the

1910s and 1920s. While the immodesty and physical intimacy of "un-dressed, scantily dressed, and fully clothed people mixed together in one big confusion" often shocked traditional sensibilities, warm summer Sundays nonetheless brought such large crowds of young men and women to public beaches that popular wit soon dubbed them "flypapers."[40]

Other popular arenas for spending leisure time included cafés and restaurants. Because of their limited resources, young women typically sought out places that served coffee and dessert rather than full meals. Yet because they were generally inclined to spend more time than money in such places, young women were often made to feel unwelcome. "If you knew the waiter, he would sometimes let you sit over the same cup of coffee all night long," Inger-Marie Rasmussen recalled, "but most often that was not possible. When a haughty waiter came by and asked if 'there was anything else?' for the second or third time, you knew it was time to go."[41] Besides, the presence of men who might be willing to pay the bill in exchange for female companionship made such places more precarious arenas for young women concerned about their sexual reputations.

While straining limited budgets, an afternoon or evening in an amusement park was often easier to negotiate. Having paid a small entrance fee, visitors were free to stroll around, look at the various booths and rides, and enjoy free musical and theater performances, occasional fireworks, and other attractions without additional expenses. Although some amusement parks were scorned by middle-class families because of their rowdy working-class clientele, others—such as the Tivoli Gardens in Copenhagen—were entirely respectable sites of entertainment for families as well as young, single people.

Various forms of theatrical entertainment also appealed to young women. In community halls and neighborhood theaters, they enjoyed cheap slapstick comedies and amateur performances starring local talent and would-be actors. In addition, hotels and restaurants frequently sought to lure customers into their businesses by offering some kind of stage performance as the opening act to an evening of dancing. The most popular form of theatrical entertainment was presented by the revue and vaudeville theaters that flourished in the 1910s and 1920s.[42] Featuring evening programs of comical sketches, singing, and dancing, replete with chorus girls, lavish costumes, and elaborate stage settings, vaudeville shows attracted both young men and women looking for a good time, an easy laugh, and a spectacle of glamour and luxury. Yet young women's participation was generally more limited than men's. Often the price of admission precluded them from attending, and sometimes the sexually suggestive character of songs and acts made them feel uncomfortable.[43] Nonetheless, most young women managed to stay remarkably well-informed about the glamorous costumes, the musical hits, and new dance steps they generated.

However, given the opportunity to choose freely among all available forms of fun and entertainment, most young women would probably not have opted for any of the amusements just mentioned. In the vast majority of cases, dancing topped their list of attractive recreational pursuits. When, for example, the popular women's magazine *Vore Damer* in 1925 queried its readers about their favorite leisure activities, fully 72 percent of the respondents listed dancing as their first choice.[44] Similarly, of the fifty-nine women interviewed for this project, at least fifty-four mentioned dancing as the favorite leisure activity of their youth. It is hardly surprising, then, that the rapidly expanding numbers of restaurants, cafés, hotels, inns, night clubs, and other establishments that offered dancing attracted vast numbers of young women.[45]

Nevertheless, public dance places remained highly controversial public settings for young women throughout the 1910s and 1920s. Like other forms of entertainment that did not encourage community-based, intergenerational sociability, these settings were viewed with suspicion by older generations. The fact that crowded dance floors and lively music facilitated, even encouraged, easy and spontaneous physical intimacy between young men and women only heightened this suspicion. As a result, public dance places constituted an exciting, but also an especially dangerous and difficult terrain for modern young women eager to have fun without jeopardizing their reputations. The tension between excitement and respectability was not unique to public dance places. The mixed-gender clientele and unsupervised mingling of city streets, skating rinks, public beaches, movie theaters, amusement parks, and variety shows could also throw into question the respectability of female participants. Therefore, public dance places merely represented the end point on a spectrum of controversial arenas for female leisure activities, simply heightening the conflicts young women experienced individually and in groups whenever they entered public space.

Although the companionship of female friends provided some measure of protection against potential dangers and missteps, it did not provide them with an inviolable safeguard. Even if young women trusted and depended on each other, there was always the nagging doubt that judgment calls of female friends might be wrong. As Meta Hansen poignantly remarked, "Having a girlfriend meant that you wouldn't get into trouble by yourself. It didn't mean you wouldn't get into trouble."[46] Without female companionship, the likelihood of getting into trouble was simply too great for most young women to risk venturing out, but even the presence of female friends did not ensure safety. To avoid making mistakes and more permanently minimize the risk of getting into trouble, young

Fig. 15. In the mid-1920s, concerns about public morality prompted Copenhagen Mayor Ernst Kaper to undertake an elaborate investigation of the city's nightlife. In spite of the damper his presence apparently placed on public entertainment, the Mayor was shocked by the intimacy among dance partners. (Reproduced from *Blæksprutten*, 1926)

women therefore eagerly sought to determine what constituted appropriate and inappropriate behavior and activities. Throughout the 1910s and 1920s, they continually struggled to define the difference between the two, hoping to establish a set of rules that would ensure protection from moral reproach without sacrificing newfound possibilities for fun and excitement.

Determining what constituted acceptable public behavior and activities was complicated by the fact that only a few public places and activities were entirely off limits for respectable woman. Therefore, simply determining the respectable from the disreputable—and placing oneself on the right side of that line—was not an easy task. Going alone to a restaurant in the afternoon might be perfectly acceptable, for example, but enjoying a cup of coffee in the very same location at ten o'clock at night would be considered highly inappropriate. Waltzing with a young man on the skating rink was one thing; tangoing with him in a night club quite another. Similarly, if watching the latest movie release in a local theater or enjoying oneself in an amusement park in the company of girlfriends provoked only few raised eyebrows, going there alone or in the company of a man to whom one was not officially engaged was likely to generate both gossip and criticism.

"It wasn't so much what you did," Gerda Nybrandt declared when asked to explain what constituted proper behavior in her youth in Aarhus in the 1920s. "It was whom you did it with, and where you did it, and when you did it."[47] Offering an almost identical explanation, Anna Eriksen remarked that "as long as it was daytime, people seemed to think that nothing immoral could take place. Doing the exact same thing when it was dark—now that was a different matter."[48] Agnete Andersen recalled the code of conduct to which she adhered in a very similar way. "Well, how should I explain it?" she mused. "It was just like—you couldn't do this, but you could do that. It all depended on circumstances, whom you were out with, where you were and so on."[49]

While in retrospect these three women maintained that "you just sort of knew" the boundary between acceptable and inappropriate public behavior, other evidence suggests that many young women at the time found determining that line an exceedingly difficult task. The fact that reliable sources of guidance were hard to come by only compounded the problem. Certainly, given their already contentious relationship, most young women did not turn to their parents for advice, and those daughters who did seek their guidance often found the older generation as confused and uncertain as they were themselves. Since the vast majority of young women were already out of school, advice from teachers was rarely an option available to them, and adult leaders of youth clubs, concerned about their standing with parents, were generally cautious and restrictive in their counsel. Writers, intellectuals, and newspaper editors steeped in older traditions of female domesticity also seemed unqualified to guide their path. And especially in urban areas, where organized religion already had lost much of its grip on young people, the prospect of going to a minister for advice never seemed to enter their minds.

In this void, young women tended instead to look to self-proclaimed etiquette experts and advice columnists for suggestions on how to negotiate public behavior and city life. The sheer quantity of letters to women's magazines and advice columns about proper behavior speaks both to the uncertainty women felt and to the significance they attributed to knowing the limits of their new freedoms. In letter after letter, young women consulted these self-proclaimed experts both about the appropriate nature of planned events and about the specific restrictions they ought to place on their escapades. Could a young woman go out alone at night, they wondered? If so, could she casually stroll city streets without being taken for a street walker? Could she smoke cigarettes in public? Could she wear makeup? What about high heels? Could she go to a movie theater? If so, how late? And how frequently? What about an amusement park? A restaurant? What if the restaurant featured live music and dancing? Could she go out alone if she returned home before a certain time? If so, at what time ought she be safely indoors?

In response, editors of women's magazines and advice columnists generally offered very specific guidance, usually in the form of strict, inflexible directives. "No, a young lady may not go to a restaurant alone at night," one columnist warned.[50] "A nice girl should always be home by 11 P.M.," another enjoined her female readers.[51] And no, a respectable young woman could "absolutely not under any circumstances" wear makeup in public—aside from "lipstick and perhaps a touch of rouge."[52]

Often, however, the logic that guided advice columnists' directives seemed incoherent, even arbitrary, and frequently their answers seemed to lack a systematic pattern. When, for instance, one advice columnist maintained that "it is perfectly acceptable for two young girls to go for an evening walk, but a group of girls strolling the streets after dark is an unfortunate phenomenon," she might very well have added to the confusion and uncertainty her readers already felt.[53]

Moreover, while generally encouraging women to avoid being alone in public and being out too late, the advice columnists frequently differed among themselves in their assessment of what constituted proper behavior. When asked almost identical questions in 1928, *Søndags B.T.* declared that a young woman could absolutely not go to the theater alone, while *Ugebladet* found it perfectly admissible "as long as [she] makes sure to sit in the front of the theater and leaves immediately after the show."[54] Such disparate pieces of advice in publications that did not otherwise represent different political and cultural perspectives underscore how confusing and unsettled the standards for women's public behavior remained throughout most of the 1920s and how difficult it was for young women to find the kind of guidance they were seeking. Paradoxically, the only rule constantly reiterated was the one young women already knew and worried about—namely, that there was a boundary between respectable and disreputable behavior and that stepping over that boundary would have consequences that even young women who insisted on being "modern" and leading "modern" lives were not willing to risk.

YOUNG WOMEN AND THE BOUNDARIES
FOR RESPECTABLE BEHAVIOR

Without adequate, consistent, or useful advice from parents, relatives, teachers, experts, or other adults, young women were largely left to themselves to figure out where the line for appropriate public conduct was drawn. Although male intellectuals of the day wasted no time ridiculing their concerns as laughably trivial, this was for young women a serious matter integral to their happiness, physical safety, and general well-being.[55] As most young women knew, simply being in the wrong place at the wrong time could mean exposing oneself to more serious moral questioning than most were willing to risk. Being in the wrong company could have even graver consequences. By spending an evening in the Tivoli Gardens in the company of a girlfriend and a couple of young men who had treated them to coffee and sandwiches, one young woman had inadvertently committed such a blunder. "All of a sudden my fiancé was standing in front of us," she explained in a heart-broken letter to an advice columnist. "Pale with anger, he stared at us, then turned his back on us. . . . The next day he sent back my ring."[56] Occasionally, even women's livelihoods were at stake. When, for example, Inger-Marie Rasmussen allowed her boyfriend to pick her up outside the Copenhagen office where she worked in the late 1920s, she was fired for acting inappropriately even though she "didn't even know [she] had done anything wrong."[57] For obvious reasons, young women therefore went to great lengths in their efforts to determine where and how far they could go without endangering themselves, their reputations, or their general well-being.

Failing to define an unambiguous behavioral code, young women sought an alternative source of protection in asserting their steadfast commitment to moral propriety. In fact, the vast majority of women who came of age in the 1910s and 1920s sought to strike a balance between excitement and the preservation of their reputations through an ideological and rhetorical construction of themselves as "nice girls." In public discourse and private settings they claimed legitimacy for their participation in new forms of public leisure and entertainment by insisting on their innocent intentions and their commitment to notions of female respectability. "We're Just Nice Girls," one newspaper headline thus quoted a young woman.[58] After interviewing a cross-section of "nice young girls," another paper seemed relieved to report that "they just want to have fun."[59] "We're two nice girls, and we wouldn't want to do anything wrong," Ella and Ellen assured an advice columnist.[60] "I'm a nice girl," another correspondent began her inquiry about the etiquette of interaction among casual acquaintances. In private, young women made similar claims. "My family always trusts me when I tell them that I am a nice girl," one young woman wrote in a popular magazine in 1923.[61] "I used to remind my parents that I was a nice girl," Margrethe Jensen recalled.[62]

Young women typically bolstered these rhetorical claims with various concessions in their manners and styles. Though pioneers of new female fashions, they were, for example, extremely cautious about their personal appearances. "Many older people still thought short dresses were a horrible thing, the end of the world or something, so you had to be careful," Dora Ingvardsen explained, adding that in the absence of such care, one might inadvertently throw one's reputation into question.[63] Clearly, the line between acceptable modern femininity and unacceptable tartiness was easily crossed. "Most of all you wanted to make sure that you didn't look cheap," Agnes Sejr recalled.[64] Because conspicuous dress or appearances signaled anything but propriety when measured by nineteenth-century standards, most young women therefore refrained from gaudy colors, shiny fabrics, and extravagant trimmings. They also avoided the most prominent hallmarks of the classic "bad girl," namely, smoking, drinking, and wearing (too much) makeup in public. "Lipstick was all right," Agnes Lundgaard recalled, "as long as it wasn't too much or too red, but painted eyes, we didn't do that. That was not something nice girls did."[65]

In addition, most young women were very cautious about their public comportment around men. Despite their otherwise widely divergent definitions of what constituted proper behavior, all the women interviewed for this project agreed that female respectability not only demanded that a woman never engage in premarital sex, but also that a woman never indicate sexual interest in a man. Being seen as "chasing after men" or as "boy-crazy" would inevitably ruin a woman's reputation.[66] As a result, even decidedly "modern" girls took great pains to avoid any behavior that might be construed in this way.

Paradoxically, then, young women sought to legitimize their participation in new forms of public fun and entertainment by clinging to traditional divisions between "good girls" and "bad girls." Keenly aware that the safest, and possibly the only way to vindicate the right of women to be on the streets and in other public places alone at night was to insist on their own virtue and morality, young women built their case on exactly these grounds. Therefore, rather than challenging the continued division of women into the pure and the fallen and possibly develop a competing politic to the good girl/bad girl distinction, they actively supported it.

The strategy of insisting on being nice girls and of making certain concessions in manners and styles did not succeed entirely in silencing public condemnation of young women's collective morality. Neither did the fact that the number of children born outside of marriage declined dramatically in the early years of the twentieth century. In Copenhagen, for example, only half as many unmarried women gave birth in 1930 as did in 1900.[67] But rather than interpreting such good news as evidence of higher moral standards among female youths, most older contemporaries remained suspicious. As they well knew, various forms of birth control were becoming more easily available in the 1920s, and abortions, although illegal and very difficult to obtain, were not unheard of.[68] Therefore, whether young women as a group were as good as they claimed remained in their minds an unanswered question.

Nevertheless, at least on the individual level, insisting on being a nice girl did seem to prove a surprisingly effective shield against the brunt of moral criticism. Clearly, young women's professed allegiance to respectability fed into the hopes and desires of many older adults. Ironically, it also seemed to resonate with their experiences. Certainly, most older people seemed willing to testify to the morality of young women in their own social circles, and generally they were much less alarmed by the activities of young women they knew personally than by the alleged improprieties of the group as a whole. Many older adults simply seemed to have a hard time envisioning their own relatives and acquaintances as licentious rebels and sex radicals. Symptomatically, the mother of one of the scandalous Langelinie girls thus defended her offspring by insisting that "she really is a nice girl. She just likes to have fun."[69] Undoubtedly, many other people were also willing, even eager, to trust their own daughters, sisters, cousins, friends, neighbors, and coworkers to be nothing but young girls looking for a good time. As a strategy to counteract individual criticisms, young women's acknowledgment of the divide between good girls and bad girls, and their frequently repeated commitment not to cross that divide, was therefore quite successful. On the immediate level, it served to appease many postwar parents and other older contemporaries, and ultimately it functioned to decrease the suspicion that surrounded young women in the public arena.

Laying claims to respectability had another advantage as well. As historian Brian Harrison has pointed out in his study of the British working class around the turn of the twentieth century, respectability "was never a fixed position."[70] Particularly in a society in flux, where understandings of exactly what separated a good girl from a bad girl varied, almost all young women were therefore able to place themselves within this broad category. This is not to say that all young women had the same chances at being recognized as respectable girls—class status clearly played a role in how their behavior was perceived—but rather than functioning as a rigidly normative and restrictive set of rules, the very malleability of the concept allowed for multiple understandings of proper conduct, and as a result it could potentially include a very broad range of behaviors.[71] This was exactly how young women were able to use the concept to their own advantage.

GOOD GIRL STATUS—BAD GIRL BEHAVIOR

Among the women I interviewed, every single person who described herself as having been "modern" in her youth also insisted on having been a "nice girl." But characteristic of the profoundly subjective nature of that category, they defined the meaning of the term very differently. Some narrators established their respectability on the basis of their class status, frequently juxtaposing themselves with other (groups of) women. "Oh yes, I was a nice girl, came from a nice family. I even went to the university," Emma Gregersen declared.[72] "I was a teacher," Hedvig Sommersted explained. "It was different from working in an office or a shop. Those girls were more, you know, 'free' [in their morals and manners] and could do what they wanted."[73] Yet, Emilie Johansen, who worked as a secretary for several years before she married, did not consider herself particularly "free." "Office girls were nice girls," she pointed out, "at least all the ones I knew, and that was what most other people thought too, but factory girls, *they* were not nice girls. It wasn't that *I* thought that—I'm sure they were perfectly nice girls—but that was what people thought back then."[74] Yet at the bottom of this occupational hierarchy of respectability, female factory workers also considered themselves nice girls, refuting (middle-) class status as the only, or even the most important, marker of respectability. As Karla Skovgaard explained, "I worked all day, lived at home, gave my mother money when she needed it, didn't go out too much—yes, I would say I was a nice girl."[75] Viola Nørlev, who worked in a soap factory from the time she was fourteen, agreed. "Yes, I think I was a nice girl. I guess that is really up to others to decide, but I think I was. And so were the other girls I worked with, all nice girls, but as we used to say back then: 'As long as our bellies don't betray us, we all remain nice girls.' "[76]

More typically, women tied their respectability to personal behavior rather than class status. Henny Nedergaard, who grew up in a very protective upper-middle class family, explained that she "certainly was [a nice girl]. I never had a chance to be anything else. Until I married in 1926, I was hardly ever allowed to go anywhere without my mother's or my sister's company."[77] Jutta Vestergaard recalled that "I was very shy and not very adventurous. Mostly I liked to stay at home and read, so, yes, you could say that I was a very nice girl."[78] Unlike these two women, Gerda Nybrandt frequently went out with friends, but she nevertheless counted herself among the respectable because "we only went to the nice places, mostly in the afternoon."[79] Growing up in the countryside, Magda Gammelgaard Jensen had fewer choices. She went to dances whenever and wherever they were offered, but because she was accompanied by a large group of friends, she did not consider it inappropriate.[80] Similarly, Anna Eriksen preferred to go out with a circle of friends, but occasionally she would venture out by herself. "But I never went to night clubs or dance halls, only private dances or dances sponsored by different clubs or organizations," she explained.[81] In comparison, Ernestine P. Poulsen was much more adventurous. She admitted that she preferred "to go out alone because then you would meet new people . . . sometimes young men." But, she hastened to add, "I never drank alcohol, just coffee and perhaps a small glass of sherry."[82]

The placement of such dramatically different forms of behavior under the shared rubric of respectability underscores the very flexibility of the category itself. It also illustrates how the absence of one single, cultural standard for respectable and disreputable behavior allowed young women continually to redraw the boundary between the two always to include themselves. The unwavering understanding of the bad girl as "Other" even permitted Rosa Jensen, who at the age of seventeen had a child outside of marriage, to consider herself "basically a nice girl."[83] Moreover, because respectability was such a fluid concept under which a broad range of behaviors could be categorized, young women's participation in activities that were by their own admission not entirely proper, or even slightly risqué, did not necessarily challenge their identity and perception of themselves as fundamentally nice girls.

Public dancing constituted one such activity. Because modern dances encouraged heightened bodily expression, lingering close contact, and un-heard-of intimacy between dance partners, they remained highly suspicious throughout the 1910s and 1920s. If they were carried out in arenas already associated with lower-class immorality, such as the dance hall, they became decidedly unacceptable. Consequently, going to dance halls was one of the few public leisure activities in which no respectable young woman could take part. Nevertheless, with three exceptions, all the women interviewed for this project admitted to having spent at least one evening in a dance hall. When asked to explain this contradiction between their good girl status and bad girl behavior, they typically pointed to subtle distinctions that differentiated their own behavior from that of other, less respectable women, thereby restoring their own respectability. Gerda Eriksen, for example, claimed that "I have never been to such a place. Never. Never at all. Well, that's not entirely true, because once one of my co-workers invited me and we went. She liked it, but I found it too rough."[84] Agnete Andersen declared that "I went sometimes, but not very often. . . . A lot of young girls went almost every night."[85] Rosa Jensen confessed that she frequently went to dance halls, but, she defended herself, "I mostly went there just to have company. I didn't dance very much. You know, some young girls just danced with anybody. I wasn't like that."[86] Similarly, Karla Skovgaard justified her occasional visits to Phønix, a dance hall that by her own admission "did not have a very good reputation," with her desire for adventure and need for companionship in an unfamiliar city. "It wasn't that I went there usually," she explained. "I didn't go there, like that, but of course I wanted to try everything, and I didn't have any home so I had to make sure to have somebody to talk to."[87] Regitze Nielsen, on the other hand, patronized dance halls specifically in order to dance, but she "only danced with nice young men, and

I didn't let them get away with anything. Once you made that clear, you didn't have any problems. Or at least *I* didn't have any."[88]

Thus, by claiming that they were essentially nice girls—even despite behavior that might indicate otherwise—young women were not only able to take part in somewhat dubious activities, but through their individual acts, they, in effect, also constantly redrew the boundaries for what was deemed socially acceptable for young women as a group. By continually seeking to determine how far a "good girl" could go without becoming a "bad girl" and by pushing at the limits they encountered, young women gradually managed to expand the scope of socially acceptable activities for women and to place entirely new, and more flexible, categories of behavior under the rubric of female respectability.

In the course of the 1920s, "modern" young women secured for themselves new personal freedoms, including the right to leisure and participation in commercial entertainment. Because most unmarried women continued to live with their parents, these rights were not won without conflict. In most homes parents were leery about giving up control and authority over their children, even as they became adolescents and young adults. Mothers, who were simultaneously hurt by what they saw as their daughters' rejection of their advice and example and concerned about the physical and moral dangers associated with the public arena, were particularly averse to daughters' independence, and as a result mother–daughter relationships were often deeply strained.

But even though mothers tended to consider their daughters reckless when they ventured out in public, and despite the fact that most older contemporaries interpreted their insistence on fun and excitement beyond the private arena as evidence of eroding morals, young women were deeply concerned about the issue of propriety. With little available guidance, they sought to negotiate ways of being "at home in the city," but because moral categories remained important to them, they sought to do so in a manner that would not endanger their status and reputation as good girls.[89] Interwoven in their rebellious insistence on the right to participate in public leisure and consumer culture was therefore a more traditional acceptance of cultural demands for female sexual virtue. Nevertheless, through the process of social and sexual experimentation in which they engaged, young women managed to challenge the boundaries for acceptable female behavior. By the end of the 1920s, a good girl could certainly get away with things that would not have been possible just ten years earlier.

CHAPTER 4

Beauties and Boyfriends,
Bitches and Brutes

THE RIGHT to participate in public leisure and commercial entertainment constituted an important part of what adolescent girls and young women understood to be a "modern" life in the 1920s, but just as important to their vision of female modernity was the freedom to pursue male companionship and cross-gender camaraderie. In direct violation of older norms and traditions according to which respectable women socialized mostly with other women, typically in and around the home, "modern" young women insisted on enjoying themselves in the company of men, outside the home and without chaperons and adult supervision. Declaring gender segregation and single-sex entertainment a thing of the past—unwarranted, stilted, and simply dull—they envisioned informal socializing across gender lines as part and parcel of the freer, more exciting life they hoped to create for themselves. Voicing what seemed the sentiment of many young women in the postwar decade, seventeen-year-old Lissie P. explained that such heterosocial interaction simply made "everything livelier, much more enjoyable."[1] According to Else C., girlfriends were "fine," but men were "a thrill."[2]

Not surprisingly, such unabashed enthusiasm for mingling with men elicited much commentary in the postwar decade. The gloomiest critics saw it as yet another sign of young women's declining morals; other warned against the general disorder and confusion such socializing would produce. Advice columnists chimed into this chorus, cautioning their female readers that easy availability of feminine companionship might put a damper on young men's interest in marriage and family life. Many employers complained that young women's seeming obsession with "having fun with the young men they meet at night" affected their ability to perform their work.[3] Some feminists even suggested that young women's disappointing failure to show any interest in women's organizations despite elaborate efforts to recruit them might lead to future reversals of some of the gains women had already made.[4]

None of these concerns seemed to have much effect on young women's fondness for male companionship. Already used to being criticized for practically every aspect of their appearances and behavior, some simply turned a deaf ear on their elders. Others dismissed their worries as hysteri-

Fig. 16. As part of their rebellion against older norms and conventions, young women eagerly pursued cross-gender camaraderie, but unlike the two women in this amateur photo, most refrained from drinking alcohol with male friends, fearing that this might compromise their respectability. (Reproduced from *Vore Damer*, 1922)

cal overreactions. Tired of constantly having to defend themselves, a few even tried to turn the tables on the older generation. It was entirely natural for young men and women to spend time together, they insisted. Claiming otherwise, they continued, was not only hopelessly old-fashioned but also the sign of a "twisted" mind.[5] Under all circumstances, they were not willing to relinquish the excitement they associated with mixed-sex sociability.

Still, young women remained deeply concerned about their reputations, and given the fact that few people in the early twentieth century believed that men and women actually could be platonic friends, they had to pursue male companionship extremely carefully.[6] That there were in early twentieth-century Denmark only few socially acceptable spaces where informal socializing between men and women might take place only made matters worse. Coeducational institutions offered one such possibility, but because the vast majority of Danish youths left school in early adolescence, such settings never became the primary sites for heterosexual adventure and social experimentation. Unlike in the United States, where high schools and college campuses became the laboratories for new forms of mixed-gender sociability in the 1920s, in Denmark such youthful experimentation had to unfold elsewhere.[7] Instead, young men and women typically met in more informal arenas, such as private homes, workplaces, public parks, city streets, youth and sports clubs, and a variety of commercial establishments, most of which were deeply problematic for young women who had their reputations and their safety to consider.

GETTING TOGETHER: ARENAS FOR CROSS-GENDER SOCIALIZING

In general, the more private or exclusive the setting, the easier it was for a young woman to negotiate. Socializing in private homes therefore proved the safest space for young women. Even the most conservative parents rarely objected to such get-togethers, especially if the guests included brothers and childhood friends, and few people questioned the propriety of parties that took place under adult surveillance. Yet for adventurous young women there were also obvious drawbacks to these settings. As Anne Kirstine Munk phrased it, the people you met at home were "always the same, and sometimes you wanted to meet someone different."[8]

But going out "to meet someone different" carried its load of difficulties. Public arenas in urban areas were an obvious place to meet new acquaintances, but the more unfamiliar and easily accessible a setting was, the more cautious women had to be. The most public of places, namely city streets, were therefore also the most problematic arena for socializing with men. Throughout the 1910s and 1920s, advice columnists and etiquette experts repeatedly cautioned young women against talking to strangers. In anonymous urban settings it was impossible, they warned, to determine what sort of man a stranger was. As a result, careless young women might inadvertently end up in bad or dangerous company.

Navigating between the poles of safe but confining private amusements and more perilous but also more exciting public activities was no easy task. Understandably, many young women therefore sought companionship in the broad range of gender-mixed clubs and youth organizations that sprang up across the country in the early decades of the twentieth century. Such settings provided an attractive intermediary space between public and private socializing. While offering the possibility of cross-gender camaraderie, adult leadership and surveillance provided at least some protection against undesirable company and unwanted attention.

Organizations that officially purported to have other goals than merely socializing were particularly attractive to young women who wanted male companionship without endangering their reputations. Sports clubs, for example, provided arenas in which young men and women could meet and mingle without having their motives questioned. Although actual sports activities were gender-segregated, most clubs sponsored Christmas parties, end-of-season dances, and other forms of evening and weekend entertainment for all members.[9]

Youth clubs of the major political parties had similar advantages, and like sports clubs their memberships soared in the postwar years.[10] That such growth hardly reflected a new interest in party politics is evidenced in the writings of the leadership of such organizations. Over and over again, party officials expressed their irritation over members' blatant lack of enthusiasm for political lectures and discussion. K. Mathiasen, the president of Conservative Youth, for example, complained that the rank-and-file had "absolutely no interest in politics. [They] only belong to our organization for the sake of the parties."[11] An equally exasperated conservative organizer bemoaned the outcome of a meeting where dinner and dancing were scheduled to follow a political lecture. "Unfortunately," she wrote, "not many had assembled for the lecture. . . . When we got to the dinner, the number of young people had increased considerably. By the time of the dance, the number had grown even more." "This seems to indicate," she reasonably concluded, "that the young people were only interested in the dance. Never mind the lecture."[12] Liberal and Social Democratic leaders struggled with similar problems. Unfortunately, they complained, political discussion much too frequently took the back seat to dancing at organizational meetings. Only occasionally did local chapters remember their true political purpose "and then they engage a speaker," noted one distraught Social Democrat, adding "all I can say is:

Poor man! As soon as he appears on the podium, you will see members taking flight for the door. Only a few people remain seated . . . and throughout the lecture, those eager to dance impatiently peek in the door from time to other. Is he still speaking? Will he never stop?"[13] If Dora Ingvardsen was a typical member of such youth groups, organizational leaders were right to worry. "I was a member of the Liberal Party," she recalled, adding matter-of-factly, "I wasn't a Liberal, but they always had the best parties."[14]

If some young women felt most comfortable socializing with men in organizations that officially had other purposes, others joined youth clubs whose sole objective was to provide a space for cross-gender interaction. Organized by young people themselves and typically sporting self-consciously "modern" names such as The Future, Free Youth, Broad-Minded Youth, and The Gay Friends, these clubs organized dances, dinners, theater performances, carnivals, picnics, bicycle rides, and other forms of outings and excursions. Members usually paid a low monthly fee to offset the cost of rented rooms, and admission policies were quite liberal. The Social Youth Club of 1916, for example, was open to all men and women between the ages of sixteen and thirty years, while The Social Club of 1925 welcomed anybody with an "unblemished reputation."[15] Yet despite their liberal admission policies, the fact that enrollments were usually capped at fifty to one hundred people ensured a certain familiarity among members and made it easier to enforce internal rules of etiquette and proper behavior. Therefore, one member claimed, "Parents who are skeptical about permitting their daughter to go to an open-admission dance" ought not worry about club activities.[16]

But even though clubs and organizations granted a certain legitimacy and provided at least some protection for young women, they were rarely able to compete with the glamour and appeal of commercial establishments. "Unfortunately, even many of our own members prefer to go elsewhere," the president of the Social Club of 1918 had to admit after a poorly attended New Year's party.[17] In retrospect, it was certainly movie theaters, cafés, restaurants, dance halls, and amusement parks that women described as their preferred arenas for fun and mixed-gender sociability. "When we really wanted to have fun and when we wanted to meet young men," Netta Nielsen explained, "we went to a café."[18] "I always liked the Kilden [restaurant]," Regitze Nielsen concurred. "It was such a beautiful place, so festive and so much fun. And it was a good place to meet other young people."[19]

In such easily accessible public settings that allowed for informal, unsupervised interaction among strangers, young women always had to tread carefully. As a result, they typically visited such places as part of a group. Sometimes these groups consisted of women only, but frequently they

Fig. 17. In an effort to maintain a reputation as respectable establishments where "nice" girls did not have to fear being accosted by strangers, some restaurants and dance places posted notices prohibiting guests seated at one table from inviting guests from other tables to dance. Apparently, such prohibitions had limited impact. (Reproduced from *Vore Damer*, 1926)

included brothers, cousins, and other long-standing male acquaintances who functioned as informal chaperons. "I much preferred when there were a number of us," recalled Johanne Nørgaard. "Sometimes I went out with my girlfriend, just the two of us, but I liked it better when there were a crowd of people I knew."[20]

Being part of a group provided an important layer of protection against moral questioning and unwanted attention. It also served another, equally important purpose. It created the possibility for monitored, and therefore relatively safe, contact between young men and women who did not know each other in advance. In these cases, social surveillance curbed at least some of the dangers and difficulties associated with mixed-gender sociability, and it granted women an attractive combination of freedom and protection. With friends nearby, always ready to step in and ward off troublesome men and potentially dangerous situations, they were able to shed some of the caution that always accompanied their forays into the world of cross-gender socializing.

Through experimentation and the use of good sense, young women thus managed to find ways and spaces that allowed them to mingle with men while still protecting as much as possible their safety and reputations. But the prudence and canniness they displayed in the process were not what struck most contemporaries. Watching from the sidelines, they saw only carefree, informal interactions between the sexes, leading many of them to believe that they were living in an age of unprecedented freedom and sexual liberation. Speaking for many people of his generation, one elderly journalist thus insisted that "young people nowadays do exactly what they want . . . without restrictions and without any consideration of what is appropriate."[21]

In the years since then, this perception has lingered. In the popular imagination and in some scholarly accounts of the era, the postwar years are still identified as the decade in which young men and women finally threw off the yoke of Victorian prudery, broke down artificial barriers between the sexes, and emancipated themselves from antiquated notions of gender difference. As they socialized, danced, flirted, and played together, young people allegedly laid the groundwork for freer, more "modern," and satisfying relations between men and women. And whether they did so in New York, Paris, Berlin, or Copenhagen, they supposedly enjoyed themselves immensely in the process.[22]

Yet despite this popular image of uninhibited, carefree, and harmonious heterosexual experimentation, the relations between young men and women were not always particularly congenial in the 1920s. While parents and other older observers might have seen only fun and familiarity among young people, their interactions were always complicated, and beneath the surface of lighthearted camaraderie loomed tension and ambivalence that often erupted into anger and conflict. To uncover this dimension of postwar youth culture, one needs only to listen to the voices of the young men and women who may have enjoyed "wriggling and twisting and waltzing" with each other, but never quite seemed to do so without struggling for the lead and stepping on each others' toes.[23] Figuring out when and where to socialize with men was therefore not the only problem young women encountered in their efforts to create suitably "modern" lives for themselves.

"A CLIMATE OF MINGLED LOVE AND MISTRUST"

Although popular perceptions have remained intact, feminist scholarship has already undercut this image of the roaring, good-time1920s. While acknowledging the emergence of new forms of informal and often fun-filled interaction among young people in public arenas, a series of studies have documented the existence of a darker side to this supposedly Golden Age. In his study of German literature produced during and after the war, Klaus Theweleit, for example, documented a virulent misogyny among male writers.[24] Similarly, Sandra Gilbert and Susan Gubar uncovered in British literature a strong current of gender antagonism and misogynist resentment over what appeared to be unfair gains made by women while men were off fighting the war.[25] In addition, Brian Harrison and Susan Kingsley Kent have described how the alienation of returning British soldiers manifested itself in violent verbal and physical attacks on women.[26] France witnessed similar problems in the wake of the war. According to Mary Louise Roberts, French public discourse was saturated with male voices venting their anger at young women who supposedly had "lived it up" while they were away at the front.[27] According to these authors, dramatically different wartime experiences had created an emotional gulf between men and women that strained gender relations in the 1920s.

Because Denmark had not been directly involved in the war, Danish men and women did not have to struggle to overcome this gulf. While many men had been called up for the national reserve for brief periods of time, they had never been forced into battle, and while daily life had been difficult because of rationing and shortages, women had not been drafted into the labor market and the kinds of jobs that had previously been the preserve of men. Some of the fundamental issues that caused strife and hostility between men and women in other European countries at the end of the war were therefore absent in the Danish context. Young men and women thus had, at least theoretically, a better chance of establishing new forms of camaraderie between the sexes.

Nevertheless, interactions between young men and women were as difficult in the Danish case as elsewhere in Europe. Like their counterparts abroad, Danish youth socialized in what the historian Françoise Barret-Ducrocq has called "a climate of mingled love and mistrust."[28] As elsewhere, contemporary sources spill over with evidence of resentment, frustration, confusion, disappointment, and outright hostility between young men and women. Letters to advice columnists bristle with self-righteous anger over perceived insults and injustices. Popular magazines are filled with young people's furious indictments of the opposite sex, along with articles such as "What I Don't Understand about Women" and "What I Don't Understand about Men."[29] Mainstream literature and popular publications contain unmediated misogynist diatribes, and newspaper articles document ceaseless street harassment and women's incensed reactions.

In fact, gender conflicts were so common in the postwar years that they became a theme in popular culture. Brutish oafs, deceitful boyfriends, ruthless Don Juans, mindless party girls, seductive sexpots, and brazen young women are all staples of 1920s cartoon humor. In 1918, the American film *The Woman Hater* drew large crowds, and in 1925 a British film with the same title met with equal enthusiasm.[30] A few years later, one of the smash hits of the annual Tivoli Cabaret was a male duo singing "We Hate Women."[31] The opening line of another popular cabaret song certainly captured part of the cultural reality when it bluntly pointed out that "Danish men and women do not always get along."[32]

Obviously, it was not only gender-specific wartime experiences that produced conflicts between men and women in the 1920s. Instead, much of the gender antagonism that plagued the postwar years was rooted in other, more specific conflicts over the relative rights that young men and women could claim when they met in unfamiliar settings and circumstances. With few guidelines to follow, they had to determine a new set of rules for proper interaction, and because these rules would reflect men's and women's status vis-à-vis each other, the process of delineating them was tension filled, to say the least.

NEW RULES FOR A NEW TIME?

Because informal camaraderie between the sexes was an unfamiliar phenomenon, figuring out how to relate to each other was a complicated matter for both men and women. As one young man noted in 1924, "Nowadays when a woman goes everywhere and does everything, it is very difficult for a man to figure out how to treat her."[33] "How is a man to know how to treat a woman anymore?" asked another bewildered soul.[34] Obviously, these and other young men were at a loss when it came to relating to women as friends and companions. Did female companionship mean, they wondered, that men had to be courteous and gentlemanly at all times? Would they have to refine their language and manners in order not to offend female sensibilities? Or should young women simply to be treated as men would each other? Most often they found no clear answers to these questions, and they had a hard time imagining new ways of behaving. "No matter what I do," grumbled one young man, "I never seem to do the right [thing]."[35]

Young women seemed equally unsure about how to interact with the opposite sex. On the one hand, they longed for frank conversations and easy rapport. On the other, they did not need advice columnists and etiquette experts, or their mothers, to remind them that "nothing is as delicate as a woman's reputation."[36] As they well knew, simply seeming too anxious for male companionship or too careless in selecting one's company was sufficient to cast doubt on a woman's moral rectitude. Yet, showing too much reserve might mean missing out on having fun.

Their concerns were therefore of a different kind than young men's. Was it really true, they wanted to know, that men found women who went out at night by themselves to be "cheap"? Did men approve of women who wore lipstick? And under which circumstances could a woman allow a young man to walk her home? "I don't want to be prudish, but I don't know what is appropriate," one nineteen-year-old woman wrote, summarizing the dilemma she and many other young women faced.[37]

In public discourse, the uncertainty over new codes of behavior came to a head in discussions over the seemingly trivial issue of male chivalry. Throughout the 1920s, young men and women debated this matter with an astonishing passion, and for that reason alone it is worth examining. What were these discussions about? What caused them? What was it about this issue that triggered such intense feelings? And what does this tell us about the difficulties associated with establishing cross-gender camaraderie?

On the surface, the lines of conflict were clear enough. Over and over again, young women complained about what they perceived as rudeness among men. "Why are Danish men so ill-mannered?" "Femme" wanted to know in 1923.[38] "Girlie" was convinced that "chivalry and courtesy disappeared along with the crinoline."[39] Writing from Italy, another woman was sure that Scandinavian men would "die of embarrassment" if they saw the gallantry with which "even lowly dock workers on the Arno River treat a woman."[40] Adding insult to injury, one of the few Langelinie girls to speak out in public claimed that her interest in the visiting sailors stemmed solely from the fact that the foreigners were "considerate," "gentlemanly," and "chivalrous" companions who did not try to take advantage of "a decent and well-behaved young girl" like herself.[41] "A Copenhagen Girl" agreed. Since "you can use a very strong magnifying glass and still not discover even the tiniest trace of chivalry" among Danish men, she didn't find it surprising that nice girls like herself preferred the company of men like "Pierre and Giovanni, Tom and Jack."[42]

In most cases, young men declared themselves guilty as charged, but, they argued, this was only because chivalry was an outdated form of conduct entirely incompatible with the kind of camaraderie women seemed to desire. "What is it that determines that a man must always be chivalrous toward a woman?" a self-described "nonattentive gentleman" thus asked.[43] Another young man who defiantly labeled himself "nongallant" wanted to know whether "a young woman has any right to be offended because I do not pick her up before a dance but ask her to meet me at a trolley stop?"[44] "Mack and Jack" were equally annoyed by what they saw as unreasonable demands on the part of female companions. "We are two young men," they wrote to an advice columnist in 1923, "who would like to hear your opinion about the behavior of two young ladies. The other night after we had been out dancing together, the young ladies wanted us to escort them home, but we live at the opposite end of town and escorting them home would have taken more than an hour out of our night's sleep, so we refused. Now they don't want to see us again."[45]

The unmistakable tone of anger, resentment, and indignation that runs through this discourse suggests that more than etiquette was at stake in the controversies over chivalry. When young people debated whether men ought to open doors, assist with overcoats, carry packages, offer cigarette lighters, give up their seats in trolley cars, and walk companions home, they were, of course, trying to determine what constituted proper behavior in an era when gender norms were being redefined. That in itself was fraught with difficulty, and the confusion they expressed was genuine. But because both men and women perceived chivalry as a source of power and control, their "conversations" are therefore best understood as part of a much larger struggle over the relative status of men and women in a changing cultural context. For that reason it became such an intensely contested issue.[46]

Certainly, women's insistence on male chivalry was not merely motivated by a desire to indulge in the pleasures that spring from a companion's service and attentiveness. In their eyes, chivalrous behavior indicated, among other things, a certain level of male regard. After all, it had in the past only been disreputable women who could not legitimately demand such treatment. Insufficient male chivalry was therefore seen, even among many self-proclaimed "modern" young women, as an insulting sign of disrespect.

More importantly, young women also perceived chivalry as a sort of sexual safety mechanism. At the heart of the ideology of chivalry lay the notion that men were responsible for serving and protecting women.[47] Therefore, as long as women could hold men to a code of behavior that emphasized courtesy and (sexual) self-control, their ability to protect themselves from physical and moral danger seemed all the greater. And if this potentially greater degree of safety came at the expense of what seemed more egalitarian companionship, that was a price worth paying for most women.

Besides, despite their modernity, young women were not out to eradicate gender-differentiated forms of behavior. While they were eager to assert their independence from older patterns of social interaction and to develop new forms of camaraderie with men, they still insisted on their femininity and on having that femininity acknowledged by male companions. "It might well be," one women poignantly argued, "that women in this country have reached their goal in terms of equality with men, but that does not mean that they have stopped being women."[48]

That sexual equality and continued male chivalry were demands not incongruous with each other was a claim many men found hard to accept. "We don't understand how young girls can demand to be equals and at the same time demand to be treated as ladies," two male friends explained.[49] "Women have by now for many years sought equality with men," another man elaborated, "and it is therefore my infallible [*sic*!] opinion that the ladies must either be entirely independent in all matters and renounce gentlemanly gallantry, or they must relinquish their equality with men."[50]

With such comments, young men laid bare what was for them at the heart of this matter. Clearly, they expected women to reciprocate for the favors and attentions they received with a certain degree of modesty and deference. As Karen Dubinsky has pointed out, the flip side of chivalry and protection is power and control.[51] When men no longer felt they had power and control over women, they were, as they repeatedly stressed, no longer willing to respect a code of conduct that endowed them with a specific set of duties and responsibilities.

Underlying the controversies over the issue of chivalry were therefore much more profound conflicts, most of which derived from young men's resentment over losing a set of gendered privileges and an authority over women that older generations of men had been able to claim. Even though many young men were attracted, at least in principle, to the idea of having fun and enjoying themselves in the company of female peers, they were also deeply ambivalent about young women's entry into what had previously been male territory and their encroachment on what had traditionally been male prerogatives. As one newspaper columnist complained in 1921, "Women have forced their way through every door—into the labor market, into politics, and into entertainment. They are getting more and more rights—rights to this and rights to that—but what about us men? We don't seem to be getting any more rights."[52]

Many young men also took offense at women's relative independence in public arenas. As long as young women had money of their own, they did not have to depend on male companions in order to partake in public entertainment. Although most men had greater earnings and more spending money than their female peers, even those women with the most limited funds were usually able to afford a movie ticket, the admission to an amusement park, or a cup of coffee in a restaurant, and unlike in the United States, for example, young Danish women typically paid their own way when they went out with male companions, at least as long as they were not engaged or going steady.[53] "Of course, we paid for ourselves when we went out," insisted Stine Petersen.[54] "Yes, naturally! Naturally, we paid for ourselves," exclaimed Netta Nielsen, seemingly surprised at the suggestion that men might pay for female companions.[55] While hard on their pocket books, such financial self-reliance had several advantages for young women. First, it allowed them, as Michael Curtin has pointed out, to signal that "the relation between themselves and [male companions] were of a public and egalitarian nature, not romantic as between lovers."[56] Perhaps more importantly, it released them from any obligation to male peers and from the moral suspicion that surrounded any woman who accepted gifts and treats from men who were relative strangers. Besides, paying one's own way also protected young women from ending up, as Nikoline Sørensen phrased it, in an "awkward position" where men "might expect things" in return for their generosity.[57] But rather than appreciating the potential for egalitarian friendships that such practices produced, most young men resented the self-reliance of their female peers, perceiving it as a challenge to male initiative and a lessening of their power.

Finally, and perhaps most importantly, much of young men's resentment grew from their sense that women were in fact not only becoming less dependent, but were also acquiring a whole new kind of power over men. "What are men to do? How can they protect themselves against these attractive, scantily dressed young girls? We are under their spell," a twenty-two-year old man complained in a statement that interwove two of the most common strands in male discourse on postwar gender relations.[58] First, men of all classes and ages spoke of young women as increasingly bewitching and seductive. Whether it was their short skirts, deep necklines, freer body language, or seeming flirtatiousness that led men to this conclusion, they generally agreed that the new generation of women possessed an unprecedented degree of sexual allure. Second, they constantly complained that women were using their wiles, their charms and their bodies as unfair means to gain control over men, who were ill-equipped to withstand such an onslaught. "This is the last and final battle in the war between the sexes," one observer declared in 1924. "After suffrage and all the other rights women have obtained, they are now plotting their final assault. With their physical allure, they are striving to master men who are, after all, only men."[59]

In this light, young men's unwillingness to behave chivalrously begins to take on its deeper meaning. In a situation in which many young men believed that women were gaining the upper hand, they were less than eager to engage in behavior that smacked of servitude to women. In earlier generations, a man who fetched a woman's coat or carried her packages had discreetly underlined his own masculinity through a show of physical ability. By the 1920s, the very same gestures seemed to many young men simply to demonstrate service and subordination to a new generation of women who already possessed too much power over them. Quite understandably, they therefore resisted any involvement in such behavior.

Although the debates over chivalry are revealing of the underlying conflicts that seriously circumscribed any effort to create more frank and egalitarian relationships between young men and young women, they may ultimately be read as fairly innocuous. After all, having to fetch one's own coat is at most an inconvenience, and while ungentlemanly behavior

Fig. 18. Throughout the 1920s, men repeatedly complained that young women were gaining the upper hand in the ongoing battle of the sexes. Sexy, self-confident, and scantily clad, they supposedly left men unable to defend themselves in the face of such a feminine onslaught. (Cover page reproduced from *Flirt*, 1922)

might offend a woman's sensibilities it hardly impairs her autonomy or her freedom of movement. But because (sexual) self-control was a central component of the ideology of chivalry, young men's increasing unwillingness to adhere to this long-standing code of conduct had more serious consequences.[60] Predictably, although unfortunately, it led to an unprecedented level of physical and sexual danger for all women who ventured into public arenas.

SEXUALITY AND MALE POWER IN PUBLIC ARENAS

Like most contemporaries, young men assumed that women's interest in their companionship was at least in part of a sexual nature. In contrast to earlier generations, who had denied that sexuality played a significant role in women's lives, they embraced the more modern belief that women, like men, were endowed with sexual desire, and as their remarks about female dress and appearance suggest, they frequently spoke not only of women's erotic interest in men, but also of their sexual aggressiveness. According to one young man, he and his peers were in fact so mercilessly pursued by young women that they felt like "game without a closed season."[61]

But if young men subscribed to new beliefs about female sexuality, they held on to the long-standing conception of male sexuality as passionate, instinctive, compulsive, and scarcely containable. These were the norms and beliefs with which young men had been raised, and rather than questioning such understandings they reinforced them, constantly pointing to the "inherent" difficulties men had in controlling their sexual nature. In the 1920s, such understandings would complicate interaction between the sexes immensely, and whether or not young men intended it as such, they would function to reassert male power in public arenas and significantly limit female freedoms.

In its crudest form, the doctrine of uncontrollable male sexuality was used by young men to warn women against becoming too "liberated." They also used it to justify any behavior on their part. "As long as nice young girls are indistinguishable in appearance from streetwalkers, and as long as they patronize the same places, a young man ought to be excused if he takes one for the other," one newspaper reporter insisted.[62] Echoing this sentiment, another man argued that "when a woman dresses like a harlot, she should expect to be treated as such. There is no reason to blame men for female excesses."[63] "Women can of course go wherever they please and wear whatever they want," a journalist added in 1925, "but they should be aware of the risks. A man is after all a man, and he will not always be able to control his natural instincts."[64]

Even more moderate young men insisted that women were fundamentally responsible for male sexual behavior. In fact, by the early 1920s, young men seemed to have exempted themselves entirely from any obligation to exercise sexual self-control, placing the responsibility for sexual transgressions squarely on the shoulders of women. Succinctly describing the view that had become prevalent by the mid-1920s, one man thus argued, "A man will seek to take advantage of any opportunity he is given, but a woman can always decide the nature of a relationship. If a man goes too far, it is her fault."[65] In an open letter to Copenhagen's female youth, another man explained that "in the face of truly refined femininity a man's brutality, rudeness and vulgarity will naturally vanish. Therefore, young ladies, do try to be natural and womanly."[66]

The notion that women were responsible for setting sexual limits was of course nothing new in the postwar years. Certainly, nineteenth-century gender ideology held respectable women responsible for controlling and limiting sexual expression. What was new in the 1920s was the notion that *all* women, irrespective of circumstances, class position, or personal reputation, were seen as directly responsible for male behavior. In the past, a man who violated the wishes of a virtuous and/or middle-class woman would have lost his standing as a respectable (gentle)man. By the 1920s, this was less and less frequently the case. In a cultural context that increasingly acknowledged the existence of female sexual desire without challenging popular assumptions about men's unruly sexual nature (or enforcing chivalry as the norm for masculine behavior), young women of all classes were therefore more vulnerable than ever before. Because they were assumed to have an active sexual interest in men, all young single women became fair game, and even middle-class women were losing the protection that their class status had previously granted them.

In practice, this translated into open harassment of women in public arenas, from workplaces to dance halls to city streets. Over and over again, young women repeatedly complained about men's unwanted advances. In furious letters to advice columns, young women wanted to know what to do in order to be "left alone, once and for all," how to "get rid of an annoying man," how to avoid "being bothered in the street," and how to behave around men "who do not want to leave us alone even though we have asked them to do so on several occasions."[67] But besides such efforts at determining how best to avoid "male pests," young women seemed at a loss about what to do, and as a result they often felt deeply vulnerable when out by themselves.[68]

Even more seriously, beliefs about women's sexual interest in men and their responsibility for arousing male companions entered courtrooms and influenced legal decisions. When, for example, the twenty-six-year-old Karl P. pleaded innocent to charges of sexual assault against a fourteen-year-old girl, claiming that the encounter had been consensual since "he had met the girl when she was out walking late in the evening, and she had led him on with her loose talk," he succeeded in sowing sufficient doubt about the girl's morals for the court to dismiss the case.[69] Consequently, in the course of the postwar decade, sexual danger became an ever more present accompaniment for all women in public, and even though crime statistics can be interpreted in a variety of ways, it is symptomatic that the annual number of reported sexual assaults almost doubled in the course of the 1920s, rising from a total of 1190 in 1922 to 2028 in 1932.[70]

Obviously, then, the Golden Twenties had their darker side. Despite young women's enthusiasm for male companionship and despite many valiant attempts to create more informal and fun-filled connections across gender lines, relations between young men and young women were strained. More often than not, misunderstandings and mistrust permeated their interactions, and tensions often erupted into full-scale anger and hostility. The emergence of a new discourse that justified sexual violence against women only exacerbated the situation. Not only did this endanger young women's virtue and physical safety, but it further undercut any chance of creating the kind of free and frank, egalitarian camaraderie between the sexes that women had set out to create in the first place.

HETEROSEXUAL ROMANCE AND COURTSHIP

In this context of gender antagonism and gender conflict, one might reasonably expect romantic relationships between men and women to have been elusive and beset with difficulties. Surprisingly, however, this does not seem to have been the case. Despite, or quite possibly because of, the pronounced tension between unattached men and women, postwar youths demonstrated a striking enthusiasm for permanent relationships, and even though stories about courtships rarely enter the historical record, the available evidence suggests that romantic relationships were much less conflicted than other forms of interaction between young men and women.

The reason for this was not that courtship and romantic interactions took place in different arenas than other forms of cross-gender interaction. From the early decades of the twentieth century, public arenas had slowly begun to replace the home and the immediate neighborhood as the preferred locations for courtship activities for both working-class and middle-class youth, and the expansion of leisure time facilitated the development of romantic relationships in settings beyond family surveillance and control.[71] By the 1920s, most older adults seemed to have accepted this change. Although some parents complained that young people met and parted much too casually and others lamented what they saw as the death of true romance when "young girls no longer spend time eagerly awaiting a letter or a call from a suitor," most did not interfere directly in the amorous pursuits of their sons and daughters.[72] There was in fact among older generations much less concern about youthful courtships than there was about young women's insistence on going out. While parents worried about their daughters' safety and reputation when out in public, they did not seem to suspect them of explicitly sexual behavior. Whether it was because parents actually trusted their daughters to be good girls or because romantic relationships most often were played out in public arenas where possibilities for sexual intimacy were rather limited, they did not seem alarmed over this issue.

As a result, romantic relationships were in the postwar era initiated, shaped, and negotiated almost exclusively by young men and women themselves. Some romances started in the workplace, but they were typically cultivated in other arenas. Sports clubs, political organizations, and youth groups also provided opportunities for meeting and getting to know potential partners. In addition, dance halls, community halls, amusement parks, restaurants, and cafés allowed young people to become acquainted. In the countryside, young people took bicycle rides and went on picnics together, and in urban areas, city streets, town squares, and public parks became meeting places for young men and women. Apparently, just about the only location where postwar youths did not seek romantic partners was at home. Although statistically insignificant, it is at least telling that none of the women interviewed in connection with this project met their future spouses in family settings. With few exceptions, they found their partners through work or leisure activities outside the home, and it was only after a significant period of courtship that partners were brought home to meet parents.

But if the arena for courtship activities shifted in the early twentieth century, those observers who assumed that there were no longer any rules regulating courtship and that young men and women were equally free to pursue romantic interests were clearly mistaken. Even though settings for courtship changed, many older rules for romantic interaction did not. Romantic initiative, for example, remained the exclusive prerogative of men throughout the 1910s and 1920s. For young women to initiate contact or pursue romantic interests directly was neither respectable nor appropriately feminine. As Agnes Sejr recalled, " 'No man will ever want a girl who chases after him'—that was what my mother always told me."[73] Anne Kirstine Munk had been given similar advice. "It just didn't look good when a young girl chased after a man," she explained, and on this one issue she and other young women seemed to trust their mothers.[74]

Popular fiction echoed such norms. Paperback novels and short stories printed in women's magazines typically featured the modest, self-effacing young woman as heroine. It was she, these narratives contended, who won praise, attention, and, most importantly, men's hearts. In comparison, flashier or more assertive women might go out more and have more fun, but their virtue was often questionable, and, at least in these stories, their path to the altar was generally long and exceedingly troublesome.[75] Advice columnists and etiquette experts also repeated this message. When one young woman in 1923 timidly asked whether it would be considered inappropriate "to return the smile of a very nice young man whom I see every morning on my way to work," she was given a stern lecture about the unsuitability of such behavior.[76] So were the two young women who asked "whether there is something wrong in inviting two young men to a dance? We would like to go, but we have no dance partners. Would that be considered too forward?"[77]

Even after protracted periods of courtship, young women were not supposed to push the development of a relationship. Instead, they were constantly admonished to curb any show of assertiveness since "men do not in any way care for aggressive women."[78] The young woman who signed herself "Impatient" fared even worse when she asked for advice after six months of courtship. "He picks me up after work and walks me home every day, and he always walks me home after a dance, but when we reach my front door, he simply shakes my hand and briskly walks away. He has never even tried to kiss me, even though he says he loves me," she wrote, adding "since I am afraid that he will never get around to it, I would like to know whether I can kiss him first?" Even her hastily added postscript that "I am a nice girl and hope to marry this man," did not save her from a scolding by the editor of the advice column who warned her that "no, absolutely not under any circumstances" was she allowed to kiss her timid boyfriend.[79]

Whether and to what extent young women actually followed such advice is of course difficult to determine. Some young women probably did more than merely contemplate taking romantic initiative, and as young woman well knew, they could always encourage the development of a relationship in other ways. "A way that always works well," confided "the experienced woman," "is to make sure to cross paths with him wearing your finest fashions, apparently without noticing his existence and without even glancing at him until you're sure that he has noticed you. At that point you can bestow upon him a brief glance."[80] Other options included a friendly, though not flirtatious, manner, signaling that attention would be welcome. Surely, young women were, as Anne Kirstine Munk pointed out, "not just flowers to be picked [by men]. You had your ways of letting them know if you were interested."[81]

Still, there is a striking contrast between young women's bold insistence on going out and having fun with friends of both sexes and their timid behavior when it came to romantic relationships. Even women who otherwise tended to revel in gleeful memories of their own spunky personalities when young did not describe themselves as having played a particularly active role in attracting their husbands or determining the course of their courtship. "We met in the spring of 1928 at a dance. He asked me to dance. We were married a year later," Thora Smed explained.[82] Emma Gregersen's much abridged version of her life story after the age of twenty-three sounded quite similar. "Then I met my husband," she recalled. "He would walk me home from work. Then we got engaged, were married and had three children."[83] Mary Ellen Madsen had equally little to tell. "We met and got married," she summarized. When asked to elaborate, she merely added, "Well, he asked me out for walks. Sometimes we went to the movies. Then he asked me to marry him."[84] In retrospect these narrators insisted that successful courtships depended on male initiative and an otherwise unusual meekness and unassertiveness on the part of young women.[85]

Scattered contemporary evidence points in the same direction. Although unsuccessful courtships are difficult to trace, some young women described the failure of their relationships in letters to legal experts employed by women's magazines, hoping to take advantage of legislation that entitled women to compensation for financial losses they might have incurred as a direct result of their engagement.[86] At least some of these letters suggest that a young woman's show of independence could have serious consequences for her courtship. Maren H.'s fiancé, for example, broke their engagement after he encountered her in a movie theater in the company of a young man whom she insisted was merely a friend.[87] "A despondent young girl" suffered the same fate after going by herself to a dance sponsored by the Social Democratic Youth Club.[88]

Evidence of male initiative and female passivity as prerequisites for successful courtship can also be found in letters to advice columnists from young women in long-term relationships. "Missy," for example, was uncertain whether it was appropriate to talk to her fiancé "about his thoughts on marriage" even though the couple had been engaged for more than two years.[89] Another young woman found herself in doubt about the same thing. "When one is engaged to a man and one does not know if he intends to get married," she wrote, "is it then permissible to ask in order to get his opinion?"[90]

A number of factors might account for young women's conspicuous timidity vis-à-vis the men they wished to marry. Some women probably realized that if assertiveness and self-assurance were requirements for entering into unfamiliar public territory, such independence was not necessarily appreciated in a potential spouse, and even if a man was initially attracted to a woman's spunk, exuberance, and feistiness, he might have reservations about marrying a "party girl." Young women themselves may also have found different kinds of behavior appropriate for different circumstances. If going out at night called for a certain daring, self-confidence, and ability to fend for oneself, contemplating marriage required a different, more conciliatory attitude. Young women's independence may also have been tempered by the fact that in couples who were "going steady," men were more likely to pay for women when they were out together. Although some couples split restaurant bills and paid for movie tickets separately, many men took pride in being able to pay for an evening out, and some young women may have reciprocated such generosity by a show of acquiescence. If paying their own way had permitted young women a certain independence in public arenas, being paid for put an obvious damper on that independence.

It should also be noted that even those young women who struggled with parents and furiously defended their right to participation in public leisure activities did not see themselves as rebels against the greater social and sexual order, and they certainly did not wish to forego the prospect of marriage. When they feuded with men of their own age, it was not over principles of sexual equality but about their right to be seen and treated as respectable women despite their public activities, and what infuriated them most were men's failure to acknowledge their status as "nice girls" and behave accordingly. While they insisted on having some of the same rights as men, they never challenged the different standards by which men and women would be judged. Once they entered into a romantic relationship, this translated into a concern about not being seen as too pushy, too forward, or in any way sexually aggressive, all characteristics deemed incompatible with respectable, and respect-worthy, womanhood. As a result, romantic relationships retained many of their older characteristics even as "modern" young women made their way into the public arena and began to cultivate new kinds of friendships with men.

In the course of the 1920s, two competing trends thus manifested themselves in the relations among Danish adolescents and young adults. One the one hand, the decade witnessed unprecedented efforts at integration between the sexes. In public and private settings young men and women met and socialized more freely and frequently than their parents and grandparents had ever done, and particularly in group settings, where the presence of friends provided a certain surveillance and social control, they often did so with considerable enjoyment. On the other hand, these encounters were often plagued by tension and conflict. Young women who simultaneously insisted on being treated as "ladies" and on being seen as "pals" left many young men confused. Even more detrimental to the attempt to create frank camaraderie between the sexes was young men's sense of having traditional male privileges and authority challenged by young women's entry into male territory and their relative economic independence of male companions. As they countered these challenges with a new rhetoric of sexual danger for women outside male control and protection, they further undercut the possibility for creating egalitarian friendships between men and women. Symptomatically, it was only in romantic relationships where young women were more willing to forego their personal independence and assertiveness that gender conflicts seemed uncommon.

Still, this did not mean that gender relations among adolescents and young adults did not change in the course of the 1920s, but it did mean that these changes came more slowly and were much more contested than young women had ever imagined. Moreover, even though "modern" young women seemed much less assertive and much more pliant in their romantic relationships with men than in other forms of cross-gender interaction, this also did not mean that they envisioned their marriages to be characterized by the same kind of sexual inequality that had characterized their parents' lives. On the contrary, they left their lives as single women convinced that they would create marital relationships that would be as new and "modern" as their unmarried lives had been.

PART III

"A Great New Task": The Modernization of Marriage and Domestic Life

IN 1923, when physical educator Karen Hansen announced her engagement and upcoming marriage to the prominent Copenhagen businessman Knud Saxtorph, her colleagues in the Female Sports Association were less than enthusiastic. It was not that they doubted her choice of a mate, but in their shower of well wishes was more than a sprinkle of resentment over the impending "loss of this great teacher." Her students were equally ambivalent about the news. While congratulating her, they simultaneously expressed their mournful gratitude for "everything you were for us young girls."[1]

That a wedding announcement would prompt such eulogizing was not uncommon in the early years of the twentieth century, and it is in many ways understandable that female friends reacted with mixed emotions.[2] In the 1910s and 1920s, a woman's entry into marriage marked the end of an era in her life. In most cases, it meant a departure from the labor market and a retreat from activities outside the home. Once married, independent outings came to an end, going to the movies became a rare occurrence, memberships of sports clubs were dropped, and evenings out on the town tapered off. After an independent, often adventurous, life before marriage most brides settled into responsible, domestic adulthood centered around husbands and children.

For "modern" young women this would seem a difficult transition in their lives. After years of wage-earning and relative economic independence, they once again found themselves in the home, financially dependent on others. After having fought for the right to public leisure, they gave up these activities. And after having spent their adolescence and early adulthood breaking boundaries and creating new

Fig. 19. Modern bride surrounded by female friends and relatives, 1919.
(Courtesy of the Danish Women's Photo Archives, Copenhagen)

styles of womanhood, they became wives and housekeepers much like their mothers and grandmothers before them.

Nonetheless, few young women seemed to harbor any serious reservation about getting married. From the mid-1910s, the annual number of marriages rose steadily, growing by more than 46 percent between 1914 and 1930.[3] According to the 1921 census, almost two-thirds of all women had married by the age of twenty-five. By the age of thirty, this number had increased to 75 percent, and of the cohort of women born between 1900 and 1905, only 13 percent never married.[4] Undoubtedly, many women simply saw marriage as a natural part of their life trajectory, never contemplating the alternatives. Some looked forward to motherhood and to having a home of their own. Others were eager to escape the pressures of low-paying, monotonous jobs and to enter into what they hoped to be a financially secure life where they would be provided for by their husbands. Unplanned pregnancies and the birth of out-of-wedlock children also prompted their share of weddings. And some women probably saw their premarital activities as youthful escapades destined to come to an end with the onset of "serious" adulthood.

But getting married was for the majority of young women an issue of neither tradition nor pragmatism. In their minds it did not signify a retreat from modernity or a return to conventionality. On the contrary, it signaled the commencement of yet another new and exciting project that would be exactly as "modern" as the rest of their lives. As Agnete Andersen explained, "It was a new time. Young girls were different. We were modern, and that didn't just end on the day you got married."[5] Contrasting themselves with older generations of women, young wives insisted that they wanted more out of marriage than security, protection, and social respectability. They were not going to settle for husbands who merely brought home the paycheck and provided little else. They were certainly not going to tolerate tyrannical mates. Unlike their mothers, they would not be submissive wives. Theirs were not going to be hierarchical relationships. As the first generations in history, they were going to create loving, respectful, egalitarian relationships between spouses.

Even the prospect of becoming full-time housewives did not seem to faze young wives. Although they scoffed at their mothers' supposedly tedious and dull lives, they did not see housewifery as inherently incompatible with female modernity. But much like marriage, housewifery needed to be updated. Up against widespread perceptions of domestic labor as unskilled and unproductive, they sought to recast women's work in the home as a modern profession, worthy of the same kind of status and respect as that bestowed upon other professions.

The following two chapters investigate the ways in which young women sought to come to terms with the realities of marriage and female domesticity without relinquishing their notion of female modernity. In the course of the 1920s, they struggled to transform both marriage and housework in ways that would allow them to maintain their sense of self. And even though they were not always successful in their efforts, they did manage to alter contemporary ideals of marriage and heighten the status of housewifery sufficiently to ease the tension between being "modern" and leading lives that would appear, at least on the surface, so very much like their mothers'.

CHAPTER 5

From Pragmatic Unions to
Romantic Partnerships?

IN THE EARLY twentieth century, when the social sciences were in their infancy and opinion polls still a rarity, the press frequently sought to gauge public opinion by inviting ordinary readers to comment on a variety of cultural and political matters of the day. Usually all answers were welcome, but in 1921, the Copenhagen daily *Politiken* decided to solicit specifically women's opinions. "What do you think about marriage?" the paper asked its female readers.[1]

After spending a few weeks sorting through the many responses, the editorial staff was pleased to report the results of its query. "Young girls still dream of getting married," the paper joyfully announced. Based on their letters, the editors were quite confident that a husband and a home remained most young women's goal in life. Despite their unconventional manners and styles, young women were, the paper concluded, "really not that different."[2]

Still, the editors could not help noticing a trend that set young correspondents apart from older letter writers. Even though the younger generation seemed eager to marry, they clearly did not expect their marriages to follow the patterns laid out by previous generations. Nineteen-year-old Emma P., for example, believed that "in the old days, the husband decided everything," and that was certainly not how she wanted her life to be.[3] Another young woman insisted that she was not "going to let my husband be the boss. That is much too old-fashioned."[4] Lis and Lise agreed. In their joint letter they proclaimed that they would "only marry husbands who treat us as human beings, not just as their wives."[5] If these women were to have their way, marital relationships were, the paper predicted, "in for a major overhaul."[6]

In the course of the 1920s, Danish marriage would in fact undergo considerable change. Not only would legislative reform establish for the first time ever complete legal equality between spouses, but by the end of the decade a new marital ideal that stressed intimacy and egalitarianism had largely replaced older understandings of proper relations between spouses. Among the most eager advocates of these changes were the women who came of age in the 1910s and 1920s, and in retrospect they would often claim much of the credit for having initiated them. In the words of Emma Gregersen, for example, her cohort "was really the first [generation of women] who didn't just say 'yes' and 'amen' to everything men said. We were really the first ones to change things."[7] In reality, matters were a bit more complicated. While young women did play a crucial role in popularizing, and to some extent implementing, the new marital ideals, the legal changes that laid the foundations for a new kind of egalitarian marriage were hardly their accomplishment. Rather, women who came of age in the postwar decade were in this matter the beneficiaries of long-standing efforts to improve married women's status.

A "NECESSARY ADJUSTMENT"? THE PASSAGE OF MARRIAGE REFORM LEGISLATION

By the time the postwar generation came of age, older women had already long voiced their criticisms of marriage. When asked, for example, by a newspaper in 1915 whether they were "happy in marriage," every single female correspondents had answered in the negative.[8] In letters to newspaper and popular magazines, women had for decades upbraided their husbands for being at best cold, insensitive, and self-absorbed, and at worst aggressive, sexually demanding, and physically abusive. At least since the turn of the century, popular literature, written by and for women, had frequently featured stories about idealistic young wives whose love and hopes of marital happiness were crushed by boorish, tyrannical husbands and the decidedly unromantic realities of daily life.[9]

To this chorus of individual comments feminists had added another, more political dimension to the public discourse on marriage. Already in the late nineteenth century they had managed to push through reform legislation that gave wives the right to dispose of independent earnings and limited husbands' control over joint property.[10] After the turn of the century, they had continued their attacks on married women's legal subordination, arguing that such treatment degraded women and lowered them to the status of servants and children. The gradual enfranchisement of women that took place between 1903 and 1915 only intensified their campaigns. As Danish women were first granted the right to vote for parish councils and later the right to vote for Social Aid Boards and city councils before gaining full suffrage in 1915, the discrepancy between their new political rights and their continued subordination within marriage had become more and more glaring—a fact feminists were quick to point out.[11] How could an enfranchised woman, they asked, be expected to tolerate legal subordination to her husband? If women were to be equal with men outside the home, why not in the home as well? And how could women be expected to marry if it meant giving up fundamental rights?

The message was clear: If married women's legal status was not improved, many women might simply abandon marriage altogether.[12]

Claiming, as women who came of age in the postwar years so often did, that theirs was the first generation to challenge patriarchal authority and female subordination in marriage was therefore an overstatement, to say the least. Long before they were born, a diverse group of women had protested against inequalities between spouses, and they had done this so loudly that male politicians had begun to contemplate marriage reform legislation even before World War I. Especially after women had been granted the right to partake in political decision making on the local level, many contemporaries had come to see women's legal subordination to their husbands as anachronistic.

Under pressure from feminists, a majority of parliamentary members had therefore already in the early years of the twentieth century decided that it was time to appoint an investigative committee that would examine the existing marriage legislation and suggest possible reforms in two areas, namely, "the contracting and dissolution of marriage and the financial and personal relations between spouses."[13] In neighboring Norway and Sweden, feminists had put similar pressure on their governments, and because the Scandinavian countries had a long tradition of comparable family legislation, the result was the establishment in 1910 of the international Nordic Commission on Family Law, popularly known as the Marriage Commission, under the chairmanship of University of Copenhagen law professor Viggo Bentzen.[14]

Between 1910 and 1913, this all-male commission of legal scholars from Norway, Sweden, and Denmark had reviewed marriage and divorce legislation before issuing its first report. Having accomplished this, the same commission, supplemented with one female representative from each country, had begun discussions of how to revise the legal relationship between husbands and wives. In 1918, this work culminated with the release of a second report in which the commission laid out its recommendation for legislative reform.

Even before the commission released its reports, several indicators suggested that change was indeed underway. In 1912, the Danish assembly of bishops had, entirely unexpectedly, decided to revise the wedding vows customarily used in the Lutheran state church. No longer would brides have to commit themselves to obeying their husbands. Instead, brides and grooms would be asked to pledge identical vows that affirmed unity, solidarity, and mutual rights and responsibilities.[15]

The recommendations of the Marriage Commission therefore came as no surprise. In both of its reports, the commission urged the Scandinavian parliaments to adopt legislation that promoted a new kind of sexual equality between husbands and wives. Dismissing the older, religious notion of marriage as a sacred engagement in which a man and a woman relinquished their separate identities to create a new familial unit headed by the husband, the commission instead recommended that marriage be redefined as a legal bond that joined two equal partners without depriving either of them of their individual rights. Within marriage, spouses would have equal obligations to contribute to the maintenance of the household through their labor. Whether this labor took place inside or outside the home, it was to be considered of equal value, and it would therefore justify equal power and status in all decisions regarding the well-being of the household. Moreover, because unpaid labor in the home was to be considered of equal value to paid labor, the commission recommended that housewives be granted the legal right to a fair share of their husbands' income. Finally, spouses were to be given equal rights over children. In case either spouse did not adhere to this, the commission recommended that the aggrieved party might seek assistance from public officials who were to be given the authority to settle disagreements. And should this fail, divorce ought to be made easier and less expensive to obtain.

According to the members of the commission, these recommendations were merely the product of pragmatic considerations. There was, they assured the public, nothing feminist about them. After all, the reports had been drafted by "reasonable, conservative men" committed to the preservation of marriage.[16] Instead, they urged that the recommendations be understood as necessary and timely adjustments, a way to bring marriage in alignment with the requirements of a new age. As Viggo Bentzen, the chairman of the commission, noted in his defense of the proposal, "Women have been granted political equality, which makes the married woman's subordination to her husband particularly irrational. . . . Now we must subscribe to the principle, legally and in our daily lives, that man and woman are equal in marriage, and that marriage is built by two free, equal, ethical individuals." In his eyes, the proposed legislation was therefore "only a confirmation of the development in personal, social, and legal beliefs that has already taken place."[17] H. G. Bechman, a Copenhagen city judge and the secretary of the commission, concurred, insisting that the reforms would simply adjust marriage and divorce legislation better to fit already existing trends toward greater individual freedom and sexual equality. "The vast majority of women and many men consider the present marriage legislation outdated," he argued, adding that the existing legislation "which at one point may have been appropriate, is by now harmful and unfair."[18]

Despite such carefully phrased arguments that deliberately sought to allay public fears and to disassociate the proposed reforms from feminism, which remained controversial, many conservatives still interpreted the recommendations as a ferocious attack on conventional family patterns and sexual hierarchies. Vinding Kruse, a University of Copenhagen law professor, for example, described the report as a "terrifying example of abstract principles applied . . . with no consideration of human nature and the undeniable differences between man and woman."[19] His colleague Knud Berlin found it "indelibly marked by having been prepared by dogmatic women's rights women."[20] Archdeacon Henry Ussing described it as "the last nail in the coffin for marriage,"[21] and the conservative cultural critic Harald Nielsen called it "a bad omen" and a threat against "the natural relationship between the sexes."[22]

These were serious criticisms voiced by powerful men, but the Scandinavian parliaments nevertheless by and large decided to comply with the recommendations of the Marriage Commission. In Denmark, the reform legislation was passed in two phases. Law no. 276 of June 30, 1922, on the Contraction and Dissolution of Marriage eased access to divorce and established rules for spouses' mutual obligations in case of separation and divorce. Simultaneously, Law no. 277 of June 30, 1922, on Minority and Guardianship established parents' equal rights over children born within marriage. Three years later, Law no. 56 of March 18, 1925, on the Legal Effects of Marriage formally established complete legal equality between spouses. This latter part of the legislation specifically stipulated that "husband and wife shall support each other and jointly they shall be responsible for the well-being of the family."[23] In addition, it delineated a new economic relationship between spouses. According to the new legislation, both spouses were obligated "through monetary payments, through activity in the home, or in other ways" to contribute to the economic well-being of the household.[24] Having recognized domestic work as an economic contribution equal to wage work, the law went on to acknowledge married women's economic equality with their husbands and their right to independent funds and equal participation in financial decision making.

For Scandinavian women the legislation constituted a remarkable gain in terms of civil rights. No longer would husbands legally rule over wives and children, and no longer would they have absolute rights in the home. Nonetheless, the legislation was passed in all Nordic countries by overwhelmingly male legislatures, and it garnered support from conservative as well as liberal and left-leaning politicians. Over the objections of angry (male) voters, lawmakers cast their ballot in favor of legislation that in fact eliminated their own privileges as men, raising the intriguing question of why male legislators would actively support the abolishment of rights that they, in the words of one contemporary, "did not exactly appreciate relinquishing."[25]

One reasonable assumption might be that feminists and women's rights advocates had in fact managed to convince legislators of the merit of sexual equality as a political principle; another, that a new constituency of recently enfranchised women voters was able to exercise sufficient control to force politicians' hands. There is, however, very little historical evidence to substantiate such hypotheses. Few elected politicians, male or female, expressed any feminist sympathies, and by the early 1920s, it was already clear that the 1915 enfranchisement of women would not significantly alter the political balance of power.[26] Besides, as was the case in so many other Western nations in the 1920s, the Danish women's movement was floundering after the passage of female suffrage, and the membership of feminist organizations was plummeting as an older generation of activists retired and few young women joined. If feminists had played a crucial role in the early years of the century in terms of having the Marriage Commission appointed, they were therefore far less central in actually having the legislation passed a decade later.

Instead, as was made clear in parliamentary debates, the legislation won the majority of political votes simply because it seemed to most lawmakers the best measure to shore up marriage at what they believed to be a critical juncture in its history. Even if the women's movement was losing steam, politicians were not oblivious to the criticism of marriage that feminists and other women had long voiced. And by the early 1920s two new phenomena made them ever more attentive to the issue. First, there was the widely announced increase in divorce rates. Although the actual figures remained small, the fact that the annual number of divorces more than tripled in the first two decades of the twentieth century—rising from a total of 383 divorces in 1900 to 749 in 1910 and 1294 in 1919—seemed to support feminist claims that something needed to be done if marriage was to survive.[27] Second, the existence of a new generation of young women who seemed to revel in their financial independence and unprecedented personal freedoms weighed heavily on legislators' minds. Like most of their contemporaries, they were convinced that these young women would be hesitant about marrying. Despite statistical evidence that clearly indicated that marriage rates were going up, not down, they still believed that if young women were to be enticed into marriage, legal reforms were a necessity.

These anxieties were clearly reflected in the parliamentary debates that preceded the passage of the legislation. When the liberal prime minister C. Th. Zahle introduced the bill, he specifically noted its potential to increase the popularity of marriage among young women. "We are in a situation where unmarried women have obtained equality with men in society," he argued. "Given this fact, it is only natural that we grant married women the same rights, particularly if we are to counteract the present inclination among young women to prefer concubinage over marriage."[28] Prominent Social Democrat K. K. Steincke agreed, explaining that he considered it "of utmost importance for society to bow in respect to the wife and mother since the welfare of society depends on the number of good homes."[29] The only way to carry marriage "safely through the troubled times in which we are living" was, according to the conservative Inger Gautier Schmit, one of the few women to hold a parliamentary seat, "to bring it into accordance with the modern age, with societal progress, and with women's wishes and demands."[30]

Ultimately, then, it was concern about how best to preserve marriage that launched the new legislation. Rather than a principled effort to promote sexual equality, the laws reflected contemporary concern about the future of marriage in the light of new forms of female modernity and independence. Judging marriage to be at a crossroads, legislators spanning the political spectrum resolved to update the institution in order to make it more attractive to women. By enhancing married women's legal status and acknowledging their economic contributions as homemakers, they hoped to entice young women into marriage, appease dissatisfied wives, curb the escalating divorce rates, and prevent female flight from the home.

Ironically, however, the young women who played such a crucial role in propelling legislators into action did not seem particularly interested in the issue. In public discourse they never voiced their opinions on the matter, and not once was the legislation mentioned in popular magazines aimed at young women. When feminists celebrated what they saw as a victory for all women, young women were conspicuously absent. Expressing what seemed a common sentiment among many young women in the early 1920s, Jutta Vestergaard, who married just a few days before the legislation went into effect, laconically recalled that "for me, it didn't make one bit of a difference."[31]

Many of the assumptions that informed legislators' decisions were therefore fundamentally misguided. Even though many young women did enjoy their status as independent wage earners, few seemed to have any reservations about marriage as an institution. On the contrary, remaining unmarried past a certain age held little appeal for young women. Not only had lifelong spinsterhood by the 1920s become associated with the kind of old-fashioned prudery and repression from which they were actively seeking to distance themselves,[32] but more importantly, social and sexual intimacy with men had become part of young women's understanding of what it meant to be "modern," and marriage was therefore an integral part of their vision for the future.

Still, the remarkable lack of interest in the marriage reform legislation that most young women demonstrated did not mean that they did not care about sexual equality in marriage. They shared with feminists the dream of egalitarian marriage, but they did not share the feminist belief in the importance of legislative change. In the minds of the vast majority of young women, egalitarian relationships were created by individual partners, not by the law. Consequently, they strove to reform the emotional dimensions of marriage and the daily patterns of interactions between spouses, believing that the specific and concrete ways husbands and wives interacted were more important than the legal formalities that circumscribed their relationship. In the end it was lifestyle, not politics, that was their concern.

"COMPANIONATE MARRIAGE": THE EMERGENCE OF A NEW IDEAL

The ideal relationship that young women in the postwar decade were hoping for was what historians have dubbed "companionate marriage." The term is usually used to describe a marital ideal that incorporates characteristics such as companionship, mutual affection, and respect between spouses. In the early twentieth century, this was certainly not a new notion. According to some historians, the idea that marriage should be based at least in part upon affection and mutuality has been a feature of Western beliefs ever since the Reformation.[33] Yet in the early decades of the twentieth century the significance ascribed to emotional ties between spouses grew to unprecedented heights. Simultaneously, new ideas about the role of sexuality in marriage came to replace older ones, and popular understandings of what constituted proper behavior for husbands and wives began to shift. In that sense, the era witnessed the emergence of a new marital ideal, and among its key advocates was the generation of women who came of age in the 1910s and 1920s.

At the core of these young women's marital ideals were trust, sharing, and companionship. Much like generations before them, they envisioned the ideal marriage as a partnership, but in contrast to their mothers and grandmothers they rejected gender difference and gender complementarity as the basis for this partnership. While they expected husbands and wives to fulfill gender-specific roles and responsibilities within marriage, they defined the ideal relationship as one of equal and fundamentally similar partners who shared a deep emotional intimacy. As one young woman noted six months before her wedding in 1920, "I would . . . only want to marry a man who sees me as his beloved, his companion and friend, a participant and advisor in all that life brings."[34] Using similar language, another young woman expressed the same hopes for her marriage. "The thought of sitting with my dearest friend in our own home, enjoying each other's company, quietly pondering the events of the day—that is one of the things I look so much forward to," she confided in a letter to her sister a few months before her wedding in 1924. "I will want to hear everything that is on his mind. [I will want to be] his friend, his assistant, his fellow conspirator on our journey through life."[35]

Further differentiating their beliefs from nineteenth-century notions of an ideal marriage was the emphasis young women placed on physical intimacy. If their parents' generation had shied away from displays of physical affection, young women defined the ideal relationship as one characterized by emotional expressiveness, romance, and affection. In the words of one "happily married young wife," "tenderness and caresses— those are the things that sustain a marriage." Never, she counseled other women, should they "be stingy with or embarrassed by your love."[36]

By the 1920s, new sexual ideologies had also filtered into young women's consciousness. By then, references to Freudian psychology and the writing of European sexologists were common even in popular magazines, and Danish sex reformers had already for years insisted on the importance of sexual enjoyment for both spouses in marriage.[37] Not surprisingly, young women therefore incorporated pleasurable sexual relations as a key component in their marital ideal. As one young wife argued in 1920, "Marital relations, the complete giving of oneself to the other" ought to be the foundation for "a deep and beautiful shared life."[38] According to another young woman, marital success depended on "physical passion, a deep, mutual longing toward complete intimacy and abandonment of oneself to the other." "If this [passion] is not present," she continued, "it is not advisable to enter into marriage since [sexual relations] otherwise easily will make the woman feel degraded, the man disappointed, and daily life together will start crumbling."[39] By the late 1920s, the notion that sexual passion was essential to marital success had become so widely accepted that when the Copenhagen newspaper B.T. in 1930 invited its readers to submit their answers to the question "What makes a marriage happy?" the winning essay emphasized exactly this aspect. "It is important that the two [spouses] are erotically compatible," the prize winners "A. L. and wife" noted. "Otherwise," they added, "their happiness will collapse sooner or later."[40]

Understandably, the generation of women who had insisted on being pals with men before marriage also carried this ideal with them after their weddings. In contrast to older patterns of separate, gender-segregated work and leisure activities for husbands and wives, they conceived of the ideal marriage as one in which spouses led deeply intertwined lives, sharing not only bed and board but also free time, hobbies, and interests. "A husband and a wife should share with each other every aspect of their life . . . and in a good marriage they will naturally want to do so," "Mrs. Marie" declared in 1925.[41] Other women agreed, arguing that a "good marriage is built on true friendship. Shared interests allow a husband and

Fig. 20. Young women typically envisioned the ideal marriage as one characterized by romance, intimacy, and communication, and most brides hoped to be their husbands' equal partner and companion. (Courtesy of the Danish Women's Photo Archives, Copenhagen)

a wife to continue to be good friends. . . . It is therefore of vital impor-tance for a marriage that spouses have good interests in common."[42]

In the course of the postwar decade, then, young women, bent on freer, more exciting lives than those of their mothers, came to conceive of the ideal marriage as an intimate, egalitarian, sexually pleasurable partner-ship between like-minded individuals sharing, and enjoying, their lives to the greatest extent possible.

"A GREAT NEW LABOR OF LOVE"

If women who came of age in the postwar decade were particularly enthu-siastic in their embrace of this marital ideal, the ideal itself did not neces-sarily derive from within their circles. In the 1910 and 1920s popular writers, journalists, psychologists, sexologists, advice columnists, and marriage counselors across the Western world promoted this vision of an ideal marriage.[43] In their eyes, the norms and values that had shaped nineteenth-century marriages had simply become obsolete. Not only did asceticism and self-control seem increasingly old-fashioned in an emerg-ing consumer culture, but patriarchal authority also seemed to violate new, more modern sensibilities. The gradual decline of separate spheres and experiments with cross-gender camaraderie had made emotional dis-tance between spouses inappropriate. And in the light of new knowledge about the human mind and the human body, the kind of sexual repression that supposedly characterized nineteenth- century marriages had become outdated. In the twentieth century, such behaviors no longer had their place, and like the Scandinavian legislators who passed the marriage re-form bills, they believed it necessary that marriages be reformed if the institution was to survive. Up against older norms, they therefore champi-oned intimacy, romance, and camaraderie as the true foundations for a happy marriage, and young women adopted many of their ideas from these sources.[44]

Surely, some young men must have been as interested as their female peers in this new marital ideal, but if that were the case, it was not some-thing to which its many advocates paid much attention. Instead, the vast majority of the experts who played such a crucial role in the conceptual-ization of the new ideal seemed to rely almost entirely on women to carry out their vision. With few exceptions, they directed their counsel toward wives—not husbands or even couples—implicitly delegating to women the responsibility for translating the new ideal into reality. In part, this reflected conventional expectations of women as patrons and regulators of emotional life. As one advice columnist explained, "It is, after all, a good wife who holds the key to family happiness."[45] But by focusing their

attention on women, marriage reformers also acknowledged that wives
had a particular interest in promoting change. While companionate marriage was supposed to promote greater satisfaction for both spouses, they
were keenly aware that women had more at stake in this issue. As one
marriage counselor astutely noted, "Because the husband will have to give
up some of the privileges he has previously had in the home, he can in
most cases not be expected to lead the effort."[46]

In many ways, young women and professional experts therefore depended upon each other in their efforts to reform marriage. Throughout
the postwar decade, young women eagerly read their tracts and listened
to their recommendations, and the woman who wrote to an advice columnist, "I have asked my husband to read your answers," was certainly not
the only one who sought to take advantage of professional expertise.[47]
Experts, on the other hand, quickly realized that even husbands who professed an interest in freer, more egalitarian relationships did not necessarily feel the same urgency about realizing these ideals as the women whey
married, and wisely enough, they therefore turned their attention toward
female audiences, commending them for their willingness to take on what
one journalist solemnly called "this great new labor of love."[48]

But despite such occasional praise, marriage reformers tended to be
more critical than supportive of the women who shared their ideals. Having delegated to them the responsibility for creating new marital relationships, they quickly proceeded to translate that responsibility into a duty
and obligation, and when marriages failed, they typically placed the
blame on wives. As one marriage counselor lectured young brides, "A
husband's love . . . is a fragile flower that must be tended by gentle hands.
If all women owned such gentle hands, marriage would not be such an
unstable enterprise."[49]

Because of their alleged responsibility in this area, women were, for
example, more and more frequently made to bear the brunt of criticism
when husbands lost interest in their wives. As one 1923 headline in a
women's magazine asked, "Whose Is the Fault? Doesn't the Reason for
the Many Divorces Often Lie in Women's Lack of Ability to Renew Themselves?"[50] Over and over again, experts identified wives' carelessness with
their looks as a key source of marital problems. Describing the near demise of one marriage, one magazine columnist typically noted that "during her engagement [the wife was] always dressed up, and her hair was
always waved and carefully set." After the wedding she "slackened off"
and began to appear "at the breakfast table with greasy cold cream on
her face, curlers in her hair and wearing slippers," inevitably alienating
her husband's affections. Only because she mended her ways, insisted the
writer, did the marriage survive.[51] As a result, marriage manuals often

included beauty advice, and beauty experts often presented themselves as substitute marriage counselors.[52]

In addition, women were repeatedly reminded to retain their appeal as partners in conversation. This entailed, experts argued, a general open-mindedness and at least some knowledge of events outside the domestic sphere. "A woman might possess plenty of admirable qualities," one magazine cautioned, "but if she cannot talk about anything besides her household, if she does not read anything, and if she does not know anything beyond the grind of everyday life, then no intelligent man will be able to stand her in the long run."[53] When one young wife somewhat indignantly asked an advice columnist whether "a husband has the right to be disgruntled just because his wife is mostly preoccupied with housework," she should therefore have expected the lecture she was about to receive. "Your husband is right," the editor of the column answered her.

> Today, a wife's duty extends far beyond cooking, baking, and washing. Like her husband, she ought to be interested in all forms of cultural enrichment available to her. She should not just be a washboard, a broomstick, and a wooden ladle. It is her responsibility to be her husband's intellectual match, and she should be interested in those cultural aspects that give life depth and nourishment and provide material for conversations that move beyond ordinary everyday nonsense. . . . In the end, it is the latter that creates the foundation for good fellowship—for marriage itself.[54]

Obviously, married women were not encouraged to expand their minds because of the gratification they might find in this, but because of the pleasure it would bring their husbands.[55] In the blunt words of one columnist, "[A] wife should be interested in the world outside the home if she wants her husband to be interested in her."[56]

Simultaneously, wives were encouraged to tone down their own problems and concerns. Specifically, they should never talk about housekeeping. "Meet him with a bright smile and a loving welcome," one marriage counselor suggested. "Do not immediately launch into a detailed description of all your worries and calamities."[57] Adding to this general advice, another writer explained that "when a husband goes out frequently, it is because he is bored to death of listening to an endless monologue about the butcher and the baker and the grocer and the high prices on everything and about the children who always fight etc. in one never-ending gray monotony. No men like to listen to all that. . . . The wise wife therefore keeps her worries and troubles to herself."[58] Obviously, if wives were to engage their husbands in the kind of intimate conversation they were longing for it would be on terms set by men. Only if they adopted interests and issues deriving from men's world and experiences could they with some justification expect their cooperation.

Popular magazines, marriage manuals, and advice columns soon added yet another requirement to the list of criteria for being an attractive wife. From the mid-1920s, they began to bring up the issue of marital sexuality, reminding women of the importance of being active and interested sexual partners for their husbands. In itself, this emphasis on sexual pleasure in marriage was not entirely new. Since the beginning of the twentieth century, sexuality had generally been presented as a positive feature of marriage for both spouses.[59] What was remarkable about the postwar discourse on marital sexuality was the change in tone. Prior to the 1920s, marriage and sex manuals had been aimed at men, typically giving them advice about how best to initiate young wives into marital sexuality without alienating their affection or crushing their desires.[60] In the course of the 1920s, advice givers shifted their focus from men to women, admonishing wives not to neglect their sexual duties. From the mid-1920s, women were repeatedly reminded of their obligation to retain their spouses' erotic interest or suffer the consequences. If a husband fell in love with another woman, "saving his affection and politeness for her and taking his bad temper out on his wife," it was, one expert warned, most likely "because [the wife] no longer dresses up to please him."[61] A modern wife should, others claimed, "also be a mistress" and "at all times seek to captivate her husband."[62] "Never be cold, indifferent or unwilling to give yourself to your husband if you want to preserve his love," one advice columnist warned. "It will alienate [him] and only bring unhappiness into your home."[63] By the end of the decade, wives were not only expected to engage in marital sexuality with pleasure, but had in fact been accorded the responsibility for maintaining an erotic atmosphere within the home and providing sexual fulfillment for their husbands.[64]

In the course of the 1920s, experts of all kinds thus heaped a dizzying array of new duties and responsibilities on married women. In addition to being in charge of children and the home, they were increasingly expected to be charming, youthful, sexually attractive, interesting, and informed companions for their husbands. In comparison, men met with few requirements. Occasionally, an advice columnist would encourage husbands to "take part in your wife's minor worries and joys" or remind them not to "skimp on a gentle word, a kind glance, or an occasional caress," but generally men were expected to offer little beyond a minimum of cooperation with their wives.[65] Quite ironically, given the emphasis on mutuality in the new marital ideas, experts obviously believed that any modernization of marriage would come through women's efforts, and through women's efforts only. It was therefore on their shoulders that the responsibility for marriages rested, and for that reason they were more often censured for their failures than praised for their efforts.

IDEALS AND REALITIES IN POSTWAR MARRIAGES

When young women entered marriage in the postwar years, it was therefore both with great hopes for the future and with an immense burden of taxing new responsibilities. Fortunately, however, experts were not always necessarily correct in their assumption that the creation of a "modern" marriage would be the concern of wives only. Occasionally, young men would write advice columnists, typically with questions about how to approach an impending marriage, and *Vore Herrer*, a magazine for young men, periodically featured articles about the new marital ideals. Oral history interviews also suggest that at least some husbands were as eager as their wives to be part of a more intimate and egalitarian marriage. "From the moment I met him, he was my best friend," Viola Nørlev recalled of her late husband whom she married in the early 1920s after a brief, but intense courtship. "Always from then on—my best friend. Throughout our marriage, always someone I could count on and trust. We always agreed about things. Always my best friend."[66] Hedvig Sommersted had similarly fond memories of her husband of more than forty years. "From the very start of our marriage, we always shared everything, told each other everything."[67] And Inga Suhr confirmed that her husband "didn't want to have a marriage like our parents either. We agreed that we wanted more out of life. And he did his part."[68]

Still, historical evidence of postwar marriages that were happy, enjoyable, and fulfilling for both spouses is scarce. In the available source material, ranging from municipal and court records to popular magazines and personal writing, postwar brides express their disappointment, bitterness, and frustrations much more frequently than they do their contentment, and husbands criticize their wives more often than they praise them. Because happy marriages generally leave much less of a record than those racked with difficulties and conflicts, this does, of course, not necessarily indicate that most (or even the majority of) marriages failed to live up to spouses' expectations, but an examination of these records does yield important insights into private efforts to realize the new marital ideals.

Most importantly, these records reveal how ardently many postwar brides struggled to bring their ideals and realities into alignment. They also demonstrate that young wives did not necessarily take on the full responsibility (or blame) for the state of their marriages. They expected husbands to be more than reluctant participants in their efforts to create the kind of egalitarian partnerships they were longing for, and when men failed to live up to their expectations, they did not hesitate to criticize them. In addition, these records confirm the claims that new hopes and expectations of marital happiness meant greater potential for failure and frustration and that heightened expectations produced new areas of con-

Fig. 21. While romance and intimacy eluded many young wives, at least a minority succeeded in translating their marital expectations into reality. Kaia Breslau, kissing her husband in the couple's backyard in 1926, was apparently among them. (Courtesy of the Danish Women's Photo Archives)

flicts between spouses.[69] Not surprisingly, when young wives complained about their husbands in the postwar years, it was typically because they violated their new expectations of romance, companionship, and egalitarianism in marriage.

For women who had hoped to be part of a affectionate and emotionally expressive relationship, the absence of romance and passion, for example, was a critical issue. "My husband is seldom kind and never loving anymore," one twenty-eight-year-old wife lamented in 1925. "Even our wedding anniversary has apparently been erased from his memory, and it would never occur to him to bring home flowers."[70] The way husbands seemed to abandon all interest in their own physical appearance also irked many wives. "Before we were married he was always well-groomed, lively, and considerate, but now he always comes home weary and exhausted, barely willing to wash up before dinner," one woman complained.[71] "Even during the Christmas holidays he never washed, shaved, or put on nice clothes," another wife disapprovingly wrote, "and when I ask him, he tells me that there is really no need [to do that], and if he can't even relax in his own home, where can he relax then? Besides, he claims that a man should not be judged on his exterior. Nevertheless, his untidiness bothers me, and I find him rather unappealing when unshaven and in slippers."[72] In striking contrast to the stern lectures they gave women who let their appearances slide, advice columnists tended to side with husbands on this issue, but that did not prevent "The modern Eve" from concluding that "the husband, the typical Danish husband . . . with his big, round stomach, sloping shoulders, unfortunate looking mustache and his thin hair . . . bears little resemblance to the prince of our dreams."[73]

In addition, many women complained that their attentive and charming suitors unfortunately turned into petty, dour, discourteous mates much too quickly after the wedding. "When we were engaged, he was cheerful and kind, obliging and generous," "Ragnhild" recalled after a few years of marriage. "Now he is taciturn and sullen."[74] Another wife angrily complained about the discrepancy between her husband's public and private behaviors. "When we go out, other women will tell me what a wonderful and charming husband I have," she fumed. "If they saw him at home, they would certainly change their minds. [He is] sour and temperamental . . . and rages over the smallest, most insignificant things."[75]

Besides unkempt appearances and moodiness, wives frequently complained about their husbands' unwillingness or inability to communicate.[76] After courtships during which intimate conversations had fueled mutual love and adoration and confirmed young women in their choice of a mate, wives resented when husbands stopped confiding in them and receded into scarce utterances or silence. "The wonderful conversations we used to have . . . have been reduced to a few words muttered between mouthfuls of dinner," noted one disappointed wife after a few years of marriage.[77] "When I ask him questions, he barely answers me," another frustrated wife wrote. "Night after night, he snores on the couch."[78] Considering their home a place of rest and relaxation, some husbands sought to defend themselves against these criticisms, arguing that "a man has a right to just be himself after a long day of work. He shouldn't have to entertain his wife."[79] But for most wives who expected intimacy and companionship in marriage, such claims did not carry much weight. "If all a man wants is a housekeeper, he should hire a housekeeper!" seethed one woman. "He should certainly not marry."[80]

The more firmly women believed in marriage as a relationship between equals who shared interests and decision making, the more difficult it was for them to tolerate their tongue-tied husbands. Not only did the absence of intimate conversation render evenings, weekends, and holidays long and monotonous, but it also undermined in a more fundamental way their ideal of partnership. As a result, one of the most commonly voiced complaints about husbands was their indifference to wives' thoughts and ideas. "As long as [she] is beautiful, or at least good-looking, the average man is satisfied. Her soul she can keep to herself, what would he do with that? That would only be an inconvenience," one woman caustically wrote.[81] Husbands who had the means to provide their wives with a sheltered existence and insisted on female idleness especially triggered the anger and exasperation of women who saw themselves as decidedly "modern" and did not want to be confined to such a narrow position.[82] In one of the many fictionalized accounts of such conflicts published in women's magazines in the 1920s, "Mrs. Inga Beck" realized after three years of marriage that "she could be so much more for her husband if she were only allowed, but he kept her away from everything."[83] Exactly because equality, emotional intimacy, and notions of partnership were so crucial to these women's understanding of what constituted a "modern" marriage, husbands' disregard of conversation or their refusal to confide in their wives proved difficult matters.

While older generations of wives had tended to complain about their husbands' authoritarianism, brutishness, and (excessive) sexual demands, the new marital ideals thus seemed to trigger new types of conflicts between spouses.[84] Young wives eager to establish a more intimate and egalitarian marriage were often frustrated in their efforts, and repeatedly they chided husbands for not living up to their expectations and for failing to contribute emotionally to the relationship. Unlike marriage experts, they obviously assumed that the creation of "modern" marriages would be a joint effort, and even though they did not always receive much support, they nevertheless sought to use the authority of professional experts in their private struggles.

But despite all the conflicts and coaching many husbands never became ideal "modern" mates. In some cases, they were simply not willing to give up the privileges their fathers had enjoyed. In others, they found themselves more comfortable with older patterns of male authority in the family. Even men who in principle subscribed to the new ideals often turned out to be less than keen to work out the implications of these beliefs in their own lives. No matter the reason, such resistance left many young wives in a quandary. To what extent would they insist on being part of what they defined as a "modern" marriage? What consequences would they take if their dreams were not realized? Was it possible to continue their marriage despite thwarted ideals? Were their disappointments sufficient grounds for leaving their husbands?

In the minds of contemporaries there was little doubt that disillusioned young wives would seriously contemplate the possibility of marital break-up. In fact, most observers believed that it was heightened marital expectations and other "modern" phenomena that explained the increase in divorce rates in the 1910s and 1920s. Consequently, in the popular imagination, the ranks of the divorced were largely made up of demanding young women unwilling to compromise their ideals and their befuddled ex-husbands, who could not—or would not—live up to "modern" expectations.

The widespread belief that young women were so committed to the new marital ideals that they were willing to risk social ostracism by seeking a divorce indicates how endangered contemporaries considered marital stability to be. But did young women really feel that strongly about their convictions? Did they find it possible, even desirable, to lead a single life rather than stay in unsatisfactory marriages? Did they actually leave their marriages for these reasons? And how unsatisfactory did a marriage have to be for them to make such a decision?

DIVORCING TRADITION?

The following analysis is based on a sample of 1150 records from Danish separation and divorce cases from the late 1910s and 1920s.[85] As historical sources, these records proved extraordinarily rich. Not only did they provide unexpected insights into the private world of married couples, but they also contained remarkable information that in almost every aspect contradicts contemporary theories and explanations for marital breakdown in the postwar years.

First of all, in striking contrast to popular perceptions, couples who separated or divorced in the late 1910s and 1920s were not particularly young. The average age at the time of legal separation was 36.3 years for wives and 37.6 years for husbands, numbers that only varied slightly between 1914 and 1930. Evidence from the case records also undermines the notion that divorcing spouses were recently married couples who simply did not have the stamina or commitment necessary for marital success. The average length of marriage prior to separation was 8.2 years. Some marriages were admittedly only very brief, as for instance that of Irene and Axel S. After six weeks of married life, they filed for separation, claiming that "we have come to the conclusion that our temperaments are so entirely incompatible that no true happiness will ever be able to exist between us."[86] In 9 percent of the sampled cases, spouses had been married less than two years when a request for separation or divorce was submitted to the authorities. But in a substantial proportion of cases, spouses had been married for more than twenty-five years, and in 12 percent of all cases, the divorcing couple had adult children.[87]

Those who believed divorcees to be affluent, self-indulgent young men and women were also mistaken. Fewer than 5 percent of the sampled couples came from middle-class or wealthy backgrounds. In close to 65 percent of the cases, husbands reported that they were unskilled or semi-skilled blue-collar workers.[88] In an additional 8 percent of the cases, husbands were recorded as being permanently unemployed, permanently institutionalized, and/or destitute. In general, then, those couples who separated or divorced in the course of the 1910s and 1920s were older, had been married for a longer period of time, and were less financially well off than contemporaries assumed.

It was not only popular understandings of *who* divorced but also general perceptions of *why* marriages broke down that were inaccurate. While contemporaries held the emphasis on individual fulfillment and personal pleasure in marriage responsible for the rising divorce rates, very little evidence from the sampled records supports this theory. Among the 1150 examined records, there was only one example (!) of a spouse who acknowledged that thwarted expectations of marital romance and happiness were among her reasons for wanting a divorce. "He doesn't make me happy anymore," the young wife in question wrote of her husband after two years of marriage.[89] In light of the fact that "mutual incompatibility" and "lasting and profound disagreements" became official grounds for divorce after the legal reforms in 1922, this is particularly striking. Even though the law acknowledged such reasons as valid grounds for divorce, it was seldom the stated reason for marital breakdown. Moreover, close examination of the minority of cases in which spouses claimed "mutual incompatibility" as the reason for seeking a dissolution of their marriages often reveal that even then it was, in fact, not new expectations of harmonious mutuality and partnership that undermined their relationship. In one such case, the wife very tellingly disclosed what was really at issue when she explained that "my husband does not provide, and he abuses me in front of my children whereby he has caused our incompatibility."[90] Apparently, then, it was not unfulfilled expectations of personal gratification, companionship, and intimacy that typically drove spouses apart.

The pursuit of new romantic interests was not a strong motivating factor for ending a marriage, either. If husbands and wives were leaving their spouses because of, or in order to pursue, a relationship with a new partner, this was rarely recorded in the divorce proceedings. Only 8.1 percent of husbands and 12.6 percent of wives listed infidelity or actual desertion as the primary cause for the collapse of their marriages. Although some wives did request divorce because their husbands, like Frida J.'s, had "taken up with another woman who he says is a hundred times prettier than me," they remained a small minority throughout the postwar decade.[91]

In general, then, the evidence drawn from case records lends little support to contemporary theories about divorcees as representatives of elevated marital expectations or as frontrunners in a race toward a new sexual order. Rather, the records suggest that even if cultural notions of what constituted an ideal relationship were changing in the postwar years, in practice marriage seemed to remain a relationship more based on mutual obligations and responsibilities than on emotional intimacy and erotic happiness. In most cases, it was spouses' violations of what was perceived to be their gender specific duties and obligations within marriage rather than thwarted expectations of love and romance that prompted separation and divorce.

Expecting, for example, their wives to be in charge of household responsibilities and child-rearing and to provide sexual intimacy, husbands typically listed poor housewifery, neglect of children, and unwillingness to engage in sex as their reasons for requesting a separation or divorce. "The apartment is so filthy that I am afraid for my children's health, and she never cooks a decent meal," one husband complained in 1922.[92] Two years later, August A. submitted a request for separation because "my wife has neglected her home, she has repeatedly denied me intercourse, she has refused to get up and make my sandwiches, my clothes she has also refused to repair, and she has twice told me when I left for work: 'I wish you would fall and break your neck.' "[93]

Particularly when money was tight, wives' failure to be sufficiently frugal also angered husbands. After only eight months of marriage, one Copenhagen husband requested separation in 1926, claiming that he had seen his wife "throw leftovers out of the window" and put "two kinds of meat on her sandwich."[94] Another husband accused his wife of bringing food home to her parents without his permission.[95]

Wives, on the other hand, expected to be provided for, and husbands' failure to do so constituted their most frequently listed complaint. In fact, no less than 60 percent of all wives listed money-related problems as a cause for ending their marriage. "We were married last fall," one young wife explained to the authorities in 1927, "but even though he has a good job, he does not give me any money. I have to fend for myself."[96] Another woman admitted that her husband was "not a bad man," but, she added, "he doesn't bring home enough money for us to live on, and I have a son to take care of."[97]

With bread-winning designated a male responsibility, periods of unemployment, underemployment, or illness placed incredible strain on marriages. "He used to be a good husband," Inga B. wrote in her request for a separation, "but he has been out of work now for more than six months and he doesn't give me anything to live on."[98] In other cases, even relatively short jail sentences brought wives to initiate separation or divorce proceedings because incarceration prevented husbands from providing adequately.

If husbands not only failed to provide, but in effect became financial burdens, many wives found little incentive to stay in their marriages. In 1924, Ella A. requested separation from her husband after three years of marriage because he "only to an absolutely inadequate degree provides for me. Recently he has not given me anything to live on at all, but forces me to work and earn money for his alcohol."[99] Three years later, another woman complained that her husband was "good for nothing. He sits at home all day, using my gas and electricity, while I go out to work. I can no longer afford to feed him."[100]

Even though husbands' failure to provide constituted wives' most common complaint, it was rarely their only reason for ending their marriages. In most cases, physical abuse and heavy drinking were intertwined with economic deprivation. More than 70 percent of the wives who asked for separation in the late 1910s and 1920s listed at least two of these three reasons, revealing both the depth and complexity of their marital problems. Surprisingly, however, while 34 percent of wives mentioned physical abuse as a cause for requesting separation or divorce, fewer than 12 percent listed it as their only or main complaint. Even women who were severely battered often focused on their husbands' unwillingness or inability to provide rather than the abuse they experienced. One young wife who had been so seriously injured by her husband's repeated beatings that neighbors and family members felt compelled to intervene, complained, for example, only about his failure to provide. "Two years ago a storm tore part of the roof off our farmhouse, and he has still not repaired it," she explained in a letter to the local officials. "He squanders all his money on drink, and a man who cannot even keep a roof over the heads of his wife and children, I don't think that's a decent husband."[101]

Such evidence amply documents that marital breakdown in early twentieth-century Denmark was an issue related to poverty, not to the pursuit of personal pleasure. The vast majority of couples whose marriage ended in separation or divorce were poor, and in most cases the conflicts that brought them into contact with public authorities were related to money.

It is hardly surprising that when wives (and in a minority of cases, husbands) finally sought separation or divorce, they generally did so in situations of extremely urgent economic need. "Through my entire marriage I have had to work because my husband never gives me enough money," one woman complained in 1922, "but I am expecting my third child and I can no longer earn enough for us so I would like to be separated."[102] Elise K., a twenty-seven-year-old mother of five, explained in her 1924 note requesting separation that "my husband will not give me any money, and I and the children have nothing to live on, and my parents can no longer help us."[103] Pregnant and with two children under the age of three, another young wife desperately requested assistance from Aalborg county officials in November 1922, explaining that "my husband told me this past Tuesday that he can no longer afford to pay for me and the children, and he has not been home since. He has not paid the rent, and we will be evicted next week. I am expecting before Christmas, and I would like to have this taken care of as soon as possible."[104]

For economically dependent wives struggling with husbands who would not or could not provide for them and their children, approaching authorities with a request for separation or divorce often constituted their last and best hope for improving their situation. Some wives undoubtedly hoped that even the threat of leaving would strengthen their position vis-à-vis husbands who otherwise saw little reason or incentive to change, and frequently this strategy did work to their advantage. A brief note asking county officials to "please send my papers back, as my husband has promised to mend his ways," was the last entry in a large number of case records.[105] Also in other, more direct ways did wives try to gain leverage in their marriages through careful, even shrewd, use of outside intervention. "Mr. Mayor," one woman began her letter in 1927, "I am writing you to ask if you would be so kind as to call in my husband again. After the last time we were with you, he behaved better for a while, but now it is the same again. If you talk to him, I am convinced that will probably improve him."[106] Although unique in the forthright formulation of her intentions, this woman was only one of many wives who counted on the help and support of public authorities in their efforts to secure a decent life for themselves and their children.

Taking advantage of the mandatory administrative attempts to reconcile spouses, of the physical protection and moral sympathy of county officials, and of the political interest in keeping families together, many wives actually succeeded in wresting concessions from their husbands in the course of separation negotiations. Elisa J., for instance, who left home with her three small children in the summer of 1928, only agreed to return after her husband permitted that his weekly earnings be paid directly to her by his employer.[107] Once husbands promised or were ordered to hand over their paycheck for housekeeping purposes, many wives agreed to continue married life.

For other women, unwilling or unable to reconcile with their husbands, legal separation or divorce provided a way out of a bad marriage and opened the possibility of entering another, more desirable relationship. "My husband traveled to America six years ago. He was supposed to send money, but I have not heard from him since, and now I have met another man who has offered to marry and support me," one woman thus noted in 1929 in her request for a divorce.[108] Another wife who had conspired with her mother and two female friends to produce fabricated evidence of infidelity on the part of her husband explained to the police after her scheme had been exposed that "he never treats me right, he uses obscene language in front of me, and he never gives me any housekeeping money. We thought I should get another husband while I'm young and good-looking and still can."[109]

Even without new marriage prospects, legal separation or divorce held the potential of improving wives' financial situation. In close to 40 percent of all the sampled cases, husbands were ordered to pay alimony to their former wives at least during the period of legal separation. Moreover, after the legal reforms in 1922, fathers were mandated in almost all cases to pay child support for those children who remained with their mothers. In case husbands neglected these financial obligations, women were legally entitled to request the monthly payments from the state, which in turn attempted to recover its costs from the delinquent provider. For wives who during their marriages had constantly struggled with husbands over money, such regular payments obviously provided them with more autonomy and at least a minimum of financial security. With this in mind, it is hardly surprising that in 78 percent of the sampled cases, it was wives who initiated legal procedures to have their marriages dissolved, even despite the social stigma that continued to be associated with separation and divorce. "I still had to pinch and scrape and watch every penny," recalled Magda Appelgaard, who divorced her husband in 1929 after four years of marriage. "But," she continued, "for the first time since I married him, at least I knew how much money I had. I knew I would be able to pay the rent and not have to beg the landlord for a postponement every month."[110] Rosa Jensen, who was married to her first husband for five years before divorcing him in 1927, had similar memories. "His beatings—that was one thing," she explained. "Back then that wasn't something you talked about. Always having to worry about money—that was almost as bad. Never having even a penny. Never knowing how you were going to eat the next day. . . . After [the separation] I had the child support payments at least, and I got a job. We didn't have much, but it was still much better." Ironically, many poor and distraught women thus found that only by leaving their husbands were they able to secure for themselves some of the protection and financial security they had expected when they first entered their marriages.

When spouses separated or divorced in the postwar decade, it was therefore rarely for reasons new to the twentieth century. If romantic love and companionship were increasingly seen as desirable qualities in marriage, absence thereof apparently did not constitute sufficient grounds for seeking its dissolution. In the overwhelming majority of cases legal separation and divorce were measures employed by women only in the most desperate of situations when poverty and violence threatened their own and their children's physical well-being. For those young women who advocated a new marital ideal and struggled to realize it in their daily lives, failure to do so apparently remained a disappointment they chose to, or had to, accept rather than break out of their marriages.

Young women's modernity thus had its limits. In their efforts to maintain a "modern" identity, they would throw enormous energy into reforming the dynamics between spouses, and as a result new kinds of conflicts beset many postwar marriages. But left with the options of resigning themselves to less than ideal marriages or striking out on their own, even the most "modern" young wives seemed to opt for the former. Perhaps Mathilde Bang-Pedersen was right when she explained, "I think you can say that we were rebels of a kind. We did a lot of things that women weren't supposed to do back then. . . . But we weren't foolish. A man and a home weren't just something you threw away. And where would you go? It was hard to find a job, and getting divorced was a horribly embarrassing thing."[111] Clearly, material and ideological limitations continued to circumscribe women's lives, making marriage their best long-term option.

In the mid-1910s, personal advertisements printed in Danish newspapers and magazines included the following examples:

> Marriage. Businessman, forty-four years old, with permanent employment, income Dkr. 3000, seeks acquaintance for the purpose of marriage with a woman, twenty-five to sixty years of age, who owns an independent business (delicatessen shop, fashion shop or the like).[112]

> Marriage. Single, younger girl seeks marriage with a man of the middle class. Dkr. 20,000 at my disposal.[113]

Marriage with a nice man is sought by a young girl from farming background. Assets Dkr. 25,000.[114]

Marriage. A young man, thirty-four years old, seeks marriage with wealthy woman.[115]

Widow, forty years old, with beautiful furniture, some capital, seeks acquaintance and subsequently marriage with older, financially well-situated gentleman, preferably businessman.[116]

By the end of the following decade, such advertisements had changed dramatically. With very few exceptions, financial data had been eliminated, and though the dreams may not have changed, prospective marriage candidates no longer announced their desire for an affluent mate. In place of this information, description of appearance and personal qualities had become the norm. A typical sample of personal advertisements from the late 1920s reads:

Marriage. A twenty-three-year-old open-minded young man with an optimistic view on life wishes to meet an approximately eighteen-year-old, slender and charming young woman for the purpose of marriage.[117]

Personable and good-looking young woman, twenty-eight years old, seeks honest friendship and possibly later marriage with intelligent, outgoing man of the same age.[118]

Marriage. A young man of the working class, in his late twenties, handsome, stable, and reliable, seeks the friendship of a young, attractive woman of similar background. Must have a sense of humor and a pleasant character. Please send photograph with the first letter.[119]

Marriage proposal. Young businessman in his early thirties wishes to become acquainted with a pretty, charming, cultured young woman who is interested in accompanying him on travels abroad. Please include a photograph in reply.[120]

As anecdotal evidence of the shift in popular perceptions of what constituted an attractive spouse and an ideal marriage, these advertisements are instructive. In the course of the 1910s and 1920s, social, political, and economic developments undermined traditional patriarchal family patterns. Legal reforms granted women new personal and political rights, and with the introduction of the new marriage legislation in the 1920s, legal equality between spouses was formally established. Simultaneously, new ideological emphases on love, romance, and intimacy between husbands and wives undermined older understandings of marriage as primarily a financial contract. But despite the political and ideological reconstruction of marriage as an egalitarian partnership, other evidence suggests that legal equality and changing expectations had limited impact on daily realities in many marriages. While more women than ever before found it possible to leave their spouses, they only did so when poverty and physical abuse actually threatened their physical survival. Hopes of romance and personal happiness seemed to remain just that—hopes, not expectations, that were beyond compromise.

~~~~~~

CHAPTER 6

"A Most Important Profession"

IF WORKING for wages for a number a years in their youth was an experience shared by the vast majority of women who came of age in the 1910s and 1920s, so was their subsequent withdrawal from the labor market after they got married. Even though the exact numbers are difficult to determine, Danish historians and statisticians estimate that by the end of the postwar decade only 10–12 percent of married women worked outside the home.[1] For upper-class and middle-class women this was in following with tradition. As elsewhere in the Western world, prosperous Danish families had long relegated women to the domestic arena, and even though a few highly educated women kept their professional jobs after marriage, they remained the rare exception.[2] For working-class women, withdrawal from the labor market upon marriage was a more recent phenomenon. Only in the twentieth century had a substantial number of working-class families become able to survive without the income of wives, and only then had the number of married working-class women who worked for wages begun to decline.[3] By the 1920s, then, almost all brides became full-time housewives after their wedding.

If young women had any reservations about giving up their relative independence in favor of homemaking and financial dependence, it has left few historical traces. On the contrary, they seemed to approach their housewifely responsibilities with much the same enthusiasm and ambition that they approached every other aspect of their lives. Becoming housewives was certainly not something they seemed to dread. As Helene Berg explained, "Having your own home, your very own place, a place where you would be able to make the decisions, that was so exciting."[4] There is also very little evidence that young women saw housewifery as incompatible with their identities as "modern" women. Even if it appeared to put them in the same position as many older, more conventional women, they still envisioned their future lives as qualitatively different than those of previous generations. Half a century later, Emilie Buhl was still quite adamant about this. Referring to the joylessness she believed to have characterized her mother's domestic life, she insisted that "no, that was not how it was going to be. I wanted more than that . . . not all that toil and moil."[5]

By the 1920s, this was an ambition whose fulfillment did not seem entirely unfeasible. Certainly, by the time the postwar generation came of age a number of long-term social and economic changes had already begun to transform domestic life. Fertility rates, for example, had steadily declined since the late nineteenth century.[6] In the 1880s, a bride could expect to give birth to five or six children. By the 1910s, only a minority had more than two or three.[7] During those same years, the number of live-in servants had dropped dramatically, and so had the number of people who resided as borders in private homes.[8] As a result, the size of the average household declined, and by the 1920s, it had typically come to consist of parents and their children only.[9]

During those same years, women's work in the home had also changed, especially in urban areas. Even though farm wives continued to produce most of the things their families needed, many other housewives were taking advantage of new mass-produced goods.[10] From the turn of the century, ready-made clothes had begun to replace homemade garments, leaving fewer women with the daunting responsibilities of producing entire wardrobes. Simultaneously, industrially produced housewares were making many domestic crafts obsolete, and manufactured food stuffs were slowly eliminated other time-consuming tasks. While tempered by tradition, most urban homes were therefore becoming consumer households, increasingly dependent on market exchange for most of its supplies and services, and in many ways this move was making women's lives less burdensome.[11] Simultaneously, the gradual improvement of the infrastructure of many urban homes to include running water and electricity had also contributed to lessening women's work. As several historians have noted, these developments may not ultimately have provided housewives with more free time since changing standards of hygiene, food preparation and child-rearing quickly added new responsibilities to their list of daily tasks, but nonetheless they still abolished at least some of the drudgery and back-breaking labor with which so many women of the older generations had had to contend.[12]

In general, then, young women who married in the 1920s would preside over households that were smaller and more intimate than had been the case in the past. With the exception of farm wives, they would typically be in charge of homes that were less centered around production than consumption of goods. And as standards of living rose, even working-class wives were able to avoid some of the most laborious domestic chores. Middle-class wives, on the other hand, were more likely to carry out their own housework as the number of available servants dropped, making their domestic situation more like that of working-class women than ever before. Without any efforts of their part, the lives of most postwar brides would therefore automatically be different from those of their mothers.

But early twentieth-century developments had not only bequeathed young women with such demographic and economic changes. As women's work in the home had changed, so too had the status of domestic labor—and not for the better. This was particularly the case for women who lived in urban areas. No matter how carefully and conscientiously they undertook their responsibilities, most contemporaries considered their work far less talented, skilled, and demanding than that of older generations of (rural) women. Besides, the recognition of the economic value of women's work in the home work had also declined. Already in the nineteenth century, an understanding of housework as unproductive labor had gradually developed, leading politicians, economists, and census takers to categorize married women as "dependents" along with children, the sick, the elderly, and the insane. In the early twentieth century, in an economy increasingly based on cash and consumption, where goods that could be bought and sold and quantities that could measured in monetary terms became the new arbiters of value, this trend became even more dominant. By the 1920s, women's unpaid labor in the home had therefore come to be seen as much less significant than paid work in the labor market.[13]

Making matters even worse for urban housewives, a new public discourse had begun to define domestic labor as tedious and mindless and housewifery as a lacuna for less intelligent, ambitious, or adventurous women. Wealthy women, in particular, repeatedly insisted that domestic labor offered few challenges and little personal satisfaction. Used to supervising, rather than performing, domestic work, they deeply resented when the unavailability of servants forced them to "slave like yoked animals within our own homes."[14] Except for cooking, "which isn't so deadly monotonous and dull as the rest of the daily work in the home," the well-known author Ellen Reumert, for example, found housework "both boring and tiring."[15] Similarly, Frieda Buehl, a prosperous conservative activist and newspaper columnist, argued that having to perform domestic labor placed her "on a lower stage of civilization" by turning her into "a slaving beast who never has the time to read a book and only knows art exhibits, theater, concerts, and other forms of enlightenment from hearsay and barely that."[16] According to these and many other privileged women, housework was tedious, and it made its practitioners dull. The fact that new educational opportunities drew some of the brightest and most dynamic middle-class daughters away from the home, while working-class girls eagerly fled domestic service to enter other occupations, only served to reinforce this perception.[17] And when the media occasionally applauded the accomplishments of career women, noting "the amazing changes we have seen" since the day when "the average woman had no other concerns than . . . the narrow world of the home and the trivialities of daily life," they further underscored the image of the housewife as drab, uninteresting, and behind the times.[18]

When young brides embarked on their careers as full-time housewives in the postwar years, it was therefore at a time when domestic work had undergone a notable devaluation. Even though this did not lead them to abandon, or even question, housewifery as their postmarital occupation, it was nevertheless an unpleasant reality that stared them in the face. For young women who envisioned an egalitarian marriage despite the gendered division of labor that made them financially dependent on their husband, it was crucial that their contributions as housewives be seen as equally valuable. And as "modern" young women, it was just as crucial that they find a way to avoid being counted among those seen as backward and dull.

But if these were concerns of particular urgency for young brides, they would not be alone in their efforts to reform the unflattering public image that domestic labor had acquired. Understandably, the belittling of the importance of housework also bothered many older housewives. They certainly took as much offense at being denied the possession of any skill or talent, and like young women they resented being seen as less meritorious than women who worked for wages. Eager to restore the status of housework, young brides and middle-age homemakers therefore bonded in a cross-generational alliance otherwise rare among women in the postwar decade. Through collective organizing, private efforts, and public initiatives, they collaborated in a series of efforts to recast their work as productive, rational, efficient, and highly skilled. And even though the practical realities of daily life changed relatively little in the 1920s, they nevertheless succeeded in challenging the unflattering image of the housewife, heightening the status of housework, and acquiring from husbands and society at large at least a minimum of recognition of the economic value of their work.

(RE)CLAIMING RESPECT FOR WOMEN'S DOMESTIC WORK

Of all the things the average housewife might have complained about in the early decades of twentieth century—the long hours, the myriad responsibilities, the physical strain, the poor working conditions, the lack of free time, to name just a few—it was the low, and declining, status of her work that seemed to provoke the most resentment. In newspaper articles, women's magazines, and popular periodicals, this was certainly the topic housewives raised most frequently. For young brides who had recently left the labor market, this was particularly noticeable—and particularly galling. "Until I married I held a position as a secretary in a small office. I was an esteemed and respected employee," a typical letter from a young wife to a newspaper editor began. "Now, as a wife and mother responsible for my own home and my family's happiness, I no longer receive the same kind of [respect] even though my workday is longer and my duties have multiplied."[19] "As a shop assistant I was granted much more respect than I am now," another newlywed woman complained.[20] The fact that a housewife "has to manage the household, balance the budget, attend to social obligations . . . raise the children, and make the home a pleasant place . . . does not seem to be considered work, or at least not work that requires any form of respect," protested yet another newspaper correspondent.[21] Apparently, most married women agreed with "Mrs. Andersen from Brønshøj," who concluded that "being a housewife, even a very good housewife, does not bestow much honor on a woman anymore."[22]

Undoubtedly, it was such experiences that contributed to the rapid growth of housewives' organizations in the postwar years.[23] The first such organization for urban women, the Copenhagen Housewives' Association, founded in 1917, had originally been envisioned as an employers' organization representing the interests of affluent women vis-à-vis their domestic servants, but within a year it had been transformed into a much more broad-based association of housewives specifically committed to defending housework against further cultural devaluation.[24] In the late 1910s, similar organizations sprang up across the country, and in 1920, when the national Federation of Danish Housewives' Associations was formed, thirty independent organizations joined forces. By 1925, the national membership of the federation had grown to more than ten thousand, making it one of the largest women's organizations in the country and one of the most successful in recruiting women across class and generational lines.[25]

Throughout the interwar period, the official goal of national federation was to "further the practical, economic, and social interests of the home," but in practice, its concerns were both more specific and more ambitions.[26] What first and foremost preoccupied the organization was the heightening of housewives' social status. As Carla Meyer, president of the federation, noted in 1922, "It has often been said that the self-supporting woman is more intellectually developed, and that being a housewife reduces one to a state of stupidity." Consequently, she continued, the "most pressing task" of the organization was to restore "the reputation and good name" of women who devoted their lives to housework.[27]

Despite Meyer's old-fashioned rhetoric of honor and reputation, housewives' organizations would in the course of the postwar decade attempt to do so in ways that were decidedly "modern." Instead of claiming, for example, that housework was inherently meaningful and pleasurable for women or in following with their nature, they chose a very different path. Most importantly, following the example of so many other occupational groups, they sought to transform housewifery into a profession with its own educational requirements, its own skilled practices, and its own expert knowledge. A first step in this process, and one that was particularly welcome among younger members, was the effort to promote housewifery as a deliberately chosen field of activity. Housewives, the argument went, did not just follow convention, and housewifery was not just something women stumbled into unthinkingly. "It is time to reckon with the notion that only women who are teachers, nurses, doctors etc. have decided to follow a calling," one woman thus argued, adding that "contrary to what many people seem to think, housewives are not simply like the dead fish that flow with the tide."[28] Other housewives, most of them young and ambitious, spoke of housework as a "brilliant and rewarding career" and as a "chosen vocation."[29] In itself, this rhetoric of vocation and career choice signaled anything but female conventionality. In the postwar years these were concepts rarely applied to women, and claiming them for ordinary housewives was bound to bolster their sense of self-worth and modernity.

Still, the distinguishing feature of any profession is the possession of a particular set of skills, and if housewives were to succeed in their efforts to recast their work as a profession, they would have to counter the public image of (urban) housework as unskilled labor. In a context where household production had all but vanished, this was no easy task. In comparison with rural housewives who still baked and butchered, wove and sewed, urban wives seemed to master preciously few "real" skills. What was left of housework—shopping, cooking, cleaning, and caring for children—struck most contemporaries as simply "natural" to women and therefore hardly worthy of praise.

Because most housewives, including the youngest among them, shared with other contemporaries the assumption that men and women were inherently different, this posed a difficult dilemma: How were they to maintain that housework was a skilled profession if what women did in the home was really just "natural" to them? Caught between essentialist notions of women's nature and their desire to professionalize housework, organized housewives adopted the only stance possible. Even though women might have "natural" talents for housekeeping and child-rearing, this was not sufficient, they argued, especially given the complexity and significance of their task. "It has been assumed," one housewife thus argued in 1918, "that taking care of home, husband, and children does not require any particular training for a woman," but, she continued, even natural talent needs to be refined.[30] Karen Braae, the president of the Copenhagen Housewives' Association, whole-heartedly agreed. "The notion," she wrote in 1922, "that someone with a natural talent does not need to develop it . . . is completely paradoxical."[31] Certainly, housewives argued over and over again, housework was not something any woman could just fall back on in case everything else failed.[32] To be a good housewife, training was needed, "no matter how naturally talented one has been born."[33]

Modeling themselves on other professions, the leadership of housewives' organizations therefore called for formal training of girls and women who entered their field of work. By the 1920s, this was not an entirely new concept. Since the late nineteenth century, many female reformers had been calling for the recognition of domestic labor as a skilled trade, and feminist organizations had lobbied for the establishment of trade schools and university courses in housekeeping. A few women had even founded their own home economics schools.[34] What distinguished postwar campaigns from these earlier efforts was the scope of their ambition. While the intention behind university courses and housekeeping schools had been to provide women for whom housekeeping was to be a life-long source of paid employment with skills and expertise, housewives' organizations advocated formal education in housewifery for a much broader group, namely, the vast majority of all women who would marry and become responsible for their own households.[35]

Ideally, this training would commence already in early childhood, but it would not take place through the traditional passing of knowledge from mother to daughter. If the efforts to elevate housewifery to the status of a skilled profession were to succeed, such an arrangement would not suffice. Not only did such informal and unregulated training seem too old-fashioned and haphazard, but in an era of rapid change the traditional housekeeper had supposedly ceased to be a useful teacher for her daughter. As Social Democratic Minister of Education Nina Bang noted in her keynote address to the 1926 annual meeting of Federation of Danish Housewives' Associations, "nobody knows yet exactly how to handle the new kind of housekeeping that primarily rests on manufactured goods. The present generation of housewives has not learned it, and therefore, they are not able to teach the next generation."[36] Instruction in housework would therefore have to be transferred from the home to the public school system, where trained professionals would oversee girls' education.[37]

There is no evidence to suggest that young housewives in any way disagreed with this emphasis on formal education for girls, but unlike the organizational leadership, they seemed at least as concerned about the more immediate task of promoting a new image of housewifery as a dynamic and constantly changing field of work. Of course, married women had to provide their families with many of the same basic goods and services as previous generations, but this was, young wives typically argued, where the similarities between nineteenth- and twentieth-century housewifery stopped. "Modern" housewives like themselves—upbeat, energetic, and always eager to face a new challenge—did not rely on tradition, handed-down advice, and common sense, and they did not learn their profession once and for all.[38] On the contrary, a "modern" housewife was continually striving to keep her knowledge and skills up-to-date, and just as she would not dream a wearing last year's fashions, she would not allow her housekeeping to fall "behind the times."[39]

No wonder, then, that young wives were particularly eager to take advantage of the many opportunities for staying abreast with the latest developments in their field of work that housewives' organizations offered their members. Most popular among these were the large annual fairs where thousands of housewives were treated to cooking classes, brief lectures, demonstrations of new housekeeping techniques, displays of the latest household technologies, educational literature, and free coffee. In addition, the organization published a monthly periodical, and from the early 1920s it hired several educators and consultants who traveled across the country offering courses, lectures, and evening classes on everything from proper lighting, economical bread-baking, efficient dishwashing, and innovative ways of stretching raw materials to the latest techniques for preserving food stuffs, preventing vermin infestations, and avoiding household injuries.[40] Specialist literature produced by housekeeping experts provided yet another means to "acquire a thorough knowledge of the more and more complicated questions and difficult issues" that housewives encountered in their homes.[41] Given the popularity of such instruction, the leadership of the national federation was probably correct in its assessment that "our housewives, and especially our young housewives" went to great lengths to improve their knowledge and skills.[42]

But despite all their efforts, housewives never succeeded in acquiring the ultimate characteristic of a profession, namely, the right and ability to control access to its ranks. Any woman could still become a housewife, and despite their efforts to make all girls and young women go through formal training in housewifery, many entered marriage with only the knowledge they had picked up from their mothers at home. Still, the strategy of professionalization was not without its merits. In the public eye, it certainly contributed to the image of a new, more "modern," and up-to-date housewife. As one newspaper columnist begrudgingly had to admit, "The housewife of today does not have the same skills as her mother, but she is efficient and perhaps more in sync with the time."[43] Besides, the association of housework with expertise and professionalism seemed to grant women's work in the home new significance, and it gave many housewives a renewed sense of pride and satisfaction in their work. For young wives who struggled to maintain their identities as "modern" women within marriage, professionalization carried additional appeal.

Fig. 22. Evening class in modern housekeeping, Copenhagen, mid-1920s. (Courtesy of the Danish Women's Photo Archives)

Even though the emphasis on continual learning added new responsibilities, it also endowed the mundane tasks of everyday life with an air of modernity, and for them, this may well have been the most attractive aspect of the efforts to recast housework as a freely chosen, highly skilled profession.

NOT YOUR MOTHER'S HOUSEHOLD

When housewives' organizations began to emphasize formal training and professional expertise as integral to their work, they were obviously adopting concepts and ideas from the world of work outside the home, hoping that this would bestow upon their work the same kind of status and respect that was allocated other occupations. But the notion of professionalism was not the only imprint that developments in the labor market left on housewifery in the postwar era. Because organized housewives were deeply concerned about seeming "modern" and up-to-date in their daily work and because they knew that status and respect came easier to occupational groups with direct links to the labor market, they closely

Fig. 23. Carla Meyer, the president of the Federation of Danish Housewives' Associations, publicly spearheaded many of the efforts to recast housewifery as a decidedly "modern" enterprise, informed by scientific research. (Courtesy of the Royal Library, Copenhagen)

monitored all developments in business and industry, and as these enterprises changed, so did their conceptions of what constituted good housekeeping.

As was the case in other parts of Western Europe and the United States, this led, among other things, to an emphasis on the importance of scientific knowledge. Throughout the 1920s, publications aimed at housewives brimmed with articles about calories and vitamins, encouraging them to adhere to modern nutritional principles. Women were also counseled about the necessity of acquiring at least a basic knowledge of biology, chemistry, and medicine, and the federation's monthly magazine featured column after column explaining the latest research in human health and hygiene. As advocates of "modern" housewifery saw it, putting this knowledge to practical use had twin purposes. While improving the well-being of households, it might also finally lay to rest the unflattering image of the housewife as an old-fashioned drudge and allow the entirely "modern" domestic scientist to take her place.

To further bolster the perception of housewifery as a modern undertaking accomplished "first and foremost with the brain and only secondly with the hands," Danish housekeeping experts also encouraged housewives to adopt new styles of work.[44] Rationalization of the labor process and scientific time management were, they argued much like their counterparts abroad, not just principles that applied to business and industry.[45] On the contrary, the home needed to be administered just as efficiently and systematically as any other workplace. As one expert reminded housewives, "Experiences from trade and industry have already shown that rational planning produces the best results. We must keep this in mind also in our profession [because] all enterprises, big and small, are subject to the same rules."[46] Housewives ought therefore always strive to develop "the best, fastest, and most practical way of getting things done."[47] To accomplish this task, they were encouraged to develop elaborate work plans for all "the thousands of little details" of which housework consisted.[48] Only by partitioning housekeeping into a series of clearly defined tasks to be carried out at specific times on a daily, weekly, or monthly basis would the most competent and practical running of the home be ensured. Or, as Carla Meyer tellingly phrased it, only then would "the entire machinery run as smoothly as it ought to."[49]

This attempt to represent the home as an elaborate machine under the supervision of conscientious household managers was not unique in the 1920s. In yet another attempt to bring housework into alignment with industrial practices, organized housewives and housekeeping experts reveled in such rhetoric in the postwar decade. Ironically, however, this was about as close as many housewives ever came to the world of modern technology. Despite the popular image of the 1920s as an era in which household appliances, kitchen implements, and a variety of other labor-saving consumer goods revolutionized domestic life, most of these products remained in Europe throughout the 1920s a privilege for the very few.[50] Gas ovens and stoves, for example, only made their way into Danish homes in the 1930s and 1940s, and vacuum cleaners, electrical irons, and refrigerators remained virtually unknown until after World War II. Even basic improvements came slowly. In 1925, only 1–2 percent of Copenhagen apartments were equipped with hot running water.[51] That same year, merely 66 percent of Copenhagen households and 46 percent of households in provincial towns had indoor plumbing. In rural areas even fewer households boasted this luxury.[52]

These were, of course, realities well-known to organized housewives and housekeeping experts, and as a result they practically never included technological advances in their vision of "modern" housework.[53] Bent on creating a more modern and respected style of housewifery—even in the absence of material change—they focused instead almost exclusively on the introduction of new housekeeping practices and work procedures. Though borne of necessity, such efforts promised to bring housework in line with the times while requiring little but talent, ambition, and perseverance. At least in theory, all housewives, irrespective of their class and social status, would therefore be able to create the kind of "modern" households that supposedly would bring them status and respect.

The extent to which ordinary housewives actually sought to pattern their daily practices in accordance with these new domestic ideals remains unclear. Even though housekeeping experts promised them that it would make a woman "boss in her own home" rather than a slave of her daily chores, reading scientific literature and developing elaborate work schedules may well have seemed just another task.[54] Nonetheless, the effort to promote housework as a rationally organized, highly skilled profession was certainly welcome. Not only did it begin to counter the perception of housework as utterly prosaic and mundane, but it also provided a set of arguments to legitimate the demand that housekeeping be granted the same status and respect as paid occupations in the labor market. And by describing housework as a positive career choice rather than an apathetic adherence to convention, it made it easier for young brides to reconcile their status as housewives with their identity as "modern" women.

Still, professionalization and rationalization of housework hardly solved all the problems housewives faced in the postwar years. No matter what they said or did, paid labor still retained its privileged position over unpaid work in the home. Even if housewives updated their household practices and managed to gain more respect, it did not change the fact that housework generally was seen as economically insignificant. It also did not alter the fact that they were financially dependent on their husbands and subject to men's will in economic matters. Especially for young women who had entered marriage with an expectation of spousal equality, this posed a difficult problem. How were they to create the kind of egalitarian marriage they longed for if only husbands' work was seen as valuable? How were they to maintain their status as equal partners if their contributions to the partnership were seen as inferior to those of their husbands? And how were they to create a married life that was more egalitarian than that of previous generations if their work was not even granted the same economic significance as their mothers'? These were issues that even the most successful efforts to upgrade the image of the housewife were never going to solve. In addition to their attempts at professionalization and rationalization, housewives therefore had to develop strategies that would address this complicated issue.

MONEY MATTERS

Even if most women in the 1920s expected to be provided for by their husbands, being without an income of their own often proved an adjustment for young brides. As Henny Nedergaard recalled, "Not having any money of your own, that was hard. You had gotten used to having your own money, had gotten used to spending your own money without having to ask anybody about it."[55] More importantly, the economically dependent role in which this gendered division of labor placed them sat uncomfortably with many young brides. In the words of Meta Hansen, "It wasn't just that you didn't earn your own money anymore, but all the money you had was your husband's money. He earned it so it was his money. That wasn't always easy."[56]

But young brides were not the only women to be concerned about this issue in the postwar years. Many older housewives also found husbands' authority over money hard to bear, and the leadership of housewives' organizations frequently criticized married women's economic situation. Trying to solve this problem, some of these leaders floated the idea that women actually be paid for the work they performed in the home. Elisa Møller Andersen, for example, repeatedly urged politicians to consider the possibility of "granting [housewives] some form of monetary compensation."[57] Other representatives of housewives' organizations recommended that husbands who benefited from their services should pay wives, directly and in cash, for the work they performed. These suggestions did not find much support, however. To most contemporaries, the notion of state subsidies for housework was simply too far-fetched to be realistic, and the proposition that husbands pay their wives for their services seemed too much at odds with the understanding of marriage as a cooperative undertaking.

But if few could envision a world in which housewives were paid for their work, many contemporaries did agree that housewives' economic situation needed to be strengthened. Given the general trend toward greater sexual equality in marriage, women's financial subordination to their husbands struck many as anachronistic. Even many conservatives, who feared that women might prefer financial independence to marriage if this problem was not solved, supported the notion that married women be granted some measure of financial autonomy. "If a housewife is to feel appreciated and respected," they seemed to agree, "it is simply not appropriate for her to have to ask for every little amount [of money] she needs." Being "forced to resort to cunning and roundabout methods in order to obtain it" seemed equally inappropriate and degrading.[58]

The solution proposed by these commentators was, however, a far cry from the suggestion that housewives be paid for their work. In place of this, they merely attempted to persuade husbands to share their finances more willingly. Without challenging men's fundamental right to control their income, they appealed to their sense of fairness and justice, urging them to be generous and make a practice of always "giving your wife a certain amount [of money] for her own personal consumption" in addition to the money for housekeeping purposes.[59]

Most leaders of the housewives' organizations remained dubious about the effectiveness of such pleas. In comparison, they were much more enthusiastic about the suggestion that married women's economic status be addressed through the new marriage legislation that was under way in the early 1920s. The recommendation of the Marriage Commission that paid labor outside the home and unpaid work in the home be considered equally valuable contributions to a household won their whole-hearted support. So did the proposal that married women be given a legal right to demand a part of their husband's income not only for housekeeping purposes but also for personal use. Such measures would, they assumed, much better address their concerns than would any campaign of moral persuasion.

With the political support of liberal and social democratic legislators, these recommendations were in fact written into law. When the new legislation went into effect on January 1, 1926, organized housewives were therefore able to celebrate what was seen as an important improvement in married women's economic standing vis-à-vis husbands. "Imagine," the newsletter of the Federation of Danish Housewives Associations enthused, "from now on [any married woman] is entitled to a certain sum of money for her personal expenditures. She is, for instance, completely justified in drinking a cup of coffee in a restaurant, or buying tobacco or sweets for herself, or dressing according to her economic standing."[60]

In principle these were significant gains, but in reality the impact of the new legislation was limited. Having the legal right to demand funds for housekeeping did not necessarily make it easier to get husbands to hand over the money, and the right to discretionary spending money made even less of a difference in the lives of most women. In affluent households, women already enjoyed this privilege. In most other cases limited incomes and strained budgets made it unrealistic. In itself, legislative change therefore did little to alter the financial relationship between spouses. Still, it reassured young wives, for whom this was particularly important, that their desire to create a more egalitarian relationship, also economically, with their husbands was not only legitimate, but appropriate.

Rather than putting an end to the debates about married women's economic situation, the legislation therefore provoked more and more assertive calls from housewives who insisted on changing the economic relationship between spouses, not only legally but also in daily practice. It was time, they argued, that husbands finally abandon their resistance to handing over money for housekeeping purposes. It was also time that the administration of this amount be left entirely in hands of housewives without husbands attempting to interfere with their financial decisions. Of course, generations of women before them had made similar demands, but the tone and rhetoric of the postwar debate were decidedly different. "As long as the housewife is expected to run the household efficiently and economically," one housewife thus argued, "she *must* know exactly how much [money] she has at her disposal, and she must receive that amount *weekly and without exception.*"[61] Equally self-confidently, another woman insisted that "a housewife should not have to beg for money. It is her *right* to receive the funds she needs."[62]

But many housewives, particularly of the younger generation, would not settle merely for housekeeping funds. Instead they insisted on a broader set of economic rights in their marriages. This included, among other things, having complete information about household finances. The days, they argued, when wives did not know the size of their husbands' paycheck would have to come to an end. In a "modern" marriage, it was only appropriate that a husband give his wife "full insight into his situation."[63] In addition to such knowledge, they agreed that housewives ought to be given the right to participate in financial planning and decision making on an equal footing with their husbands. When, for example, the Copenhagen daily *B.T.* queried its readers in 1925 about whether a husband should account for all his expenses, women were unanimous in their response. Without exception, they argued that since all financial decisions ought to be made jointly by husbands and wives, married women were of course entitled to such information. "If a man wants to spend money without his wife's knowledge, he does not have the correct understanding of marriage—which is [a partnership] in which they are supposed to share everything," "Annalise" argued.[64] "The idea that the wife is in charge of the money for food and clothing and the husband makes all other decisions is utterly out-of-date," another woman wrote. "They should," she added, "share [this responsibility] and discuss things together. In a marriage built on love, consideration, and understanding, that is the only natural way."[65] In the ideal world that they sought to realize, financial dependence would obviously not mean female subservience.

But for all their arguments, and despite public pleas and legal stipulations, husbands still held the purse strings. As long as they brought home the paycheck, they had the ultimate power to grant, or deny, their wives access to and control over that money. If the ideal of greater economic equality between spouses was to be translated into reality, men would necessarily have to consent. Housewives therefore had to resort to what seemed to them the only possible strategy: They set out to convince husbands that it was in their own best interests—and in the best interests of their households—to treat women as equals in financial matters.

The best way to do this, they quickly surmised, was to demonstrate in practice their talents as money managers, and since housekeeping funds were the only money entrusted to them, this was the obvious place to start. Once housewives had proven "that we are fully capable of handling [housekeeping funds] in the best, most sensible manner," men would, they somewhat naively assumed, naturally begin to treat them as equals in larger financial decisions.[66] The only question was how they might go about proving this. Generations of women before them had also administered housekeeping funds, but no matter how successful they had been in this endeavor, it had rarely led to equal status with their husbands in larger decisions about household finances. Simply going about things in the same manner as women before them was therefore not likely to produce the desired results.

Casting about for solutions to this dilemma, the leadership of the housewives' organizations and housekeeping experts settled upon what seemed to them a promising means. They encouraged women to keep record books in which they drew up detailed budgets and kept itemized accounts of all housekeeping expenditures. Although admittedly tedious, such work had several advantages, they assured women. Carefully kept accounts would, for instance, provide them with a quick overview of household expenditures, and drawing up a budget would make them more aware of their own spending habits and encourage thriftiness.[67] In addition, it might well ease marital conflicts over money. If, for instance, a husband could not or would not "understand how difficult it is for us to make ends meet," a detailed accounts of all spending would allow women to document and justify their expenses.[68] Besides, financial planning, careful budgeting, and meticulous record-keeping would also bolster the image of the housewife as a skilled professional.[69]

But in the eyes of its advocates, the greatest promise of fastidious record-keeping lay in the potential it held for gradually transforming the economic relationship between spouses. Certainly, they argued, such evidence of financial responsibility was bound to impress husbands. As wives became more and more familiar with planning and budgeting, husbands would have to notice how it made them "better able to discuss financial matters . . . in a rational and intelligent manner."[70] And, the argument continued, once a husband realized his wife's competence in this area, he would "naturally seek her advice and opinions."[71] In the words of one enthusiast, "this will teach him to appreciate his wife's judgment in financial matters."[72]

For housewives who longed for economic equality in their marriages but were unable to force their husbands into letting them share in financial planning and decision making, these were enticing arguments. If the leadership of housewives' organizations and housekeeping experts were correct in their predictions, this fairly simple measure might help them accomplish what otherwise seemed next to impossible. Willing to take the chance, large numbers of housewives therefore chose to follow their advice and take on the laborious chore of carefully recording every financial transaction.[73]

Apparently, tracking budgets and keeping account books did have an impact on married women's lives. While it did not necessarily lessen their struggles to make ends meet, it did seem to reinforce many housewives' sense of being "modern," rational, and businesslike. Keeping records also seemed to provide many women with a new sense of competence in financial matters. "Before I began keeping written accounts," one housewife explained, "I never really knew where the housekeeping money went, but now I can account for very penny [and] I am certain that I do my best."[74] With even greater self-confidence, another woman insisted that "after having kept an account book for more than four years now, I can honestly say that I know as much about money matters as my husband does."[75] Finally, record-keeping seemed to bestow upon many women a new sense of entitlement to speak their minds about financial matters. Because keeping account books had given them new insights into the proper handling of money, it was only logical, they argued, that they share this knowledge with their husbands and that they be party to all decisions about family finances.

But contrary to experts' predictions and housewives' expectations, record-keeping did not always mean that husbands automatically began to treat their wives more equally. In some households, women continued to have to struggle to get husbands to hand over any money at all. In other families, men willingly handed over funds for housekeeping purposes, but they still refused to relinquish any authority over the remaining finances.[76] In still other cases, husbands agreed to share financial decision making with their wives, only to renege on their promises if wives did not agree with them.[77] And in families where spouses carefully outlined a budget together and agreed to keep it, some husbands would still squander money, claiming it their right to do so because they were, after all, the wage earners.[78] In cases like these where husbands refused to cooperate or deliberately violated mutual agreements, financially dependent wives had little recourse. If they were not willing or able to take on employment that would ensure them an independent income, they had to contend with the fact that the ultimate power over money continued to rest with their wage-earning husbands.

Nevertheless, economic relations between spouses did begin to shift in the postwar decade, especially among younger couples. Even though more husbands than ever before were sole bread-winners, other developments were simultaneously curtailing the increased power this might have given them in the household. The new emphasis on egalitarianism in marriage functioned to undercut the cultural legitimacy of husbands' unrestrained authoritarianism in the home. So did the reforms of marriage legislation and the general consensus that married women's economic situation needed to be improved. But in the daily lives of ordinary couples, the strategy of record-keeping as a means to establish credibility as responsible and conscientious money managers, and thereby gain more of a say in the allocation of household finances, seems to have played a role as well.

According to the press, that was certainly the case. From the early 1920s, newspapers, housewives' journals, and women's magazines published letter after letter in which wives gleefully recounted their successes in this matter. "A young wife" was delighted to report, for example, that after having kept account books for a year she had finally managed to convince her husband that their household consisted of "two clearly thinking minds," and he had subsequently begun to include her in financial decision making.[79] Another woman explained that "I had to convince my husband that if I was capable of keeping accounts of housekeeping money, I would also be able to help him handle other money matters. At first, he did not want to burden me with such responsibilities, but he has since realized that I am both willing and able to take [them] on."[80] That these were not isolated incidents was the gist of many contemporary editorials. As one journalist noted, "The competence and seriousness with which our housewives approach their daily work has in recent years opened the eyes of their husbands. Nowadays they will generally consult their wives before making any major decision."[81] The president of the Federation of Danish Housewives' Associations, Carla Meyer, agreed. By 1928, she was confident that "the vast majority of our housewives who keep budgets" shared in financial decision making in their households.[82]

Whether or not Carla Meyer was correct in her assessment, organized housewives and their supporters had by end of the 1920s succeeded in altering ideal notions of what constituted proper economic relations between spouses. Even though wage-earning husbands maintained the ultimate power over family finances, they had lost both the legal and the moral right to rule dictatorially over the household income. At the same time, many ordinary housewives had managed to acquire more access to financial decision making, and in that sense they had gained more equality with their husbands. But even if some housewives managed to convince their spouses that they were both skilled enough and talented enough to be treated as their equals in the home, this was not sufficient to alleviate their more general concern about married women's social status. As long as housework continued to be seen, at least in the greater scheme of things, as economically insignificant, they knew that housewives would always be relegated to second-class status. Simultaneously with their efforts to refashion housewifery as a profession and gain more economic leverage within the household, they would therefore have to combat this understanding.

HOUSEWIFERY AND THE NATIONAL ECONOMY

In the early twentieth century, most people agreed that women's work in the home was important for the general welfare of their families. They also agreed that the welfare of families was important for the well-being of the nation. But, as historian Nancy Folbre has argued, this did not mean that housework was seem as economically significant work.[83] For housewives who realized the growing importance of participation in the market economy for personal status and respect, this was obviously a problem. In an economy based on paid labor, they were faced with the difficult task of making the case that housewives were equally productive members of society even if their work was not paid.

Fortunately, the foundation for such a claim had already been laid in the course of World War I when public attention had first been called to the importance of housewives' work. Immediately after the outbreak of the war, fear of shortages had led the Danish government to impose a ban on the export of crucial supplies such as fuel and grain. Simultaneously, price regulations and rationing had been introduced as a measure to control the domestic distribution of goods. Nevertheless, as the war proceeded, shortages of provisions, substitute products, smaller rations, and rising prices made daily life increasingly difficult. In the majority of households where husbands' income did not increase or did not increase sufficiently to offset the rising cost of living, the situation was especially trying, and family welfare often depended heavily on the ability of housewives to stretch money, food, and other goods.

During the war this produced an outpouring of appreciation for women's work in the home. The press applauded "the competent Danish housewives" who accepted their onerous task "without a murmur [of complaint]."[84] Politicians eagerly followed in their footsteps, commending women for their financial responsibility and "social spirit."[85] But if such acknowledgments filled housewives with a sense of pride, it was the new and surprising statements by economists and statisticians about the larger, economic importance of women's domestic work that attracted most of their attention. When, for instance, Jens Warming, an economist and high-ranking official in the Statistical Bureau, in the fall of 1916 published a lecture in which he described housewives as one of the financially most significant groups in society, women were, quite understandably, captivated by his ideas.[86]

Warming's argument was simple, yet convincing, and in the following years it would be repeated over and over again by housewives and many economists. Taking his point of departure in evidence from the 1911 census, he noted that there were approximately 650,000 Danish households. In the vast majority of these, he continued, women were in charge of housekeeping expenditures, totaling an estimated Dkr. 800 million annually. This meant, Warming claimed, that housewives had at their disposal a larger amount of funds than any other single occupational group besides farmers. It also meant that if housewives would succeed "in saving merely 1 percent [of their budget], this alone would come to more than Dkr. 8 million." And, he added, "it is probably possible to save much more than 1 percent."[87]

For housewives, these arguments held obvious appeal. By linking the household economy to the national economy and placing women as consumers at the nexus between these two economic spheres, it boosted housewives' status in two ways. First, it granted national importance to the household economy, and in particular to women's role as managers of housekeeping expenditures. Second, it elevated married women by placing them at the critical juncture between private domestic economies and the more highly valued and traditionally "male" national economy. It is hardly surprising then that many housewives quickly embraced such claims.

Within months, Warming's arguments reverberated through discussions in women's organizations and popular magazines. Already in January 1917, the editor of *Vore Damer* reminded female readers of "our great responsibility for our country's economy in these difficult times."[88] Two months later, an article in the feminist periodical *Kvinden og Samfundet* encouraged women to "to demonstrate our sense of social responsibility [by] managing our households in the best, most economic manner."[89] From its very inception in 1917, the Copenhagen Housewives' Association also embraced the notion of women's responsibility for the national economy.[90] Characteristically, its first major public initiative, the "Savings Exhibition" that opened in May 1917, was specifically designed to "help housewives adjust their consumption" to better comply with national economic interests.[91]

Warming's theories also seemed to spread surprisingly quickly among ordinary housewives. In a letter to the editor, printed in the first issue of *Husmoderen* in November 1918, "an economical housewife" asked, for example, about the proper use of some of the new substitute products that had been introduced in the course of the war because, as she explained, "I am not sure [how to do it], but I consider it my obligation to do my best both for my family and for the sake of our country's economy."[92] Another woman wrote to *Politiken* in the fall of 1917 that "we housewives are completely aware that the way we handle the housekeeping money is important for the welfare of our families and for our country."[93] Even separating and divorcing wives sometimes used these arguments. In 1918, when a twenty-eight-year-old woman was forced to defend herself against her husband's charges of poor housewifery, she explained to the Copenhagen authorities that "I have never not fed my husband properly . . . but I have had to do my best to stretch our money. I have been frugal and saved wherever I could. I can honestly say that I have never thrown out any food or clothes that could be repaired [because] I know it is important not just for our families, but also for our country that housewives do their best."[94] In the final years of the war, many housewives thus seemed to acquire both a new sense of their own economic importance and a new set of arguments that might help boost their standing both within their own families and in society at large.

Toward the end of the war, this new self-confidence manifested itself in a series of efforts to extend married women's sphere of economic influence beyond the home. Given the fact, housewives argued, that it was primarily their tireless efforts that kept both families and the nation afloat, it was only reasonable that they be given more of a say not only in financial decisions within their own, private households, but also in the larger national household. Only by taking advantage of female expertise would it be possible, they claimed, to "keep our country's household in the best order in these difficult times."[95] As a result, organized housewives insisted on being represented in political forums where issues related to the economic welfare of the country were discussed. In 1917, for instance, the Copenhagen Housewives' Association requested representation on all committees established by municipal authorities to address the special social and economic needs created by the war. "Being responsible for managing our homes, we are especially aware of the difficulties faced by ordinary families," they argued, "and as housewives who have to make ends meet, we have a special interest in making sure that all decisions that affect daily housekeeping are as appropriate as possible."[96] In other cities and towns across the country, women followed their example, asking to be consulted on a variety of issues ranging from price fixing to closing times for businesses.

Even though housewives presented their demands for economic representation as an exceptional measure made necessary by the war emergency, this did not mean that they simply ceased to make such demands when the war ended in 1918. As long as rationing of household goods remained in place and high prices kept taking their toll on most house-holds, organized housewives persisted in their demands.[97] But as the war receded into the past and special government commissions designed to regulate the economy were dissolved, the acknowledgment of housewives' economic importance began to slip.

After the wartime emergence during which housewives managed to ac-quire more respect for their work, it seemed that the prewar trend toward devaluation of domestic labor would reassert itself. For ordinary house-wives, who had reveled in the praise and attention they received during the war, this was of course disappointing. For the leadership of house-wives' organizations, who had succeeded in carving out a public role for themselves, it was even more disheartening. But for ambitious young brides who insisted on being equal partners with their husbands, this was especially devastating. If women's work in the home was, once again, to be seen as economically insignificant, they would have a much harder time creating the kind of egalitarian marriages they hoped for. As a result, they and many other housewives turned their attention to finding ways of maintaining the economically significant role women had been granted during the war.

Had the Danish economy boomed in the postwar years, or had it even shown signs of steady improvement, housewives might well have failed in this effort, but because economic difficulties and instability continued to plague the country, there was at least a possibility for retaining their new role. As imports escalated, the trade deficit grew, inflation soared, and unemployment rates approached 20 percent in the early 1920s, housewives seized the moment to present themselves, once again, as po-tential rescuers of the welfare of the nation. As consumers in charge of household spending, they were, they claimed, in a key position to improve the situation. Only this time, it would not be through management of scarce resources, but through responsible patterns of consumption.

In these claims, they received the backing of leading economists, who saw a curtailment of private spending as the best means to counteract the nation's troubles. While most economists would have preferred political regulation of international trade, a government committed to free trade and economic liberalism made this implausible.[98] Instead, they began to call on consumers to voluntarily restrict their spending. Thrift, they ar-gued, would put an end to the dramatic fluctuations that characterized the postwar economy. By avoiding imported products and buying Danish goods only, housewives and other ordinary people could do their part to improve the trade deficit and reduce the unemployment rates, thereby, in effect, saving the nation from economic chaos.[99]

Because the leadership of the housewives' organizations and many housekeeping experts deemed this their best opportunity to maintain the new economic role married women had held during the war years, they launched a large-scale campaign to inform ordinary housewives about basic economic principles and instruct them in proper consumer behavior. In the course of just one year, the national Federation of Danish House-wives' Associations thus sponsored fully fourteen exhibits on the virtues of Danish products. Simultaneously, housewives across the country were treated to a host of lectures with titles such as "The Fall of the Danish Krone," "The Danish Krone on Its Downward Path," "The Danish Wife and the Danish Krone," and "Women and the National Economy."[100]

While many housewives must have found such lectures perplexing and difficult to understand, not to mention plain boring, the measures they recommended seemed utterly sensible. Knowing from their own households that a balanced budget was an economic necessity, it seemed reasonable to them that the same rules would apply to the larger national household. "We all know that you cannot pay more out than you get in . . . but that is exactly what we, as a nation, have been doing during the last couple of years," Elna Asby explained in 1920. "We have been buying from abroad, carelessly sending our money out of the coun-try . . . without noticing that the same amounts were not coming in." Therefore, she continued, women now had to "demonstrate our ability and determination to take part in valuable work . . . by diminishing our consumption as much as possible."[101] "Our country lacks money," an-other women translated the economic message, "so it is now our responsi-bility to save and be frugal."[102]

In many ways, the arguments of the 1920s were simply extensions of wartime rationales, but in comparison with the claims they had made during the war, the emphasis on the importance of consumption manage-ment for the well-being of the nation granted housewives a much more lasting economic role. Crisis or not, housewives would always be in charge of large parts of household spending, and as long as household spending was seen as important to the national economy, they would play a key role. By casting themselves as rational, responsible consumers they therefore had a chance at more permanent public acknowledgment of the significance of their work.

In many ways, this strategy proved quite successful. Throughout the 1920s, economists repeatedly praised housewives for their efforts. The fact that advertising began to cater more and more directly to housewives also seemed an affirmation of their importance. Besides, after a few years of largely ignoring housewives, politicians once again began to appoint representatives of their organizations to parliamentary committees on fi-nancial issues. Even though many of these committees were only advisory, it nevertheless meant that housewives had at least to some extent suc-ceeded in establishing a new public and political role for themselves.

In the private arena, the emphasis on responsible consumption for the welfare of the nation also seemed to have its advantages for women. It certainly bestowed a new legitimacy on housewives' demand to be included in financial decision making in their own homes, and many housewives skillfully employed arguments about the (national) significance of savings and thrift to gain more access to and control over family finances. When, for example, one husband complained in 1924 that his wife attempted to "make my life as miserable as possible by always nagging me about the money I spend on tobacco and other little pleasures," she shot back that "I only try to do my best, not just for our household but also for our country."[103] With similar self-confidence, other women castigated husbands for their irresponsible and exorbitant spending habits, and when the Statistical Bureau in 1922 released a report documenting that the annual import of cigars totaled more than Dkr. 3 million and imported alcohol added another Dkr. 21 million to the national deficit, housewives wasted no time criticizing men as a whole. "What happened to the father who supposedly knows best?" one woman taunted. "What happened to the "Masters of Creation"? . . . If this is how they are going to save our country, then God bless us!"[104]

But these gains also had their price. While they contributed to heightening the status of housework and empowering housewives within the home, the emphasis on women's talents as rational economists simultaneously underscored the primacy of women's family responsibilities in financial matters. As Carla Meyer, the president of the Federation of Danish Housewives' Societies reminded housewives in 1928, "In regard to money, a woman ought always to think of the well-being of others—be it her own family or the larger societal family—first. We carry a great, new responsibility that we must never abandon. . . . This is truly the woman's cause of the twentieth century."[105] Obviously, the right to individual pleasure and consumption that many young housewives had so enjoyed before their marriages would not be part of the "modern" lives they created after their weddings.[106]

In the early decades of the twentieth century, the lives of both working-class and middle-class wives became more centered around the practical, daily responsibilities of housewifery. Yet had it not been for the simultaneous depreciation of the perceived value of housework, housewives might have found little common ground across class and generational lines. As it were, a shared frustration over the low, and declining, status of housework propelled a broad array of married women into action in the post-war decade.

The energy and determination these married women demonstrated in their efforts to create a new, more up-to-date style of housewifery and a more flattering image of the housewife speak volumes about the significance they attached to this project. For all housewives, this was a matter of respect and recognition, but for young brides it was an issue of particular urgency. If they were to maintain their identities as "modern" women and create more egalitarian relationships with their husbands despite their domesticity and economic dependency, a new style of housewifery that would bestow more status on its practitioners was a *sine qua non*. As means toward this end, they therefore embraced what seemed the quintessence of modernity in the labor market—including professionalism, scientific knowledge, and rational work processes—and applied them to housewifery. Simultaneously, they sought to restore their collective standing as productive members of society by pointing to the economic significance of rational housekeeping, both for their individual families and for the nation as a whole.

Most of these efforts were spearheaded by housewives' organizations, whose membership boomed from the late 1910s. To dismiss these organizations as conservative, even reactionary, bearers of tradition as some feminist historians have done is therefore a problematic claim.[107] While they did not challenge the sexual division of labor that placed women in the home, they played a central role in developing strategies that would enhance the status of housework. As they took on this task, they challenged popular assumptions about domestic work as unskilled and "natural" to women, and they successfully contested its designation as unproductive and economically insignificant labor. With few other means at their disposal than their ambition, housewives therefore managed to update their occupation in the course of the 1920s in a manner that enhanced the status of housework and made it much more compatible with the ideals and identities of women who saw themselves as "modern."

CONCLUSION

IN RECENT YEARS most feminist historians have leaned toward the interpretation that, ultimately, the 1920s brought little change to women's lives. As they have pointed out, women continued to occupy the lowest skilled and worst paid sectors of the economy. Despite the introduction of women's suffrage in most of the Western world, the impact of women on political decision making remained, at best, marginal. Moreover, women's access to resources, whether economic or educational, hardly expanded. And as psychologists and sexologists increasingly defined marriage and motherhood as not only a "natural" part of the female life course but as a prerequisite for female health and happiness, women's erotic choices became in some ways more circumscribed than they had been in the nineteenth century.

But many Danish women who lived through the 1920s had a very different experience. Generally, they regarded the postwar decade as an era of profound upheavals and change. In 1929, when asked by a newspaper editor to reflect on the decade that was drawing to a close, one middle-aged woman insisted that "life today is so different from the days when I was a girl."[1] Another female commentator was convinced that the postwar decade had witnessed a revolution in manners and mores and that women had obtained "so many new freedoms and rights."[2] Looking back at their youth in the 1920s, most of the women I interviewed agreed with this assessment. Their lives, they told me, had certainly been different from those of older generations of women. And they were equally sure of their own role in that process. In most cases I barely had to turn on the tape recorder before they regaled me with strikingly self-confident stories about their youthful exploits and accomplishments and about the ways in which their generation had altered the course of women's history. According to Dora Ingvardsen, for example, her generation was "the first [generation] that didn't just accept everything. Before our time women were just supposed to sit at home, but we were not willing to accept that. There was no way that we were going to be fobbed off with that little."[3] Amanda Christensen was equally convinced that "our generation really changed things for women."[4] No matter what feminist historians may think of the 1920s, these women recalled the postwar decade as an era of upheaval in women's lives, and they certainly saw themselves as important agents of change.

As this study has demonstrated, such claims are not entirely without merit. Despite considerable opposition, the postwar generation pioneered

new styles of fashionable femininity that allowed for more physical movement and greater comfort and ease for women. They also promoted a
healthy and active female physicality, and they insisted on the right to
bodily pleasures and self-expression. In the course of the 1920s, most
young women also managed to claim for themselves the right to leisure,
spending money of their own, and at least some freedom from family
surveillance and control. Driven by a desire for fun and excitement,
they made their way into the world of public leisure, where they largely
succeeded in reconciling women's participation with notions of female
propriety and respectability. As a generation, they also promoted new
kinds of cross-gender camaraderie, and they eagerly advocated the emerging ideal of romance, companionship, and egalitarianism within marriage. And even after marriage, when most of them became financially
dependent on their husbands, they went to great lengths to reinvent
housewifery in ways that would make it compatible with their identities
as "modern" women.

None of these efforts to create new styles of femininity, freer and less
formal relationships with men, greater egalitarianism and mutuality
within marriage, and more satisfying daily lives were unique to Denmark
in the 1920s. Across the Western world and beyond, young women were
engaged in similar projects of rebellion against the confines of nineteenth-
century gender arrangements. But because Denmark differed in significant
ways from many of the countries historians have typically focused on
when investigating the 1920s, an analysis of the Danish case allows new
insights into the complicated processes through which Victorian womanhood and gender relations gradually gave way to new styles, practices,
and prescriptions.

First, the Danish case throws into question assumptions about causa-
tion. Because Denmark did not experience either dramatic economic development in the early twentieth century or profound disruptions as a
result of World War I, the reasons for upheaval in gender arrangements
obviously have to be sought elsewhere. In Denmark, the impetus for
change clearly sprang from the desires and ambitions of women who came
of age in the postwar decade. Across class lines, large numbers of young
women strove to expand the boundaries that circumscribed their lives
to incorporate more personal enjoyment and satisfaction. While other
contemporaries, including most members of the older generation and
many young men, contested these efforts, seeking to reign in their rebelliousness or at least channel their behavior in acceptable directions,
opponents of change remained largely on the defensive throughout the
1920s, constantly having long-standing norms undercut and their authority challenged.

Of course, the ambitions and desires that young women so eagerly pursued did not spring from their unencumbered imaginations. They were facilitated by new representations of female modernity, largely produced by commercial mass culture, the rapidly growing film and beauty industries, and the concomitant emphasis on individual pleasure and consumption. These powerful cultural forces provided young women with alternative images of adult womanhood, from which they were able to fashion their own styles of female modernity. The Danish case therefore suggests that participation in World War I and rapid industrial development may have had much less significance for gender upheaval in the 1920s than we have previously assumed.

Still, the larger social and economic context in which these upheavals took place obviously played a role. Young women's labor market participation, for example, needs to be taken into consideration. In itself, the fact that young women worked for wages was nothing new in the early twentieth century. Throughout the nineteenth century, poor and working-class families had always sent their children out to work, and wage earning as such does therefore not explain the postwar generation's ability to assert their independence from the conventions that had previously ruled women's lives. However, as wages rose in the early decades of the century, allowing most working-class households to sustain themselves without the financial contributions of all members, grown daughters were able to claim at least a portion of the money they earned for their independent consumption. During those same years, greater numbers of middle-class daughters entered the labor force, and, like their working-class counterparts, they were generally permitted to spend part of their earnings as they wished. For the first time historically, large numbers of young women therefore had money of their own in the 1920s, and they used that money as a ticket out of the home and into the emerging world of consumer goods and commercial entertainment.[5]

Along with disposable income, the growth of a consumer culture, replete with its commercial and recreational opportunities, constituted another precondition for the creation of Danish female modernity. As this study has demonstrated, the public world of commercial leisure and entertainment not only provided much of the terrain on which new female identities were formed, but in a much broader sense it also fostered, furthered, and fortified young women's desire for change. But even though urban centers provided the greatest opportunities for partaking in this culture, the Danish case suggests that urbanization may also have been less significant for social and sexual change in the postwar decade than has previously been assumed. Throughout the interwar years, most Danes continued to live in rural areas or small villages, but that does not seem to have seriously impeded country girls' familiarity with or participation in modern consumer culture. By the 1920s, illustrated magazines, popular movies, radios, and phonographs were bringing the sights and sounds of modern life even to the most remote areas of the country, while cars, busses, and bicycles did their part to diminishing the urban–rural divide that most historians still consider a characteristic of early twentieth-century Europe.

Yet if the models of female modernity from which young women drew their inspiration largely derived from mass-produced images and consumer culture, it is important to note that "modern" female identities were not constructed exclusively, or even predominantly, through consumption. Had that been the case, it would certainly have prevented many young women from fashioning themselves as "modern." Instead, being "modern" had as much to do with personality, attitude, and body language as with particular sartorial desires and recreational preferences, and it depended as much on determination and ambition as on economic resources—a reality that helps explain why the phenomenon of female modernity could transcend class boundaries. Nowhere was this more evident than in young women's efforts to update housewifery. Even in the absence of substantial material changes, such as the introduction of new household technologies, they developed new, more "modern" styles of housekeeping, calling attention to the fact that individual female agency was a crucial component in the reorganization of Danish gender relations in the 1920s.

In comparison, the discourses of feminism seem to have played only a very small role in this process. Not only did young women generally reject feminist politics just as vehemently as they rejected their mothers' domestic and family-centered lives, but they also went out of their way to ridicule "the emancipated woman with her tailor-made suits . . . manly cigars and rigid opinions" who supposedly did her best to imitate men and in that process completely lost her feminine charm.[6] Feminists, on the other hand, also did their part to mark the distance between themselves and "modern" young women. Throughout the 1920s, they repeatedly complained that the younger generation took for granted the rights and freedoms they enjoyed and that they did not show sufficient gratitude toward women's rights advocates, whose struggles had won them those rights. They also criticized young women for their lack of political interest and involvement, for their disregard of women's organizations, and for their frivolous "obsession with fun, fashion, and dance partners."[7] Perhaps it was the latter that proved the greatest hindrance to any cooperation between these different groups of women who each in their way sought to expand the boundaries for women's lives. By scorning the politics of pleasure and the joys of beauty, style, glamour, fun, and excitement, feminists failed spectacularly in their efforts to appeal to a generation of women for whom these matters lay at the heart of their vision of the good life. In this light, young women's pronouncement that "we only want to be modern . . . not emancipated," certainly takes on a deeper political meaning, reminding us, once again, that any progressive movement always ignores such desires at its own peril.[8]

But at the same time, there is also no doubt that young women's careful distancing of themselves from feminism functioned to ease the acceptance of their rebellion, and despite its initial vehemence, public opposition against young women's efforts to reshape femininity and gender relations faded surprisingly quickly. By the end of the 1920s, public concern about women and gender relations was clearly on the wane. The heated debates about women's fashions and appearances had largely fallen silent. Critiques of their participation in sports and physical exercise had all but vanished. Even young women's insistence on the right to public leisure and their indisputable fondness of commercial entertainment and urban nightlife no longer seemed to provoke much controversy. That young people socialized in mixed-gender groups was rarely questioned. On the contrary, such socializing was generally celebrated as "healthy development" bound to eliminate "the unfortunate stiffness and unnaturalness" that supposedly had characterized relations between older generations of men and women.[9] And only a few years after the controversial marriage legislation had been passed, there was hardly anyone willing to question, at least publicly, that a marriage ought to consist of two equal partners and that wives should be allowed to take part in decision making in the home.

In the course of little more than a decade, the existence of "modern" young women—women who wore short dresses and bobbed hair, who worked during the day and enjoyed themselves at night, and who expected romance and egalitarianism within marriage—had largely been accepted. When, for example, the Copenhagen daily paper *Ekstrabladet* in 1931 invited a number of prominent men and women to comment on "the young girl of today," their enthusiasm was virtually unanimous. Without exception, they were charmed by the naturalness, vigor, and lively energy of young women. In stark contrast to the moral condemnation of new female fashions that had characterized the immediate postwar years, they were also pleased that young women "no longer hide their physical charms in strange long skirts and high-necked dresses with long sleeves."[10] They even suggested that young women's public presence had "done much to beautify our cities" and that there was "something exhilarating" about "hearing [their] giggles wherever you go."[11] Summarizing the general sentiments of those surveyed by the paper, Albert E. Koch delightedly wrote that "the young girl of today is a modern, liberated woman. But still, she has remained entirely feminine. She is coquettish and eager to please, sweet-tempered and charming. . . . She is a little girl

[in] her lover's arms, and she's a Joan of Arc when sanctimonious men and moralistic old ladies advance on her with the heavy artillery of old-fashioned morality. . . . All in all, she is wonderful."[12]

Such comments begin to explain why public criticisms of young women faded so quickly. First of all, contemporaries soon realized that "modern" young women were no less committed to femininity than their mothers had been. Gradually, they were also reassured that young women were not striving to eradicate the distinctions between men and women, and that even though the new styles displayed more of the female body than older fashions had done, this did not necessarily mean the abandonment of all decency and propriety. Although young women might look different from the generations who preceded them, they were, as one commentator concluded with considerable relief, "not really less nice girls" than "the ladies of past times."[13]

After their initial denunciations, most contemporaries gradually seemed to reach much the same conclusion with regard to young women's public leisure activities. Rather quickly it became clear to them that even though young women gained access to city streets, commercial entertainment facilities, and other public arenas and began to spend more of their free time away from parental and neighborhood control, this did not mean that they escaped social surveillance. Neither did it mean that gender hierarchies were necessarily being overturned.

Even more importantly, many contemporaries realized in the course of the 1920s that young women were, in fact, not particularly concerned with gender hierarchies as such. Their primary interest lay in having lifted some of the particular restrictions placed on their lives and in being able to pursue fun and excitement beyond the home, preferably in gender-mixed company. But even as they strove to reach these goals, they remained deeply concerned about issues of female propriety and respectability, never questioning that men's and women's behavior would be judged by different standards.

Young women's obvious enthusiasm for men and male companionship also helped dampen much of the criticism they first encountered. Even the most conservative critics were often struck by the girlish femininity and easy-going charm they seemed to exude. Especially in comparison with older generations of feminists, they certainly seemed strikingly friendly and unantagonistic toward men, and they rarely asserted the kind of moral authority that their mothers and grandmothers had felt free to claim. As one male observer mused in 1927, "Women's new freedoms seem to have made them more self-assured, but also more amicable."[14] After having queried female readers about their opinions of men, the Copenhagen daily *B.T.* reached the same conclusion in 1928. "Fortunately," the editor noted, "young girls of today have relinquished the inimical tone that characterized so many of the older women's rights women. They no longer need to elevate themselves by putting down men."[15] In light of this congenial attitude, even young women's insistence on more equality with the men in their lives seemed tolerable to many contemporaries.

Besides, those who had predicted that young women's departure from conventions was bound to cause the destruction of the family gradually had to admit that their concerns had been unfounded. Contrary to their assumptions, young women did not opt for personal independence and individual pursuit of pleasure over marriage and motherhood, and they rarely chose to pursue a career at the expense of family life. As had been the case for previous generations, the overwhelming majority of women who came of age in the decade following World War I married while in their twenties, and after marriage they generally retreated from the labor market to become full-time mothers and housewives. After a relatively adventurous youth—and despite their insistence on greater equality between spouses—even "modern" young women settled into a daily life that structurally was not very different from that of their mothers, and as the 1920s wore on, this did much to calm the initial opposition to their insistence on freer, less restrictive forms of womanhood.

Ultimately, then, the relatively swift acceptance of young women's rebellion against long-standing gender norms and conventions may therefore best be explained as the result of their contemporaries' gradual realization that these were challenges that did not pose a fundamental threat to existing gender hierarchies. As women who came of age in the 1910s and 1920s would be the first to admit, theirs was not a struggle based on an ideological commitment to sexual equality. Instead, their actions were motivated by much more immediate and individualistic concerns. In the words of Thora Smed, "We wanted to have fun, to enjoy ourselves, to go out, to have some excitement in our lives."[16]

But if the concerns that preoccupied young women in the 1920s were less overtly political than, for example, the struggle for women's suffrage or the battles over access to education and employment, this did not mean that their actions had no liberating impact on women's lives. In the course of the 1920s, many social norms and cultural practices did undergo a remarkable change, and by the end of the decade young women had successfully managed to challenge many of the restrictions that had previously been placed on women's lives. Operating within a set of social, economic, political, and ideological realities that gave men power over women, but driven by the ambition to create a life for themselves that would permit more glamour, pleasure, enjoyment, and satisfaction on the individual level, young women experimented with a range of new cultural forms that would serve this purpose. So even though young women's activities may not have succeeded in freeing women from male domination, they did at least replace older forms with an updated version of sexual hierarchy that seemed less inhibiting and restrictive to most women. As Inger-Marie Rasmussen, one of the women interviewed for this project phrased it, "I don't think you could say we got equality with men . . . but at least we had more fun, and that was sort of an improvement too."[17]

Notes

Introduction

1. Johanne Blom's diary remains in her personal possession, but she was kind enough to lend it to me after I interviewed her in Copenhagen on December 7, 1993.

2. Oral history interview, Copenhagen, Denmark, December 7, 1993.

3. Karen M. Andersen, *At højne Moralen blandt de unge. Et Foredrag* (Copenhagen, 1920), p. 4; and Ernst Kaper, "Et Forsvar for Kvinden i Hjemmet," unpublished manuscript in the Manuscript Collection, File no. Utilg. 359, "Borgmester Kapers efterladte papirer m.m.," the Royal Library, Copenhagen, Denmark.

4. For general surveys of European women's history in the opening decades of the twentieth century, see Bonnie G. Smith, "The New Woman," in *Changing Lives: Women in European History Since 1700* (Lexington, Mass., and Toronto, 1989), pp. 317–63; Renate Bridenthal, "Something Old, Something New: Women between the Two World Wars," in Renate Bridenthal and Claudia Koonz (eds.), *Becoming Visible: Women in European History* (Boston, 1977), pp. 422–44; and Marilyn J. Boxer and Jean H. Quataert, "Women in the Era of the Interventionist State," in Marilyn J. Boxer and Jean H. Quataert (eds.): *Connecting Spheres: Women in the Western World, 1500 to the Present* (New York and Oxford, 1987), pp. 187–222.

Analyses of women's experiences within particular national contexts include James F. McMillan, *Housewife or Harlot: The Place of Women in French Society 1870–1940* (New York, 1981), pp. 56–63; Michelle Perrot, "The New Eve and the Old Adam: Changes in French Women's Condition at the Turn of the Century," in Margaret Randolph Higonnet et al. (eds.), *Behind the Lines: Gender and the Two World Wars* (New Haven, Conn., and London, 1987), pp. 51–60; Ute Frevert, *Women in German History: From Bourgeois Emancipation to Sexual Liberation* (New York, 1989), pp. 149–204; and Leonore Davidoff and Belinda Westover, "From Queen Victoria to the Jazz Age: Women's World in England, 1880–1939," in Leonore Davidoff et al. (eds.), *Our Work, Our Lives, Our Words* (London, 1986), pp. 1–35.

5. For women's activities during World War I, see Gail Braybon and Penny Summerfield, *Out of the Cage: Women's Experiences in Two World Wars* (London, 1987); Gail Braybon, *Women Workers in the First World War: The British Experience* (London, 1981); Jane Lewis, *Women in England, 1870–1950* (Brighton, England, 1984); Arthur Marwick, *Women at War 1914–1918* (London, 1977); Richard Wall and Jay Winter (eds.), *The Upheaval of War: Family, Work and Welfare in Europe, 1915–1918* (Cambridge, 1988); Frevert, *Women in German History*, pp. 151–67; Jürgen Kocka, *Facing Total War: German Society 1914–1918* (Cambridge, Mass., 1984); and Edith Rigler: *Frauenleitbild und Frauenarbeit in Österreich* (Vienna, 1976).

6. Here quoted from Mary Louise Roberts, " 'This Civilization No Longer Has Sexes': La Garçonne and Cultural Crisis in France After World War I," *Gender and History*, vol. 4, no. 1 (Spring 1992), p. 49.

7. Harald Nielsen, *Moderne Ægteskab* (Copenhagen, 1919), p. 61.

8. Letter from Harald Næsgaard to Emma Knak, March 30, 1922. (Letter in the private ownership of Elisabeth Knak Sørensen, Aalborg, Denmark.)

9. Søren Pedersen-Tarp, "Kvinderne breder sig," *København*, November 3, 1921, p. 4.

10. "En ny Tid," 1919. Unidentified newspaper clipping, in the Emma Grandsgaard Collection of Newspaper Clippings, the Women's History Achieves, the State Library, Aarhus, Denmark.

11. "En ny Dag Gryer," 1920. Unidentified newspaper clipping, in the Emma Grandsgaard Collection of Newspaper Clippings, the Women's History Achieves, the State Library, Aarhus, Denmark.

12. The most (in)famous example of this type of postwar literature was Victor Margueritte's novel *La Garconne* (1922). Quickly translated from French into numerous other languages, it became a best-seller in most European countries. For a historical analysis of this controversial novel, see Mary Louise Roberts: *Civilization without Sexes: Reconstructing Gender in Postwar France* (Chicago, 1994), pp. 46–62.

13. See, for instance, William E. Leuchtenburg, *The Perils of Prosperity, 1914–1932* (Chicago, 1958), pp. 158–77; Kenneth A. Yellis, "Prosperity's Child: Some Thoughts on the Flapper," *American Quarterly*, vol. 21 (Spring 1969), pp. 44–64; and Erik Nørgaard, *Jazz, guldfeber og farlige damer* (Copenhagen, 1965).

More recently, Thorsten Borring Olesen and Nils Arne Sørensen have made similar claims in their article "Da Chaperonen forsvandt. Kærlighed, seksualitet og engelske middelklassekvinder i 1. verdenskrig," *Den jyske historiker*, no. 41 (1987), pp. 96–116.

14. Replacing the original optimistic approach, this revisionist historiography has been described by British historian Sylvia Walby as "the new Feminist pessimism." See Sylvia Walby, *Patriarchy at Work: Patriarchal and Capitalist Relations in Employment* (Cambridge, 1986), p. 156. For other discussions of the historiographical turn in the literature on gender in the 1910s and 1920s, see Angela Woollacott, *On Her Their Lives Depend: Munitions Workers in the Great War* (Berkeley, 1994), pp. 14–15; and Billie Melman (ed.), *Borderlines: Genders and Identities in War and Peace, 1870–1930* (New York and London, 1998), pp. 5–9.

15. Renate Bridenthal, "Beyond 'Kinder, Küche, Kirche': Weimar Women at Work," *Central European History*, vol. 6, no. 2 (1973), pp. 148–66; Bridenthal, "Something Old, Something New," pp. 473–98; Karin Hausen: "Unemployment Also Hits Women: The New and the Old Woman on the Dark Side of the Golden Twenties in Germany," in Peter Stachura (ed.), *Unemployment and the Great Depression in Weimar Germany* (New York, 1986), pp. 78–120; McMillan, *Housewife or Harlot*; Jane Lewis, *Women in England, 1870–1950: Sexual Divisions and Social Change* (Bloomington, Ind., 1984); and Miriam Glucksmann, *Women Assemble: Women Workers and the New Industries in Inter-War Britain* (London, 1990).

Other studies that document women's continued social and sexual subordination throughout the interwar years include Davidoff and Westover, "From Queen Victoria to the Jazz Age," pp. 1–35; Braybon and Summerfield, *Out of the Cage*; Jean H. Quataert, "Women's Work and Worth: The Persistence of Stereotype Attitudes in the German Free Trade Unions, 1890–1929," in Norbert C. Soldon (ed.), *The World of Women's Trade Unionism: Comparative Historical Essays*, (Westport, Conn., 1985), pp. 93–124; Atina Grossman, "'Satisfaction Is Domestic Happiness': Mass Working-Class Sex Reform Organizations in the Weimar Republic," in Michael N. Dobkowski and Isidor Wallimann (eds.), *Towards the Holocaust: The Social and Economic Collapse of the Weimar Republic* (Westport, Conn., 1983), pp. 265–93; Atina Grossmann: "'Girlkultur' or Thoroughly Rationalized Female: A New Woman in Weimar Germany," in Judith Friedlander et al. (eds.), *Women in Culture and Politics: A Century of Change* (Bloomington, Ind., 1986), pp. 62–80; and Tim Mason, "Women in Germany, 1925–1940: Family, Welfare and Work," parts I and II, *History Workshop* (Spring 1976 and Autumn 1976), pp. 74–113, 5–32.

16. See, for instance, Susan Kingsley Kent, *Making Peace: The Reconstruction of Gender in Interwar Britain* (Princeton, N.J., 1994); Sheila Jeffreys, *The Spinster and Her Enemies: Feminism and Sexuality 1880–1930* (London, 1985); Sheila Jeffreys, "Sex Reform and Antifeminism in the 1920s," in The London Feminist History Group (eds.), *The Sexual Dynamics of History: Men's Power, Women's Resistance* (London, 1983), pp. 177–202; Martha Vicinus, *Independent Women: Work and Community for Single Women 1850–1920* (Chicago and London, 1985); and Michelle Perrot, "The New Eve and the Old Adam: Changes in French Women's Condition at the Turn of the Century," in Margaret Randolph Higonnet et al. (eds.), *Behind the Lines: Gender and the Two World Wars* (New Haven and London, 1987), pp. 51–60.

Some studies of the American case have drawn similar conclusions. See, for instance, Rayna Rapp and Ellen Ross, "The 1920s: Feminism, Consumerism, and Political Backlash in the United States," in Friedlander et al. (eds.), *Women in Culture and Politics*, pp. 52–61.

17. See, for instance, Jeffreys, *The Spinster and Her Enemies*; Christina Simmons, "Modern Sexuality and the Myth of Victorian Repression," in Kathy Peiss and Christina Simmons (eds.), *Passion and Power: Sexuality in History* (Philadelphia, 1989), pp. 157–77; and Margaret Jackson, "Sexual Liberation or Social Control? Some Aspects of the Relationship between Feminism and the Social Construction of Sexual Knowledge in the Early Twentieth Century," *Women's Studies International Forum*, vol. 6, no. 1 (1983), pp. 1–17.

18. Roberts, *Civilization without Sexes*, p. 6. As Millie Melman has suggested, paying attention to the contemporary sense of upheaval may have the added advantage of moving the historiography on women and gender in the 1920s beyond the debate on change or nonchange in women's lives. See Melman, *Borderlines*, p. 6.

19. Joan W. Scott was among the first to make this claim in her influential essay, "Gender: A Useful Category of Historical Analysis," *American Historical Review*, vol. 91, no. 5 (1986), pp. 1053–75.

20. Roberts, *Civilization without Sexes*; Kent, *Making Peace*; and Billie Melman, *Women and the Popular Imagination in the 1920s: Flappers and Nymphs* (London and New York, 1988).

21. In many ways this study can therefore be seen as a response to German historian Atina Grossman's call for an analysis of "the New Woman as producer and not only consumer, as an agent of constructing a new identity." See Atina Grossman, "Girlkultur or Thoroughly Rationalized Female," p. 64.

22. Braybon and Summerfield, *Out of the Cage*. See also Woollacott, *On Her Their Lives Depend*; and Ute von Gersdorff, *Frauen im Kriegsdienst 1914–1945* (Stuttgart, 1969).

23. See, for instance, Sandra M. Gilbert, "Soldier's Heart: Literary Men, Literary Women, and the Great War," in Marilyn J. Boxer and Jean H. Quataert (eds.), *Connecting Spheres: Women in the Western World, 1500 to the Present* (New York and Oxford, 1987), pp. 232–45; and Klaus Theweleit, *Male Fantasies*, vols. 1–2 (Cambridge, Mass., 1987–89).

For a less pessimistic analysis of the impact of war on men's view of women, see Joanna Bourke, *Dismembering the Male: Men's Bodies, Britain and the Great War* (Chicago, 1996).

24. See, for instance, Roberts, *Civilization without Sexes*; and Kent, *Making Peace*.

25. See, for instance, Frevert, *Women in German History*, pp. 131–204; and Deborah Thom, *Nice Girls and Rude Girls: Women Workers in World War I* (London and New York, 1998).

26. See, for instance, Susan K. Besse, *Restructuring Patriarchy: The Modernization of Gender Inequality in Brazil, 1914–1940* (Chapel Hill, N.C., and London, 1996); and Sueann Caulfield: "Getting into Trouble: Dishonest Women, Modern Girls, and Women-Men in the Conceptual Language of *Vida Policial*, 1925–1927," *Signs*, vol. 19, no. 1 (1993), pp. 146–76.

27. See Barbara Hamill Sato, "The *Moga* Sensation: Perceptions of the *Modan Garu* in Japanese Intellectual Circles During the 1920s," *Gender and History*, vol. 5, no. 3 (1993), pp. 363–81; Miriam Silverberg, "The Modern Girl as Militant," in Gail Lee Bernstein (ed.), *Recreating Japanese Women, 1600–1935* (Berkeley, Calif., 1991), pp. 239–66; and Miriam Silverberg, "Constructing the Japanese Ethnography of Modernity," *Journal of Asian Studies*, vol. 51, no. 1 (1992), pp. 30–54.

28. Vivian Ng, "The Reconstruction of Gender in China, 1897–1911." Unpublished paper presented at the Department of History, University of Minnesota, October 16, 1989.

29. For general histories of Denmark in English, see W. Glyn Jones, *Denmark: A Modern History* (London, 1986); Steward Oakley, *A Short History of Denmark* (New York, 1972); Kenneth E. Miller, *Government and Politics in Denmark* (Boston, 1968); Erik Kjersgaard, *A History of Denmark* (Copenhagen, 1974); and John Danstrup, *A History of Denmark* (Copenhagen, 1947).

30. See, for instance, Sune Aakerman, "Internal Migration, Industrialization and Urbanization," *Scandinavian Economic History Review*, vol. 23, no. 2 (1975), pp. 149–58.

31. "Folkemængden 1. Februar 1921 i Kongeriget Danmark," *Statistiske Meddelelser*, series 4, vol. 63, no. 1 (1921), p. 4.

32. "Folkemængden 1. February 1921," p. 6.

33. Hans Chr. Johansen (ed.), *Dansk historisk statistik 1814-1980* (Copenhagen, 1985), pp. 34–35.

34. In 1920, a national total of 4500 industrial enterprises employed only 160,000 Danish workers out of a work force of 1,360,000 people. See B. R. Mitchell (ed.), *European Historical Statistics, 1750–1970* (New York, 1975), p. 154. For histories of Danish economic development, see Karl Gunnar Persson (ed.), *The Economic Development of Denmark and Norway since 1870* (Hants, England, 1993); Svend Aage Hansen, *Økonomisk vækst i Danmark 1720–1983* (Copenhagen, 1984); and Ole Hyldtoft, *Københavns industrialisering 1840–1914* (Copenhagen, 1984).

35. See Svend Aage Hansen, *Early Industrialization in Denmark* (Copenhagen, 1970), p. 7

36. For a history of the Danish wartime economy, see Einar Cohn, *Danmark under den store Krig. En økonomisk Oversigt* (Copenhagen, 1928).

37. Johansen (ed.), *Dansk historisk statistik, 1814–1980*, p. 295.
In most sections of the economy, wages would continue to increase in the immediate postwar years. For skilled male workers employed in industry or manufacturing, wages grew by 365 percent between 1914 and 1920. For unskilled industrial workers, male and female, the increase was almost 400 percent. See Arbejdsløn i Haandværk og Industri," *Statistisk Aarbog 1920* (Copenhagen 1921), p. 149.

38. Søren Mørch, *Den ny Danmarkshistorie 1880–1960* (Copenhagen, 1982), p. 96.
Household budgets collected by the Danish Statistical Bureau in the 1910s and 1920s document this rising standard of living. While in 1911 a working-class family typically spent up to 70 percent of its total income on food and housing, this percentage had dropped to 55 in 1921, allowing more money to be spent on furniture, books and newspapers, entertainment, and other forms of recreation. See "Husholdningsbudgetter for 1911, 1916, 1921 og 1926," *Nationaløkonomisk Tidsskrift* (1932), pp. 74–118.

39. According to census findings, the percentage of economically active women out of the total female population was 27.2 in 1911, 24.1 in 1921, and 26.9 in 1930. The proportion of women in the work force also remained unchanged. In 1911, women constituted 31.3 percent of the entire work force; in 1921, 29.7 percent; and in 1930, 30.5 percent. Here cited from Bridenthal, "Something Old, Something New," p. 476.

40. See Mitchell (ed.), *European Historical Statistics, 1750–1970*, p. 154; and Tinne Vammen, *Rent og urent. Hovedstadens Piger og Fruer 1880–1920* (Copenhagen, 1986), pp. 49–80.

41. See Kirsten Geertsen, *Arbejderkvinder i Danmark 1914–1924* (Grenaa, 1977), p. 46; and Ole Markussen, "Danish Industry, 1920–1939: Technology, Rationalization and Modernization," *Scandinavian Journal of History*, vol. 13 (1988), pp. 240–41.

42. Mitchell (ed.), *European Historical Statistics, 1750–1970*, p. 154.

43. During these years, a small number of women made their way into teaching and nursing. See Bente Rosenbeck, *Kvindekøn. Den moderne kvindeligheds historie 1880–1980* (Copenhagen, 1987), pp. 253–84; and Kirsten Geertsen, *Dannet ung Pige søges. Kvinder på kontor 1900–1940* (Copenhagen, 1990).

44. On the decline of married working-class women's labor market participation, see Kirsten Geertsen, *Arbejderkvinder i Danmark 1914–1924*, pp. 45–72.

45. See Drude Dahlerup, "Women's Entry into Politics: The Experience of the Danish Local and General Elections 1908–1920," *Scandinavian Political Studies*, vol. 1, no. 2–3 (1978), pp. 139–62; Aagot Lading, *Kvindens stilling i det danske samfund* (Copenhagen, 1943), pp. 102–109; and Aagot Lading, *Dansk Kvindesamfunds Arbejde gennem 25 Aar* (Copenhagen, 1939), pp. 48–65.

46. For contemporary discussions of the problems facing organized feminism after the passage of women's suffrage, see Natalie Frantzen, "Lidt om Taknemmelighed," in *Ved Festlighederne i Aarhus i Anledning af Dansk Kvindesamfunds 50 Aars Jubilæum* (Aarhus, 1921); Thyra Jensen, "Hvorfor bør vi staa i Dansk Kvindesamfund?" *Kvinden og Samfundet*, vol. 33, no. 9 (1917), p. 131; and "Er det Dansekavallerer Dansk Kvindesamfund mangler?" *Vendsyssel Tidende*, June 14, 1927, p. 2. For more general histories of the Danish women's movement, see Aagot Lading, *Dansk Kvindesamfunds Historie gennem 40 Aar* (Copenhagen, 1912); Aagot Lading, *Dansk Kvindesamfunds Arbejde gennem 25 Aar*; and Hanne Rimmen Nielsen and Eva Lous (eds.), *Kvinder undervejs. Dansk Kvindesamfund i Aarhus 1886–1986* (Aarhus, 1986).

47. "Kvinden i vor Tid," 1924. Unidentified newspaper clipping in the Emma Grandsgaard Collection of Newspaper Clippings, the Women's History Archives, the State Library, Aarhus, Denmark.

48. "Kvinderne og den moderne Stil," 1926. Unidentified newspaper clipping in the Emma Grandsgaard Collection of Newspaper Clippings, the Women's History Archives, the State Library, Aarhus, Denmark.

49. "Hjemmets Fremtid," *Aarhus Stiftstidende*, March 3, 1921, p. 7.

50. In the post–World War II era, local and national archives in Denmark have repeatedly encouraged local citizens to submit autobiographical accounts. For this project, I examined the holdings of such records in the Danish National Museum, the Copenhagen Municipal Archives, and the Local Historical Archives for Aalborg Municipality.

The oral history interviews were conducted between 1990 and 1994. In three cases I knew the women prior to the interview. The remaining fifty-six women were located through arbitrary personal contacts. All interviews were conducted in the private homes of the narrators, each lasting two to five hours. The interviews, which were tape-recorded and later transcribed for my personal use, focused on adolescent and early adult experiences in the home, the workplace, and public life in the 1910s and 1920s, but they also touched on childhood, upbringing, family, marriage, child-rearing, and many other aspects of their lives.

In eleven cases, the women requested that I use pseudonyms rather than their real names. (A complete list of narrators, and the date and place of the interviews, is included in the Select Bibliography.)

51. Approximately 20 percent of the women grew up in prosperous families, and another 20 percent came from decidedly poor households. Despite the fact

that I had to rely on arbitrary personal contacts, the women I reached thus represent a fairly broad cross-section of the Danish population.

52. As so much recent work on language, memory, and subjectivity has reminded us, personal narratives cannot be treated as unproblematic reflections of the past. Not only may memories be distorted, but they are also selective. Besides, the self is not a fixed entity but is reconstructed over time, and the particular construction at any one time depends, among other things, on the situation, the person who is listening, the questions asked, and the relationship between the narrator and the interviewer. It is therefore impossible to know how women "really" experienced and interpreted their lives at the time, and in most cases we cannot know how that might differ from their retrospective accounts.

Nonetheless, in reconstructing a history of women's lives in which subjectivity and experience is foregrounded, personal narratives offer information that few other sources do. They can bring to the surface events, phenomena, and perspectives deemed too trivial, insignificant, or commonplace to have entered the historical record elsewhere. Besides, despite their shortcomings, they are still revealing of attitudes, beliefs, and motivations. Moreover, the use of repeated refrains, key phrases, and pronouns yields at least some insight into the relationship between the narrator and her social world, and common patterns and tropes of language provide important glimpses of the social and cultural world in which narrators lived.

For particularly insightful discussions of the methodological difficulties associated with the uses of personal narratives in historical scholarship, see Carolyn Steedman, *Past Tenses: Essays on Writing, Autobiography and History* (London, 1992); Personal Narratives Group (eds.), *Interpreting Women's Lives: Feminist Theory and Personal Narratives* (Bloomington, Ind., 1989); Mary Jo Maynes, *Taking the Hard Road: Life Course in French and German Workers' Autobiographies in the Era of Industrialization* (Chapel Hill, N.C., 1995); and Luisa Passerini, "A Memory for Women's History: Problems of Method and Interpretation," *Social Science History*, vol. 16 (1992), pp. 669–92. For more specific discussions of the practice and uses of oral history, see S. B. Gluck and D. Patai (eds.), *Women's Words: The Feminist Practice of Oral History* (London, 1991); and Trevor Lummis, *Listening to History: The Authenticity of Oral Evidence* (London, 1987).

53. I have borrowed this phrase from Caulfield, "Getting into Trouble," p. 172.

Part I

1. "En Skønhedskonkurrence," 1926. Unidentified newspaper clipping in the Emma Grandsgaard Collection of Newspaper Clippings, the Women's History Archives, the State Library, Aarhus.

2. "*Vore Damers* Skønhedsstævne," *Vore Damer*, vol. 14, no. 32 (August 11, 1926), p. 12.

3. "Det første danske Skønhedsstævne aabnes," *Vore Damer*, vol. 14, no. 22 (June 3, 1926), p. 21.

4. "Det første danske Skønhedsstævne aabnes," p. 20.

5. "*Vore Damers* Skønhedsstævne," p. 12.

6. "Det store Skønhedsstævne. De første Deltagere - og Arrangementet af Stævnet," *Vore Damer*, vol. 14, no. 25 (June 23, 1926), p. 21.

7. "Edith Jørgensen. Danmarks første Skønhedsdronning," *Vore Damer*, vol. 14, no. 33 (August 18, 1926), p. 15; and "Atter lidt om Skønhedsstævnet," *Vore Damer*, vol. 14, no. 49 (December 8, 1926), p. 26–27.

8. "En Skønhedskonkurrence," 1926.

CHAPTER 1

1. Oral history interview, Copenhagen, Denmark, December 3, 1993.

2. "Moderne og den unge Pige," *Politiken*, March 22, 1914, p. 7.

3. "Tidens Mode," *Berlingske Tidende*, August 11, 1914, p. 9.

4. "Krigen og Foraarsmoden," *Politiken*, March 2, 1915, p. 7.

5. Helga Meisen, "Kvindelige Sundhedsbegreber," *Politiken*, March 28, 1915, p. 13; "De sidste Moder," *Politiken*, April 2, 1917, p. 8.

6. "Mere om Tidens Mode," *Aarhus Stiftstidende*, October 11, 1916, p. 7.

7. On women's changing fashions in the late nineteenth and early twentieth centuries, see Valerie Steele, *Paris Fashion: A Cultural History* (New York and Oxford, 1988); Elisabeth Wilson, *Adorned in Dreams: Fashion and Modernity* (London, 1985); Bonnie G. Smith, *Changing Lives: Women in European History since 1700* (Lexington, Mass., and Toronto, 1989), pp. 325–30; and Lois W. Banner, *American Beauty* (Chicago, 1983), pp. 128–74.

8. I am indebted to Valerie Steele for this description of the turn-of-the-century transformation in women's fashions. See Steele, *Paris Fashion*, p. 219.

9. In Denmark in the mid-1910s, the Copenhagen department store Magasin du Nord pioneered lavish fashion shows, where young female clerks modeled the latest styles for a select group of customers. (Information obtained from the Corporate Archives of Magasin du Nord A/S, Copenhagen, Denmark.) Others quickly followed the lead, and from the early 1920s, Copenhagen department stores such as Illum, and Crome & Goldschmidt regularly invited prosperous customers to attend presentations of spring and fall fashions.

10. On the significance of popular film for the dissemination of fashion information, see Mary Ryan, "The Projection of a New Womanhood: The Movie Moderns in the 1920s," in Jean E. Friedman and William G. Slade (eds.), *Our American Sisters: Women in American Life and Thought* (Boston, 1982), pp. 175–95; Maureen Turim, "Seduction and Elegance: The New Woman of Fashion in Silent Cinema," in Shari Benstock and Suzanne Ferriss (eds.), *On Fashion* (New Brunswick, N.J., 1994), pp. 140–58; Banner, *American Beauty*, p. 276; and Gunnar Sandfeld, *Den stumme scene. Dansk biografteater indtil lydfilmens gennembrud* (Copenhagen, 1966), p. 476.

11. Oral history interview, Randers, Denmark, April 16, 1994.

12. Deferred payment systems were first introduced in Denmark in the first decade of the twentieth century. "Why pay cash when you can pay in installments?" Thomsen's Stores in Copenhagen asked in a 1908 advertising campaign. Two years later, the prominent firm, N.C. Rasmussen, declared in an advertise-

ment that "the credit system is triumphantly sweeping the world, and nowadays anything in the world can be bought on credit." Here quoted from Erik Nørgaard, *Dansk Reklames Barndom eller Røde Næser bortfjernes med overraskende Resultat* (Copenhagen, 1973), p. 21.

Seeking to stimulate private consumption, manufacturers and businessowners eagerly promoted the new payment systems, but convincing a public accustomed to saving rather than spending often proved a difficult task. Older people especially remained staunchly opposed to the idea, as illustrated by the recollections of Sigrid Johansen. In her memoirs, she vividly recalls the misfortunes that befell her older sister when she came home for a visit dressed in the latest fashions.

> Karen was too well-dressed considering her income, and hard pressed she had to admit that she had bought on credit in [the town of] Frederikshavn [where she worked as a domestic servant.] On credit! You should think Karen had done something criminal considering my father's outrage. Karen had to accompany my father back to Frederikshavn and listen to him rebuke the store owner for *luring* young girls into buying clothes that way. He paid Karen's debt, and she was told to repay the amount at the first of the month, no excuses. That is how bad it was to buy on credit in 1919.

Quoted from unpublished memoir, file no. 1986/1126 E 3392, in the Local Historical Archives for Aalborg Municipality, Aalborg, Denmark.

13. In Scandinavia, *Nordisk Mønstertidende*, an inexpensive bimonthly pattern publication, promised to give "a completely fresh and current picture of the newest styles", in addition to being "an exceptional consultant in all questions of fashion." See "Moderne ved Aarsskiftet," *Illustreret Familiejournal*, vol. 43, no. 1 (January 2, 1919), p. 33.

14. "Tidens Tegn," *Aarhus Stiftstidende*, May 16, 1918, p. 4.

15. "Vore Døtre," *Vore Damer*, vol. 3, no. 25 (June 27, 1915).

16. Similar concerns echoed through public discourse in other Western societies in the 1920s. According to Beth Bailey, many American observers were equally distressed about this trend. See Beth Bailey, *From Front Porch to Back Seat: Courtship in Twentieth-Century America* (Baltimore, 1988), pp. 70–71.

17. Gerda Mundt, "Hvis er Skylden?" *Kristeligt Dagblad*, November 20, 1919, p. 6.

18. As Valerie Steele has noted, "A woman wearing Twenties dress was much more *touchable* than a woman in Victorian or Edwardian dress." Valerie Steele, *Fashion and Eroticism: Ideals of Feminine Beauty from the Victorian Era to the Jazz Age* (New York and Oxford, 1985), p. 239.

19. For a history of women's underwear, see C. Willett and Phillis Cunnington, *The History of Underclothes* (London and Boston, 1981), pp. 140–60.

20. I have borrowed this phrase from Edmonde Charles-Roux, *Chanel: Her Life, Her World—and the Woman behind the Legend She Herself Created* (New York, 1975), p. 157.

21. Ernst Kaper, "Storbyens Natteliv. En Renlig Sondring mellem Byens Borgerskab og dens Bundfald." Unpublished manuscript in the Manuscript Collec-

tion, File no. Utilg. 359, "Borgmester Kapers efterladte papirer m.m.," the Royal Library, Copenhagen, Denmark.

22. Ernst Kaper, "Synspunkter overfor Storbyens Moral." Manuscript in the personal papers of Ernst Kaper, file no. Utilg. 359, the Manuscript Collection, the Royal Library, Copenhagen, Denmark.

23. "Kvinde!" *Ekstrabladet*, November 19, 1919, p. 1.

24. For descriptions of 1910s and 1920s fashions as boyish, see, for example, Mary Louise Roberts: *Civilization without Sexes: Reconstructing Gender in Postwar France, 1917–1927* (Chicago, 1994), pp. 63–87; Bonnie Smith: *Changing Lives: Women in European History since 1700* (Lexington, Mass., and Toronto, 1989), pp. 416–19; and Robert Daniel, *American Women in the 20th Century: The Festival of Life* (San Diego, Calif., 1987), pp. 55–61.

At the time, the down-playing of female curves in the new fashions did not go unnoticed. If most men agreed that fashionable young women were becoming more sexy and attractive, many female observers expressed their reservations about what they called the "masculine lines" in the new fashions. See, for instance, "Smaa Vink," *Politiken*, February 21, 1915.

25. "Foraar i Byen," *Politiken*, May 23, 1921, p. 4.

26. "Kvindelige Moder," *Folkets Avis*, November 22, 1919, p. 3.

27. "Kvinde!" p. 1.

28. Ibid.

29. Carla Meyer's statement was published in most national newspapers, including *Politiken, Social Demokraten, Berlingske Tidende, Nationaltidende, Folkets Avis, Kristeligt Dagblad,* and *Ekstrabladet.* It is here quoted from *Politiken*, November 25, 1919, p. 7.

30. This statement was also published in most national newspapers. Here quoted from *Politiken*, November 27, 1919, p. 3.

31. "De halvnøgne Damekostumer," *Folkets Avis*, November 25, 1919, p. 4.

32. "Et Stormangreb mod Skøgedragten," *Klokken 5*, December 2, 1919, p. 3.

33. "De halvnøgne Damekostumer," *Politiken*, November 27, 1919, p. 6.

Unfortunately, such mean-spirited attacks on older female activists were not uncommon in the 1910s and 1920s, and they were not unique to the Danish case. According to Kathy Peiss, many films from the 1910s and 1920s "delighted in poking fun at the earnest efforts of moral reformers, temperance advocates, and other uplifters." See Kathy Peiss, *Cheap Amusements: Working Women and Leisure in Turn-of-the-Century New York* (Philadelphia, 1986), p. 157.

34. Den moderne Eva, "Typer: Min æstetiske Veninde," *Vore Herrer*, vol. 8, no. 5 (March 1, 1923).

35. This is a point also made in Linda Mizejewski, *Ziegfeld Girl: Image and Icon in Culture and Cinema* (Durham, N.C., and London, 1999), p. 78.

The portrayal of feminists, female activists, and highly educated career women as old hags who paid no attention to their appearances was obviously a mocking caricature, but despite an extensive literature on the New Woman we still do not know much about their actual self-representation, or about the politics of physical appearance that informed their choices and styles.

36. "Amerikanerinden i sit Hjem," *Vore Damer*, vol. 8, no. 1 (January 3, 1920).

37. "Moden 1924," *Illustreret Fagblad for danske Damefrisører*, vol. 11, no. 129 (February 1924), p. 3.

38. "Hvor stammer det kortklippede Damehaar fra?" *Ugens Spejl. Organ for Soignerings-, Toilet- og Sanitetsbrancherne*, vol. 14, no. 324 (July 15, 1925), p. 1.

39. "Det kortklippede Damehaar," *Ugens Spejl. Organ for Soignerings-, Toilet- og Sanitetsbrancherne*, vol. 14, no. 310 (April 8, 1925), p. 2.

40. "Fra Barberstuen," *Politiken*, May 22, 1926, p. 8; "Shinglingens Sejersgang," *Danmarks Barber- og Frisørtidende*, vol. 36, no. 16 (August 8, 1926), p. 3.

41. Oral history interview, Aarhus, Denmark, March 15, 1994.

42. Oral history interview, Copenhagen, Denmark, November 5, 1993.

43. Oral history interview, Copenhagen, Denmark, December 14, 1993.

44. Between 1900 and 1925, the number of beauty salons in Copenhagen increased from fifteen to approximately three hundred, and smaller towns around the country witnessed similar developments. See "25 Aar. Damefrisørfaget og Elektriciteten," *Illustreret Fagblad for Danske Damefrisører*, vol. 13, no. 152 (January 1926), pp. 13–14.

45. For examples of this, see, for instance, Sigfred Hjort Eriksen's recollections of events at his mother's beauty salon in the 1920s, "Min mors damefrisørsalon," in *Sådan var Aarhus: Lette Vidnesbyrd om Aarhus i 1920'erne og 1930'erne* (Aarhus, 1973), pp. 24–31.

46. Oral history interview, Aarhus, Denmark, February 27, 1990.

47. "Et Interview fra Bladet 'Klokken 5,'" *Ugens Spejl*, vol. 15, no. 386 (September 22, 1926), p. 2.

48. "Haarmoden," *Aarhus Stiftstidende*, April 22, 1926, p. 6.

49. "Er Pagehaaret ikke tækkeligt eller - ?" *Ekstra Bladet*, June 8, 1924, p. 2.

50. "Det kortklippede Damehaar," *Nyborg Avis*, August 6, 1926, p. 9.

51. Ibid.

52. Oral history interview, Copenhagen, Denmark, February 6, 1990. Aware of this widespread opposition, some young women sought to promote their long hair as an asset in the labor market. "Young girl, not bobbed hair, from a nice home, seeks a position from June 1," one job advertisement read in 1926. One mother marketed her offspring in a similar manner, advertising that "for my daughter, nineteen years old, I am seeking a position . . . preferably in the countryside; is lively and dependable. . . . *Not short hair.*" Here quoted from "Er De kortklippet," *Politiken*, May 16, 1926, p. 13.

53. See, for instance, "Hendes Haar," *Vore Damer*, vol. 14, no. 33 (August 18, 1926), p. 14; "Det bobbede Haar kræver tre Ting: Penge, Tid og Type," *Ugebladet*, vol. 4, no. 124 (August 20, 1924), pp. 10–11; and "Smaaudklip," *Ugens Spejl*, vol. 15, no. 379 (August 4, 1926), p. 4.

54. "Flirts Spørgekasse," *Flirt*, vol. 2, no. 22 (September 7, 1922), p. 9.

55. "De nye Frisurer," *Flirt*, vol. 2, no. 31 (November 9, 1922), p. 16.

56. "Den moderne frisure," *Ugebladet*, vol. 5. no. 49 (December 9, 1925), p. 18; and "Skal Frøken Garçonne tvinges til at gaa paa Barberstue?" *B.T.*, August 10, 1925, p. 11.

57. "Nogle Ord om Moden," *Illustreret Familiejournal*, vol. 48, no. 5 (January 30, 1924), p. 42.

58. "Emancipering af den kvindelige Haarmode," *Ugens Spejl*, vol. 15, no. 377 (July 21, 1926), p. 2.

59. "Kort eller langt Haar?" *B.T.*, August 15, 1925, p. 11.

60. For discussions of this "physiognomic paradigm," see Kathy Peiss: "Making Up, Making Over: Cosmetics, Consumer Culture, and Women's Identity," in Victoria de Grazia, with Ellen Furlough (eds.), *The Sex of Things: Gender and Consumption in Historical Perspective* (Berkeley, Calif., 1996), p. 313; Allan Sekula: "The Body and the Archive," *October*, no. 39 (1986), pp. 3–64; and Joanne Finkelstein: *The Fashioned Self* (Philadelphia, 1991), pp. 15–77.

61. "Det kortklippede Damehaar," *Ugens spejl*, vol. 14, no. 310 (April 8, 1925), p. 2.

62. "Kort eller langt Haar? Stor Diskussion," *B.T.*, August 21, 1925, p. 11.

63. "Haar og Skæg," *Ugens Spejl*, vol. 14, no. 329 (August 12, 1925), p. 4.

64. "Det kortklippede Damehaar," p. 2; see also "Bliver de drengeklippede Damer skaldede?" *B.T.*, October 12, 1928, p. 2.

65. "Kort eller Langt Haar? Stor Diskussion," p. 11.

66. As Karen Callaghan has pointed out, the pursuit of feminine beauty has typically been assumed to be undertaken for men's pleasure and approval. See Karen Callaghan (ed.), *Ideals of Feminine Beauty: Philosophical, Social and Cultural Dimensions* (Westport, Conn., 1994), p. ix. That was certainly the case in Denmark in the 1920s, and it was for that reason that so many critics were utterly appalled when young women ignored men's criticisms of the new styles.

67. Thit Jensen, one of the most controversial and outspoken Danish women's rights advocate of the period, proved the exception to this rule. Pushing the practicality argument one step further—and shifting the mode from defense to offense—she lashed out at men who opposed the styles, questioning their capacity as providers and accusing them of hypocrisy. "The simple truth is," she trumpeted in her provocative manner, "that the woman cuts her hair in order to have time to do the work that the man ought to do." See Thit Jensen, "Langt eller kort Haar," 1926. Unidentified newspaper clipping in the Emma Grandsgaard Collection of Newspaper Clippings, the Women's History Archives, The State Library, Aarhus, Denmark.

68. "Kort eller langt Haar? Stor Diskussion," p. 11.

69. Ibid.

70. "Kort Haar med Posticher," *Danmarks Barber- og Frisør-Tidende*, vol. 36, no. 24 (December 15, 1926), p. 3.

71. "Page-Frisuren," *Fagblad for Danske Damefrisører*, vol. 9, no. 104 (January 1922), pp. 5–6.

72. "Mandligt Pigehaar og kvindeligt Drengehaar," *Ugens Spejl*, vol. 15, no. 388 (October 6, 1926), pp. 3–4.

73. "Shinglingens Sejersgang," *Danmarks Barber- og Frisør-Tidende*, vol. 36. no. 16 (August 15, 1926), p. 3.

74. "La Garçonne eller ej?" *Ugebladet*, vol. 4, no. 114 (June 11, 1924), p. 11.

75. "Den moderne Frisure," *Ugebladet*, vol. 5, no. 49 (December 9, 1925), p. 28.

76. See, for instance, "Kvindelighedens Triumf," *Ugebladet*, vol. 8, no. 18 (April 29, 1928), p. 44.

77. Agnes Nymann, "Pariser-Model. Tekst til Modebilaget," *Illustreret Fagblad for Danske Damefrisører*, vol. 14, no. 164 (January, 1927), pp. 10–11.

78. Julie Berthelsen, for example, recalled her father's remarkable change of heart. "Like so many other young women, I had my hair cut," she told me. "When I came home, my father was furious. You should think I had done something terrible. His daughter was not going to be seen like that. He yelled and screamed. But, you know, the funny thing was that a few years later, he actually told my sister [who was growing her hair out] that her hair looked like a bird's nest, and why didn't she get it cut? . . . I guess he had gotten used to it by then." Oral history interview, Silkeborg, Denmark, March 13, 1994.

79. "Tidens Mode," *Politiken*, March 7, 1927, p. 5.

80. See, for instance, Smith, *Changing Lives*, p. 326; Steven Hause: "More Minerva Than Mars: The French Women's Rights Campaign and the First World War," in Margaret Higonnet et al. (eds.), *Behind the Lines: Gender and the Two World Wars* (New Haven, Conn., 1987), p. 102; R. Broby-Johansen, *Omrids af Modens Historie. Set fra et københavnsk modehus 1847–1947* (Copenhagen, 1948), p. 53.; and Erik Nørgaard, *Jazz, guldfeber og farlige damer* (Copenhagen, 1965), p. 16.

81. Oral history interview, Aarhus, Denmark, February 19, 1990.

82. Oral history interview, Copenhagen, Denmark, October 10, 1993.

83. Oral history interview, Copenhagen, Denmark, October 12, 1993.

84. Oral history interview, Helsingør, Denmark, November 20, 1993.

85. Oral history interview, Copenhagen, Denmark, November 3, 1993.

86. Steele, *Paris Fashion*, p. 232.

87. I have borrowed this phrase from Kim Chernin, *The Obsession: Reflections on the Tyranny of Slenderness* (New York, 1981).

88. Even though slenderness was a prerequisite for appearing elegant and graceful when wearing a modern dress, it should be noted that the new fashionable styles were not the only reason why more and more women began to strive to reduce their bodies in the early decades of the twentieth century. Equally significant was the simultaneous transformation of the social symbolism of body weight and size. As Susan Bordo has pointed out, bulging bodies were in the mid-nineteenth century "a symbol of bourgeois success, an outward manifestation of accumulated wealth." See Susan Bordo, "Reading the Slender Body," in Mary Jacobus et al. (eds.), *Body/Politics: Women and the Discourses of Science* (New York and London, 1990), p. 94. By the late nineteenth century, when social power became less dependent on the sheer accumulation of material wealth and more connected to the ability to control and manage the labor and resources of others, corpulence gradually went out of vogue for both men and women of the upper and upper-middle classes. From the turn of the century, wealthy women became accustomed to watching their bodies and appetites in order to be able to conform to changing aesthetic ideals. In this process, slenderness acquired strong moral

valuations. From the early twentieth century, excess body weight gradually came to be seen as a sign of personal and moral inadequacy, or, in the words of Bordo, the "outer indication of the state of the 'soul'" (p. 88). By the late 1910s, when slenderness had become disassociated from its original class basis and emerged as a cross-class ideal, this moral coding of fat and slender bodies was firmly in place. Being thin was no longer a designator of social status or simply a sign of fashion consciousness; it was physical manifestation of virtue.

89. "Smaa Vink," *Politiken*, February 21, 1915, p. 12.

90. "Vil De være slank?" *Aftenlæsning*, vol. 2, no. 1 (May 4, 1927), p. 16.

As the decade wore on, diet advice became stricter and stricter, and the tone in which such advice was dispensed more and more harsh. While the earliest dieting experts had been rather sympathetic to the would-be thins who occasionally capitulated to temptation and indulged in the pleasures of good and bountiful food, they gradually became more and more contemptuous of such behavior. In 1927, one advice columnist thus asserted that it was lack of will power combined with absence of a strong character that caused women to become "unshapely." See "Vil De være slank?" p. 16. Consequently, women often came to experience the relationship to their own bodies as adversarial. Women increasingly feared that their bodies, if not constantly watched, would turn on them, becoming ugly, fat, and undisciplined. In addition to narrowing the range of acceptable and attractive feminine appearance, the new cultural imagery of ideal slenderness thus functioned to impose perpetual anxieties about the body, to ensure an increased sensitivity to departure from social norms, and to engage women in an immense labor in the service of those norms.

91. See, for instance, "Hvordan man bliver slank," *Aftenlæsning*, vol. 1, no. 1 (1926), p. 9.

92. See, for instance, "Det gør Dem slank!" *Aftenlæsning*, vol. 1, no. 27 (November 3, 1926); and "Vore Herrer ynder kun de slanke. Farris er min sidste Redningsplanke" (advertisement), *Vore Herrer*, vol. 9, no. 19 (September 11, 1924), p. 44.

93. Joan Jacobs Brumberg, *The Body Project: An Intimate History of American Girls* (New York, 1997).

94. Roberts, *Civilization without Sexes*, p. 85.

95. Oral history interview, Copenhagen, Denmark, October 31, 1993.

96. Oral history interview, Helsingør, Denmark, November 20, 1993.

97. Oral history interview, Randers, Denmark, April 16, 1994.

98. Oral history interview, Aalborg, Denmark, December 22, 1993.

That female members of Conservative Youth were as likely to adopt the new styles as any other group of women is a claim substantiated by contemporary photographs of the organization's members. See, for instance, "Efteraarsudflugten," 1928. Unidentified newspaper clipping in the Emma Grandsgaard Collection of Newspaper Clippings, the Women's History Archives, the State Library, Aarhus, Denmark.

99. Oral history interview, Aarhus, Denmark, February 28, 1990.

100. Oral history interview, Copenhagen, Denmark, December 14, 1993.

101. Oral history interview, Copenhagen, Denmark, December 1, 1993.

102. Oral history interview, Copenhagen, Denmark, October 28, 1993.

103. Oral history interview, Copenhagen, Denmark, October 10, 1993.

104. Ibid.

105. Oral history interview, Copenhagen, Denmark, December 19, 1993.

That the generation of women who came of age in the late 1910s and 1920s probably spent more time and money on "looking good" than most women before them is a fact that many feminist historians of the era have noted. In the 1910s and 1920s, a burgeoning beauty industry eagerly promoted the idea that beauty could be obtained by all women, irrespective of age and class, if only they paid attention to their appearances and used the right products and treatments. However, the new democratic idea that all women *could* be beautiful soon translated into the demand that all women *should* be beautiful. From the early 1920s, variations of Helena Rubinstein's infamous claim that "there are no ugly women, only lazy ones," echoed through women's magazines, placing enormous pressure on women to take the perpetual, labor-intensive, and time-consuming project of beauty care. For a few examples from Danish magazines, see "Enhver Kvinde kan blive smuk," *Charme*, vol. 1, no. 24 (June 11, 1927), p. 28; and "Skønhedsplejens Ti Bud," *Eva. Ungdom og Skønhed*, vol. 1, no. 1 (March 10, 1925), p. 18.

Yet, as Vera Thorsen's comments suggest, the careful cultivation of beauty and appearance probably granted many women much pleasure, gratification, and self-confidence. It also provided them with a host of problems and worries. Individual procedures were tedious and time-consuming, the labor perpetual and indefinite. Beauty products and treatments, although ranging widely in price to encompass working-class as well as middle-class markets, were expensive and in constant need of replenishment. Moreover, since experts proclaimed beauty within the reach of all women, those who were not beautiful had only themselves to blame. On top of this, women who did not conform to popular definitions of beauty often had to contend with the scorn of those who believed in beauty not only as an arena of female knowledge and authority but also as each woman's personal responsibility. For analyses of the emerging beauty industry and its consequences for women, see Kathy Peiss, *Hope in a Jar: The Making of America's Beauty Industry* (New York, 1997); Kathy Peiss, "Making Faces: The Cosmetics Industry and the Cultural Construction of Gender, 1890–1930," *Genders*, vol. 7 (Spring 1990), pp. 143–69; Banner, *American Beauty*, pp. 202–25; and Brumberg, *The Body Project*, pp. 97–137. For a similar point, see also Roberts, *Civilization without Sexes*, p. 83.

106. Oral history interview, Slagelse, Denmark, November 26, 1993.

107. "Nutidens Kvinder," *Nationaltidende*, March 26, 1922, p. 5.

CHAPTER 2

1. "En Skønhedskonkurrence," 1926. Unidentified newspaper clipping in the Emma Grandsgaard Collection of Newspaper Clippings, the Women's History Archives, the State Library, Aarhus, Denmark.

2. "Nutidens unge Pige," *Politiken*, February 21, 1922, p. 9; Helge Meyer, "Københavnerinden over de femogtredive," *Vore Herrer*, vol. 9, no. 24 (November 20, 1924), p. 27.

3. "Den danske Pige af 1922," *Jyllandsposten*, May 14, 1922, pp. 9–10.

4. "Københavnerinden," *Kvinden og Samfundet*, vol. 33, no. 18 (October 30, 1917), p. 240.

5. "Badeliv," 1923. Unidentified magazine clipping in the Emma Grandsgaard Collection of Newspaper Clippings, the Women's History Archives, the State Library, Aarhus, Denmark.

6. *København ved Nat* (Copenhagen, 1923), p. 4.

7. See *Kvindelig Idrætsforening. Festskrift 1906–1931* (Copenhagen, 1931); and *De unges Idræt gennem 20 Aar, 1905–1925* (Copenhagen, 1925). For a more general history of Danish sports and athleticism, see Else Trangbæk, *Dansk idrætsliv*, vols. 1–2 (Copenhagen, 1995).

8. See, for instance, "Hockey - et glimrende Spil for Damer og Herrer," *Vore Damer*, vol. 6, no. 22 (October 24, 1918), p. 17; and *Dansk Idræt gennem 50 Aar* (Copenhagen, 1946), part II, p. 143.

9. "Kvindesporten til Lands og til Vands," *Vore Damer*, vol. 10, no. 17 (August 24, 1922), p. 19; "I Kajak langs Øresunds Kyster," *Vore Damer*, vol. 6, no. 19 (September 12, 1918), p. 12.

10. See for instance "Frøken Tennis," *Politiken*, August 15, 1915, pp. 8–9; "Fra Damernes Fægteturnering om Hasselbalch-Pokalen," *Vore Herrer*, vol. 8, no. 10 (May 10, 1923); "Den kvindelige Landmand, der vandt Damernes Mesterskab i Fægtning," *B.T.*, April 17, 1923, p. 11; and "Frk. Elsa Fischer - en Sportens Københavnerinde af Aargang 1918," *Vore Damer*, vol. 6, no. 14 (July 4, 1918), pp. 3–5.

11. See, for instance, "Der er snart ikke den Sport i Verden," *Vore Damer*, vol. 10, no. 20 (May 18, 1922), p. 19; "Moderne Damer paa Jagt," *Aftenlæsning*, vol. 1, no. 21 (September 22, 1926), p. 6; "Er det kvindeligt at øve Skydning," *Vore Damer*, vol. 14, no. 20 (May 19, 1926), p. 27; "Kræfter er godt, men man kan ogsaa faa for meget af det Gode," *Vore Herrer*, vol. 7, no. 9 (May 11, 1922); and "Nordjyllands første Motor-Sportskvinde," *B.T.* (March 21, 1923), p. 11.

12. See, for instance, " 'Tango'en kommer til København," in Axel Breidahl and Axel Kjerulf, *Københavnerliv 1912–1937* (Copenhagen, 1938), p. 44.

13. Agnes Nyrop Christensen and J. C. Gottlieb: *Hvad alle bør vide om moderne Dans* (Copenhagen, 1919), p. 38; "De moderne Danse gaar deres Sejrsgang - !" *Vore Damer*, vol. 10, no. 19 (September 21, 1922), p. 17.

14. Report by Netta Rasmussen Berg, located in the records of the Virgilia Christian Reform Society, the Manuscript Collection, the Royal Library, Copenhagen, Denmark. For a similar assessment, see also "Borgmester Kaper om Storbyens Moral," *Nationaltidende*, February 4, 1925, p. 3.

15. Oral history interview, Copenhagen, Denmark, May 27, 1991.

16. Oral history interview, Aarhus, Denmark, February 26, 1994.

17. "Hvilken Betydning har Sporten for Kvinden? En Række Interessante Udtalelser fra kendte Kvinder," *Vore Damer*, vol. 16, no. 10 (March 3, 1928), pp. 14–15.

18. "Den moderne kvinde: ung og frisk!" *Vore Damer*, vol. 14, no. 32 (August 11, 1926), pp. 7–8.

19. "Nogle Betragtninger om Tidens Ungdom," 1925. Unidentified newspaper clipping in the Emma Grandsgaard Collection of Newspaper Clippings, the Women's History Archives, the State Library, Aarhus, Denmark.

20. Oral history interview, Copenhagen, Denmark, October 12, 1993.

21. Oral history interview, Helsingør, Denmark, November 20, 1993.

22. Oral history interview, Copenhagen, Denmark, December 3, 1993.

23. Oral history interview, Aalborg, Denmark, December 22, 1993.

24. This is a point also made by Mary Louise Roberts in her study of French gender relations in the post–World War I era, *Civilization without Sexes: Reconstructing Gender in Postwar France, 1917–1927* (Chicago, 1994), p. 19.

25. "Sporten og de unge Piger," 1924. Unidentified newspaper clipping in the Emma Grandsgaard Collection of Newspaper Clippings, the Women's History Archives, the State Library, Aarhus, Denmark.

26. This made Denmark the first country in the world to introduce gymnastics in primary schools. See Else Trangbæk, "Discipline and Emancipation through Sports: The Pioneers of Women's Sport in Denmark," *Scandinavian Journal of History*, vol. 21, no. 2 (1996), p. 124. For more detailed accounts of nineteenth-century Danish sports history, see also Else Trangbæk, *Mellem leg og disciplin. Gymnastikken i Danmark i 1800–tallet* (Copenhagen, 1987); and Trangbæk, *Dansk idrætsliv*, vols. 1–2.

27. Birthe Skov Jensen, "Den tidlige kvindegymnastik," in Per Jørgensen et al. (eds.), *Idrætshistorisk Aarbog 1985* (Copenhagen, 1985), pp. 83–107.

28. Trangbæk, "Discipline and Emancipation through Sports," p. 125.

29. Jensen, "Den tidlige kvindegymnastik," p. 86.

30. This was the case not only in Denmark, but across the Western world. See Roberta J. Park, "Sport, Gender and Society in a Transatlantic Perspective," in J. A. Mangan and Roberta J. Park (eds.), *From "Fair Sex" to Feminism: Sport and the Socialization of Women in the Industrial and Post-Industrial Eras* (London, 1987), pp. 58–93.

31. Else Margrethe Kjerrumgaard-Jørgensen, "Københavnsk cyklisme i det 19. århundredes slutning," *Historiske Meddelelser om København*, series 4, no. 1 (1947–1949).

32. In 1900, a bicycle cost approximately Dkr. 250. A decade later the average cost had fallen to Dkr. 60–80. A statistical survey of household budgets has demonstrated that by 1922 at least 75 percent of all Danish households listed expenses related to bicycles. By 1931, that number had grown to 87 percent. See Hans Kryger Larsen and Carl-Axel Nilsson, "Consumption and Production of Bicycles in Denmark 1890–1980," *Scandinavian Economic History Review*, vol. 32 (1984), pp. 143–58.

33. "Der er snart ikke den Sport i Verden," *Vore Damer*, vol. 10, no. 20 (May 18, 1922), p. 19; "Sport og Kvindelighed," *B.T.*, April 7, 1923, p. 11. For similar claims, see also "Hvilken Betydning har Sporten for Kvinden?" pp. 14–15.

34. On nineteenth-century scientific understandings of the female body, see Cynthia Eagle Russett, *Sexual Science: The Victorian Construction of Womanhood* (Cambridge, Mass., 1989); Thomas Laqueur, *Making Sex: Body and Gender from the Greeks to Freud* (Cambridge, Mass., 1990), pp. 193–243; and Bente Rosenbeck, *Kroppens Politik. Om køn, kultur og videnskab* (Copenhagen, 1992).

On the relationship between the medical profession and women's physical education in the nineteenth century, see Patricia Vertinsky, *The Eternally Wounded Woman: Women, Exercise and Doctors in the Late Nineteenth Century* (Manchester, 1990); Patricia Vertinsky, "Exercise, Physical Capability, and the Eternally Wounded Woman in Late Nineteenth-Century North America," *Journal of Sport History*, vol. 14 (1987), pp. 7–27; and Patricia Vertinsky: "Body Shape: The Role of the Medical Establishment in Informing Female Exercise and Physical Education in Nineteenth-Century America," in J. A. Mangan and Roberta J. Park (eds.), *From "Fair Sex" to Feminism*, pp. 256–81.

35. "Sundt Helbred," *Aarhus Stiftstidende*, December 3, 1919, p. 4.

36. "Kvinder og Fodbold," *Hjemmet*, vol. 25, no. 5 (February 2, 1922), p. 18.

37. "Den unge Piges Helbred," *Nationaltidende*, April 4, 1918, p. 2.

38. As demonstrated in chapter 1, this concern over the potential erasure of visible gender differences would surface in public discourse once again a few years later when short hair first became popular among young women.

39. See, for instance, "Gør Sporten Kvinden smukkere?" *B.T.*, July 2, 1922, p. 8; and "Kræfter er godt, men man kan også få for meget af det gode."

40. "Unge Piger og Sportsdyrkelse," *Nationaltidende*, November 2, 1921, p. 6.

41. "Lægen raadgiver," *Illustreret Familiejournal*, vol. 42, no. 15 (April 11, 1918), p. 27.

42. "Veje til et godt Helbred," *Illustreret Familiejournal*, vol. 42, no. 2 (January 9, 1918), p. 17.

To convince potential skeptics, doctors and physical educators often interspersed their encouragement with accounts of actual improvements in women's health that had occurred as a result of their physical activity. In 1928, Johanne Næser, a well-known and highly respected female physician, announced, for example, that anemia, tuberculosis, and indigestion had been all but eliminated among her female patients. Erik Faber, the head physician at a Copenhagen hospital, added stomach catarrh to this list of physical ailments supposedly cured by fitness and exercise. See "Hvilken Betydning har Sporten for Kvinden?" pp. 14–15; and "Den moderne Kvinde. En Samtale med Dr. Med. Erik Faber," *Vore Damer*, vol. 16, no. 12 (March 21, 1928), pp. 24–25.

43. "Kvinden og Gymnastiken," *Vore Damer*, vol. 14, no. 9 (March 3, 1926), p. 3.

44. "Hvilken Betydning har Sporten for Kvinden?" pp. 14–15.

45. There is an extensive literature on the link between sport and masculinity. Danish studies include Hans Bonde, *Mandighed og sport* (Odense, 1991); and Hans Bonde: "Masculine Movements: Sport and Masculinity in Denmark at the Turn of the Century," *Scandinavian Journal of History*, vol. 21, no. 2 (1996), pp. 63–89.

46. "Typer: Sportskvinden," *Vore Herrer*, vol. 8, no. 13 (June 21, 1923), p. 12.

47. Ibid.

48. See, for instance, "Luftens Datter," *Vore Herrer*, vol. 3, no. 3 (February 7, 1918); "Kvinder og Fodbold," *Hjemmet*, vol. 25, no. 5 (February 2, 1922), p. 18; "Gør Sporten Kvinden smukkere?" p. 8; "En Kvindelig Champion i Bueskydning," *Vore Herrer*, vol. 7, no. 23 (November 23, 1922); and "En Stikprøve af Boksningen i alle dens Afarter og en Udfordring til danske Kvinder," *Vore Herrer*, vol. 7, no. 10 (May 22, 1922).

49. Here quoted from Axel Breidahl and Axel Kjerulf, *Københavnerliv gennem et halvt Aarhundrede. Gemt og glemt i Alvor og Skæmt, 1912–1937*, vol. 2 (Copenhagen, 1938), p. 382.

50. Breidahl and Kjerulf, *Københavnerliv gennem et halvt Aarhundrede*, p. 395.

51. "Hvilke Sportsgrene egner sig bedst for Kvinden?" *Vore Damer*, vol. 16, no. 10 (March 7, 1928), p. 17.

52. Already in the late nineteenth century, some physical educators had begun to develop this philosophy. In 1878 Paul Petersen, a gymnastics instructor, opened the Institute for Danish Women's Gymnastics, where he experimented with particular forms of exercise for women. See Trangbæk, "Discipline and Emancipation through Sports." For an analysis of similar developments in the United States, see Susan K. Cahn, *Coming on Strong: Gender and Sexuality in Twentieth-Century Women's Sport* (New York, 1994), pp. 7–30.

53. "Hvilke Sportsgrene egner sig bedst for Kvinden?" p. 17.

54. "Unge Damer og Sport," *Vore Damer*, vol. 14, no. 7 (July 7, 1926), p. 21.

55. For an elaboration of these arguments, see Hans Bonde, "Køn, klasser og kropskultur," *Idrætshistorisk Aarbog 1985* (Copenhagen, 1985), pp. 61–74.

56. This struggle is outlined in Julie Friis-Skotte, "Historisk Oversigt," in *Københavns Kvindelige Gymnastikforening 1886–1936* (Copenhagen, 1936), pp. 3–12.

57. Else Thomsen, "Elli Björkstén," in *Københavns Kvindelige Gymnastikforening 1886–1936*, p. 15.

58. In their development of such exercise programs, Danish physical educators were greatly influenced by Finnish exercise instructor Elli Björkstén, who insisted that women's exercise should reflect gender-specific movements and body language. On a brief visit to Denmark in 1913, she called on female physical educators to "emancipate the [female] body to be an expression of the soul. Emancipate women's exercise from male gymnastics!" See "Kvindegymnastik," *Bog og Naal*, vol. 20 (September 15, 1913), pp. 222–23; see also Elli Björkstén, "Kvinnogymnastik," *Bog og Naal*, vol. 21 (July 1, 1914), pp. 187–93; Elli Björkstén, "Kvindegymnastik," *Bog og Naal*, vol. 21 (July 15, 1914), pp. 209–15; and Thomsen, "Elli Björkstén," pp. 13–20.

The principles that guided female physical educators in the 1920s are outlined in, for example, Grete Herskind, *Den moderne Kvindegymnastik* (Copenhagen, 1929); Frede Hansen, *Dagsøvelser i Gymnastik for Kvinder* (Horsens, 1928); "Rytme," *Kvindelig Idrætsforenings Medlemsblad*, vol. 2, no. 1 (February 1, 1924), p. 1; and Else Thomsen, "Pigegymnastik," *Husmoderen*, vol. 10, no. 12 (June 24, 1927), pp. 224–27.

59. "Legemskultur," *Flirt*, vol. 2, no. 8 (April 1922), p. 13; "Typer: Sportskvinden."

60. "Hvordan bliver vi smukke?" *Vore Damer*, vol. 14, no. 8 (February 24, 1926), p. 23; "Lige Ret—," *Kvindelig Idrætsforenings Medlemsblad*, vol. 3, no. 1 (February 25, 1925), p. 1.

61. See, for example, "Mensendieck Gymnastiken," *Illustreret Familie-Journal*, vol. 48, no. 14 (April 2, 1924), p. 23; "Kvindelegemets Kultur og Økonomi,"

Vore Damer, vol. 10, no. 22 (November 3, 1922), p. 22; and "De unge Piger og Gymnastiken," *Nationaltidende*, October 10, 1923, p. 4.

62. Oral history interview, Copenhagen, Denmark, October 28, 1993.

63. "Spørgekassen," *Flirt*, vol. 2, no. 27 (October 12, 1922), p. 17.

64. See, for instance, "Intolerance," *Kvindelig Idrætsforenings Medlemsblad*, vol. 6, no. 1 (February 1, 1928), pp. 2–3.

65. Oral history interview, Aalborg, Denmark, May 14, 1991.

66. Oral history interview, Aalborg, Denmark, December 22, 1990.

67. In her analysis of the British Women's League of Health and Beauty, Jill Matthews has reached a similar conclusion. See Jill Matthews, " 'They Had Such a Lot of Fun': The Women's League of Health and Beauty," *History Workshop Journal*, issue no. 30 (1990), p. 49.

68. Eja Packness, "Kærlighedserklæring til Aalborg," in Aage Svendstorp et al. (eds.), *Ung i Aalborg. Kendte aalborgensere skriver om storbyen set i lillelivets perspektiv* (Aalborg, 1976), p. 15.

69. Herskind, *Den moderne Kvindegymnastik*, p. 4.

70. "Kvindelig Idrætsforenings Opvisning," *Kvindelig Idrætsforenings Medlemsblad*, vol. 7, no. 3 (June 15, 1929), p. 18.

71. Herskind, *Den moderne Kvindegymnastik*, p. 16.

72. The coercive aspect of the emphasis on beautiful female bodies is abundantly clear in contemporary newspapers and popular magazines. In article after article, women were reminded that their every motion and gesture ought to be scrutinized and possibly improved upon to fit the modern style. The way women walked, for instance, was pronounced in dire need of reform. "Most women walk unattractively," one headline announced. The article proceeded to advise women to "walk naturally with lowered shoulders pulled backwards, with raised head and the legs stretched straight from the hip with the toes pointed slightly outward; the arms must move naturally and freely with the body." See "En smuk Gang - De fleste Kvinder gaar grimt," *B.T.*, May 19, 1930, p. 14. Other articles instructed women in "the art of moving gracefully" and "how to carry oneself with dignity." An illustrated column from 1926 even demonstrated "the new way of shaking hands which gradually is securing a foothold [*sic*!] among ladies abroad." See "Kunsten at bevæge sig med Ynde," *Aftenlæsning*, vol. 1, no. 17 (1926), p. 8; and "Hvordan man hilser," *Aftenlæsning*, vol. 1, no. 1 (1926), p. 13.

73. For a similar argument, see Mary P. Ryan, "The Projection of Modern Womanhood: The Movie Moderns in the 1920s," in Jean E. Friedman and William G. Slade (eds.), *Our American Sisters: Women in American Life and Thought* (Boston, 1982), pp. 175–95.

74. Oral history interview, Aarhus, Denmark, March 15, 1994.

75. Oral history interview, Copenhagen, Denmark, December 1, 1993.

76. Oral history interview, Aarhus, Denmark, April 2, 1994.

This evidence seems to confirm the claim of Danish film historian Gunnar Sandfeld, who has argued that young women's movie-watching in the 1920s "soon came to influence the hair cuts, the clothing, the gait and general comportment— down to the way of smiling, laughing and crying." See Gunnar Sandfeld, *Den stumme scene: Dansh biografteater indtil lydfilmens gennembrud* (Copenhagen, 1966), p. 476.

77. The lively style of Liva Weel was illustrated, for example, in a 1926 magazine articles featuring multiple photographs of "the wonderful, charming, sparklingly talented, loved, admired and envied" actress shamelessly flirting and showing off her figure, coquettishly picking out dresses in her backstage dressing room, and gigglingly sliding down a banister! See "Liva - den vidunderlige, bedaarende, gnistrende talentfulde, elskede, beundrede og misundte," *Vore Damer*, vol. 14, no. 50 (December 15, 1926), pp. 6–7.

78. Oral history interview, Copenhagen, Denmark, October 28, 1993.

79. Oral history interview, Helsingør, Denmark, November 20, 1993.

80. Oral history interview, Køge, Denmark, November 28, 1993.

81. Although many young women seemed to believe this upbeat attitude the "natural" inclination of female stars, it was in fact, as Linda Mizejewski has pointed out, a style carefully cultivated by the entertainment industry. See Mizejewski, *Ziegfeld Girl*, p. 113.

82. Oral history interview, Roskilde, Denmark, February 11, 1990.

83. Such characterizations of popular actresses echo magazine articles and fan letters from the 1920s. In 1919, *Vore Herrer*, for example, ran a story about Ragnhild Sannom, the celebrated lead actress at one Copenhagen theater, praising her for her "indomitable cheerfulness, her charming determination and her sparkling spirit." See "Skuespillerinde Fru Ragnhild Sannom," *Vore Herrer*, vol. 4, no. 8 (April 17, 1919). When one young woman wrote to the editor of *Flirt* in 1926 requesting that the magazine publish more photographs of Mary Pickford, she described her idol in a similar manner. "I would like to see more of her cheerful smile," she explained. See "Flirts Spørgekasse," *Flirt*, vol. 2, no. 33 (November 23, 1922), p. 8. A few years later "Sonia" wanted to know whether Gloria Swanson was married and how she acquired "her positive attitude." See "Spørgekassen," *Ugebladet*, vol. 3, no. 27 (October 12, 1928), p. 12. Dreaming of a movie career, another young woman wondered how to get in contact with film producers because, as she wrote, "I have vast energy and, I think, the right kind of unfailing good spirits." See "Entr'act!" *Hvepsen*, vol. 1, no. 4 (1925).

84. For photographs of jubilant young exercising women, see, for example, "Kvinden og Gymnastiken," pp. 3–5; and G. Westergaard and N. Sodemann, "Frankrigsturen," *Kvindelig Idrætsforenings Medlemsblad*, vol. 4, no. 3 (June 25, 1926), pp. 20–22.

85. Oral history interview, Aarhus, Denmark, February 19, 1990.

86. Oral history interview, Aarhus, Denmark, February 28, 1994.

87. Oral history interview, Copenhagen, Denmark, October 10, 1993.

88. This was not a particularly Danish phenomenon. According to Judy Giles, the British popular press in general and romance fiction in particular also praised female cheerfulness in the interwar years. See Judy Giles, " 'You Meet 'Em and That's It': Working Class Women's Refusal of Romance between the Wars in Britain," in Lynne Pearce and Jackie Stacey (eds.), *Romance Revisited* (New York and London, 1995), p. 283.

89. "Nutidens unge Pige," *Klokken 5*, May 11, 1920, p. 4.

90. "Hvori bestaar den kvindelige Charme?" *Nationaltidende* (July 6, 1924), p. 14.

Most often, contemporaries referred to the new styles of femininity as the "modern temperament" or the "modern personality." However, on occasion it was referred to as the "slender temperament," clearly associating a particular body with this particular style. See, for instance, Agga Amdrup, "Frou-Frou. Toilette Camouflage. Portiere Dragten," *København*, July 27, 1919, p. 6.

The historical literature on emotion and emotional styles remains rather limited. For an interesting but nongendered discussion of the early twentieth-century shift from "character" to "personality," see Warren I. Susman, " 'Personality' and the Making of Twentieth-Century Culture," in *Culture as History: The Transformation of American Society in the Twentieth Century* (New York, 1984), pp. 271–85. For a discussion of twentieth-century emotional styles, see Peter N. Stearns, *American Cool: Constructing a Twentieth-Century Emotional Style* (New York and London, 1994). For a more general analysis, see Elizabeth Lunbeck, *The Psychiatric Persuasion: Knowledge, Gender, and Power in Modern America* (Princeton, N. J., 1994).

91. Olga Hoffmann-Canitz, *Moderne Skønhedspleje* (Copenhagen, 1917), p. 9.

92. "Hvilke Egenskaber beundrer Manden mest hos en Kvinde?" *Aftenlæsning*, vol. 1, no. 5 (1926), p. 16.

93. "Den kvindelige Kvinde," *Hjemmet*, vol. 27. no. 1 (January 2, 1924), p. 22.

94. "Hvad er Charme?" *Illustreret Tidende*, vol. 62, no. 19 (May 15, 1921), p. 230.

95. Charlotte Dalmark, *Humørhygiejne. En Vejledning for ung og gammel* (Copenhagen, 1922), p. 5.

96. "Har De Personlighed?" *B.T.*, July 1, 1925, p. 11.

97. "Skønhed og Nerver," *København*, January 18, 1920, p. 8.

98. "Damebrevkassen," *Søndags B.T.*, November 10, 1922, p. 2.

If a cheery disposition was crucial to physical beauty, it was not enough to ensure physical attractiveness. Beauty experts repeatedly reminded women that "mental and physical cosmetics [must] go hand in hand; a winning smile from a mouth with thirty-three decayed and black teeth loses somewhat of its charm, and a soulful gaze from a pair of red-rimmed eyes seems almost blasphemous." See "Hvori bestaar den kvindelige Charme?" p. 14.

99. "Sjælens Spejl," *Flirt*, vol. 3, no. 44 (February 8, 1923), p. 12.

100. "Den moderne Skønhedspleje," *Flirt*, vol. 2, no. 8 (April 1922), p. 19.

101. "Sjælens Spejl," p. 12.

102. See, for instance, "Skønhedsplejens Ti Bud," *Eva. Ungdom og Skønhed*, p. 18; and "En Time i Charme," *B.T.*, July 3, 1925, p. 11.

103. Dalmark, *Humørhygiejne*, p. 10.

104. "Godt Humør," *Hjemmet*, vol. 25, no. 29 (July 20, 1922), p. 18.

105. Fru Vera, *Amors Central. 1. Hvorledes man gør Lykke hos Herrerne. Bliver elsket, attraaet, beundret, hurtig forlovet og gift. Uundværlig Vejleder for unge Piger* (Copenhagen, 1918), p. 3.

106. "Hvori bestaar den kvindelige Charme?" p. 14.

107. Olga Hoffmann-Canitz, *Moderne Skønhedspleje* (Copenhagen, 1917), p. 8.

Part II

1. "Forholdene paa Langelinie," *Dagens Nyheder*, July 4, 1919, p. 4; "Bleg-sotig Ungdom - tomhjærnet Ungdom!" *Fremad*, vol. 13, no. 8 (July 19, 1919), pp. 1–2.
2. "Forholdene paa Langelinie," p. 4.
3. Ibid.
4. "Langelinie-Nyborg," *København*, July 4, 1919, p. 2.
5. "Forholdene paa Langelinie," p. 4
6. "Forholdene paa Langelinie. En alvorlig Advarsel til Forældrene," *Dagens Nyheder*, July 3, 1919, p. 7.
The cross-class composition of the so-called Langelinie girls were also noted by other newspapers. See, for example, "Et Tidens Tegn," *København*, July 6, 1919, p. 9; and "Skændselen paa Langelinie," *Berlingske Tidende*, July 1, 1919, p. 5.
7. "Langelinie-Nyborg," p. 2.
8. "Langelinie afspærret," *Ekstrabladet*, July 7, 1919, p. 2.
9. "Et Tidens Tegn," p. 8.

Chapter 3

1. Oral history interview, Copenhagen, Denmark, December 10, 1993.
2. Oral history interview, Copenhagen, Denmark, November 6, 1990.
3. Oral history interview, Aalborg, Denmark, February 26, 1990.
4. See Mary Jo Maynes: *Schooling in Western Europe: A Social History* (Albany, N.Y., 1985).
5. Unfortunately, only scattered evidence indicates the actual percentages of daughters who continued to live with their parents until marriage. In her study of Danish clerical workers in the early decades of the twentieth century, Kirsten Geertsen cites a 1915 investigation that concluded that 70 percent of all unmarried female clerical workers under the age of forty-five lived with their parents. Among clerical workers under twenty-four years of age, fully 83 percent lived at home. A similar investigation in 1946 found that even then less than 11 percent of single women between the ages of fifteen and twenty-four lived independently. Geertsen concludes that at least until the middle of the twentieth century, low wages prevented most working women from living independently. Even boarding houses and rented rooms remained beyond their financial reach. See Kirsten Geertsen, *Dannet ung pige søges. Kvinder på kontor 1900–1940* (Holme Olstrup, 1990), pp. 128–32.
Evidence from memoirs and oral histories supports Geertsen's claims. Carla Marie Larsen, a clerical worker, recalled that even as her salary rose, she "never had any ideas about moving away from home. You simply did not do that before marriage." From an unpublished memoir, file no. 1980/3094, in the Local Historical Archives for Aalborg Municipality, Aalborg, Denmark. Of the fifty-nine women I interviewed, only those who migrated to major urban areas to work lived away from their parents, typically receiving room and board from their employers or sharing small apartments with other young women from their hometown or work place.

6. Oral history interview, Copenhagen, Denmark, November 3, 1993.

7. Oral history interview, Copenhagen, Denmark, November 6, 1990.

8. That wage-earning impacted young women's sense of rights and obligations vis-à-vis the family is a widely documented phenomenon. Barbara Hamill Sato, for example, points out that even though the overwhelming number of young Japanese women who held jobs in the 1920s used their salaries to help supplement the family income, "the fact that young women were moving into society and earning wages by dint of their own efforts instilled a sense of independence, however slight, in women bound by the oppressive family system." See Barbara Hamill Sato, "The Moga Sensation: Perceptions of the Modan Garu in Japanese Intellectual Circles during the 1920s," *Gender and History*, vol. 5, no. 3 (1993), p. 376. For other examples of this, see also Kathy Peiss, *Cheap Amusements: Working Women and Leisure in Turn-of-the-Century New York* (Philadelphia, 1986); and Barbara Alpern Engel: *Between the Field and the City: Women, Work and Family in Russia* (Cambridge, 1994), pp. 64–100.

9. Søren Mørch, *Den ny Danmarkshistorie, 1880–1960* (Copenhagen, 1982), pp. 95–96. For a discussion of the erosion of the traditional family economy in the face of emerging industrial capitalism, see also Joan Scott and Louise Tilly: *Women, Work and Family* (New York, 1978).

10. The sexual division of leisure has been the topic of much feminist scholarship. In the Scandinavian context, it has been analyzed by Anna Jorunn Avdem and Kari Melby in their study of Norwegian women's domestic work from 1850 to the present, *Oppe først og sist i seng. Husarbeid i Norge fra 1850 til i dag* (Oslo, 1985).

11. For discussions of intrafamilial conflicts over daughters' rights and obligations, see Peiss, *Cheap Amusements*, pp. 67–72; and Karen Dubinsky, *Improper Advances: Rape and Heterosexual Conflict in Ontario, 1880–1929* (Chicago, 1993), pp. 119–22.

12. From the 1910s, the popular press began to feature advice columns in which questions related to personal and familial relationships and social etiquette were addressed. While it is difficult to gauge the mass of their readership, the fact that they appeared in almost all women's and family magazines by the middle of the decade suggests their popularity. In one rare instance, *Ugebladet* cited actual figures for incoming correspondence. According to its editor, the magazine received more than one hundred letters *daily* during the first five months of 1923. See "Ugebladets Spørgebrevkasse," *Ugebladet*, vol. 3, no. 60 (May 31, 1923), p. 19.

13. "Spørgekassen," *Flirt*, vol. 2, no. 27 (October 12, 1922), p. 12.

14. "Spørgekassen" *Flirt*, vol. 2, no. 28 (October 19, 1922), p. 14.

15. Oral history interview, Nørresundby, Denmark, December 22, 1990.

16. Oral history interview, Copenhagen, Denmark, February 10, 1990.

17. Peter Gay has described the 1920s as a decade characterized by conflicts between fathers and sons. See Peter Gay, *Weimar Culture: The Outsider as Insider* (New York, 1968), pp. 102–18. As this documents, the postwar period also witnessed considerable conflict between mothers and daughters. For other discussions of intergenerational conflicts between women in the 1920s, see, for instance, Atina Grossman, "'Girlkultur' or Thoroughly Rationalized Female: A New

Woman in Weimar Germany," in Judith Friedlander et al. (eds.), *Women in Culture and Politics: A Century of Change* (Bloomington, Ind., 1986), pp. 62–80; and Judy Giles: *Women, Identity and Private Life in Britain, 1900–1950* (New York, 1995), pp. 55–61.

18. "Vore døtre," *Vore Damer*, vol. 9, no. 22 (May 31, 1921), p. 17.

19. "Spørgebrevkassen," *Ugebladet*, vol. 8, no. 24 (June 10, 1928), p. 23.

20. "Forholdene paa Langelinie," *Nationaltidende*, July 2, 1919, p. 2.

21. Oral history interview, Aarhus, Denmark, April 2, 1994.

22. Oral history interview, Aalborg, Denmark, December 22, 1990.

23. The concern over women's public leisure activities was an international phenomenon in the early twentieth century. See, for instance, Peiss, *Cheap Amusements*; and Sueann Caulfield, "Getting into Trouble: Dishonest Women, Modern Girls, and Women-Men in the Conceptual Language of Vida Policial, 1925–1925," *Signs*, vol. 19, no. 1 (1993), pp. 146–76.

24. See, for instance, Peiss, *Cheap Amusements*; Mary P. Ryan, *Women in Public: Between Banners and Ballots, 1825–1880* (Baltimore, 1990); Elizabeth Wilson, *The Sphinx in the City: Urban Life, the Control of Disorder, and Women* (Berkeley, Calif., 1992); and Judith R. Walkowitz, *City of Dreadful Delight: Narratives of Sexual Danger in Late-Victorian London* (Chicago, 1992).

25. Walkowitz, *City of Dreadful Delight*, p. 23.

26. Peiss, *Cheap Amusements*, pp. 113–14.

27. "Dame-Brevkasse," *Søndags B.T.*, June 21, 1925, p. 13.

28. "Ugebladets Spørgekasse," *Ugebladet*, vol. 3, no. 70 (August 9, 1923), p. 15.

29. Oral history interview, Helsingør, Denmark, November 30, 1993.

30. Oral history interview, Copenhagen, Denmark, February 10, 1990.

31. Oral history interview, Copenhagen, Denmark, October 10, 1993.

32. Oral history interview, Køge, Denmark, November 28, 1993.

33. "Danse-spørge-kasse," *Flirt*, vol. 2. no. 18 (August 10, 1922), p. 11.

34. "Nutidens unge Pige," *København*, November 11, 1920, p. 4.

35. Several historians have documented the shift from a nineteenth-century homosocial world in which female friendships and networks were of crucial importance to women to a new heterosocial culture established in the early twentieth century in which relationships with men took on a new importance, thereby implying that female friendships declined in importance. See, for instance, Sheila Jeffreys, *The Spinster and Her Enemies: Feminism and Sexuality 1880–1930* (London, 1985); and Leila J. Rupp, "Feminism and the Sexual Revolution in the Early Twentieth Century: The Case of Doris Stevens," *Feminist Studies*, vol. 15 (1989), pp. 289–309. My findings suggest that while the meanings of female friendships might have changed, they remained equally important for young women.

36. See, for instance, Ejnert Gregersen, unpublished memoir, file 1980/3130; Elly Reiner Pedersen, unpublished memoir, file 1980/3129; A. Peder Nielsen, unpublished memoir, file 1980/3131; and Carla Marie Larsen, unpublished memoir, file 1980/3094, all located in The Local Historical Archives for Aalborg Municipality, Aalborg, Denmark. See also Bernhardt Jensen, *Som Aarhus morede sig. Folkelige forlystelser fra 1890'erne til 2. verdenskrig* (Aarhus, 1966); and Axel Breidahl and Axel Kjerulf, *Københavnerliv, 1912–1937* (Copenhagen, 1937).

37. See, for instance, Steffen Linvald, *København har moret sig* (Copenhagen, 1966), p. 163. See also unpublished memoir by anonymous writer, file 1980/3002, in The Local Historical Archives for Aalborg Municipality, Aalborg, Denmark.

38. See Michael B. Miller, *The Bon Marche: Bourgeois Culture and the Department Store, 1869–1920* (Princeton, N.J., 1981); Rosalind H. Williams, *Dream Worlds: Mass Consumption in Late 19th Century France* (Berkeley, Calif., 1982); William R. Leach, "Transformations in a Culture of Consumption: Women and Department Stores, 1890–1925," *Journal of American History*, vol. 71, no. 2 (1984), pp. 319–42; and Elaine S. Abelson, *When Ladies Go A-Thieving: Middle-Class Shoplifters in the Victorian Department Store* (New York and Oxford, 1989). For an early discussion of the Danish case, see Herman Bang, "Vore Stormagasiner," *Politiken*, May 3, 1886, pp. 1–2.

39. For contemporary criticisms of the movie theaters, see, for instance, Olaf Fønns, "Fra Filmens Verden," *Arbejdernes Almanak*, vol. 22 (1930), pp. 47–64. The history of the Danish film industry and the emergence of movie theaters in the early decades of the twentieth century are chronicled in Jørgen Dinnesen and Edvin Kau, *Filmen i Danmark* (Copenhagen, 1983); Gunnar Sandfeldt, *Den stumme scene; Biografteaterforeningerne 1910–1960* (Copenhagen, 1960); and Arnold Hending, "Det københavnske Hollywood," *Historiske meddelelser om København*, series IV, vol. IV (1954–47), pp. 641–88.

40. "Vort uskønne Sommer-badeliv," *Vore Damer*, vol. 6, no. 20 (September 26, 1918). See also C. F. Hansen, "Om badeanstalten 'Helgoland,'" unpublished manuscript, Ny kongelig Samling 4380, the Manuscript Collection, the Royal Library, Copenhagen; "Det muntre Badeliv paa Helgoland," *Vore Herrer*, vol. 8, no. 12 (June 7, 1923); and Jensen, *Som Aarhus morede sig*.

41. Oral history interview, Roskilde, Denmark, April 13, 1991. For a similar recollection, see Ingeborg Nielsen, unpublished memoir, file 1980/3146, the Local Historical Archives for Aalborg Municipality, Aalborg, Denmark.

42. According to entertainment tax statistics, Copenhagen's citizens had the opportunity to attend a total of 6,012 theater, revue, and vaudeville performances during the 1923–1924 theater season, and each citizen of that city spent an average of Dkr. 13.24 on theater tickets. In Aarhus, there were 593 performances that same year; in Aalborg, 700. See "Forlystelsesafgiften 1912/13–1923/24," *Statistiske Efterretninger*, vol. 18, no. 37 (December 29, 1926), pp. 230–35.

43. In 1924, when admission to a movie theater cost Dkr. 0.25, seats at the popular Scala Theater in Copenhagen, for example, ranged in prices from Dkr. 1.45 to Dkr. 9.00. That same year, the Apollo Theater, another popular Copenhagen theater, charged Dkr. 2.05–5.65 for admission. See *Damernes Bog* (Copenhagen, 1924), pp. 18–24.

44. "Den unge Pige af Idag," *Vore Damer*, vol. 13, no. 8 (February 22, 1925), pp. 23–25.

45. In the first decade of the twentieth century, dancing remained a rare phenomenon in commercial establishments. From the early 1910s, however, this began to shift. In towns and cities across the country, entrepreneurs sensitive to the widespread "dance mania" opened new restaurants and cafés that featured live music and dancing. See Jensen, *Som Aarhus morede sig*; Axel Breidal and Axel Kjerulf, *Københavnerliv gennem et halvt Aarhundrede. Gemt og glemt i*

Alvor og Skæmt, 1912–1937, vols. 1–2 (Copenhagen, 1938); Linvald, *København har moret sig;* and Erik Nørgaard, *Jazz, guldfeber og farlige damer* (Copenhagen, 1965).

46. Oral history interview, Roskilde, Denmark, February 11, 1990.

47. Oral history interview, Aarhus, Denmark, February 23, 1990.

48. Oral history interview, Copenhagen, Denmark, February 10, 1990.

49. Oral history interview, Copenhagen, Denmark, December 10, 1991.

50. "Spørgebrevkassen," *Ugebladet,* vol. 5, no. 2 (January 10, 1925), p. 17.

51. "Flirts Spørgekasse," vol. 2, no. 33 (November 23, 1922), p. 8.

52. Ibid.

53. "Spørgebrevkassen," *Vore Damer,* vol. 16, no. 8 (February 22, 1928), p. 13.

54. "Dame-brevkasse," *Søndags B.T.,* no. 41 (October 7, 1928), p. 10; "Spørgekassen," *Ugebladet,* vol. 3, no. 27 (October 12, 1928), p. 12.

55. In his 1925 novel *Ny Ungdom,* Emil Bønnelycke spent several pages despairing over the ignorance and stupidity of young women who wrote to advice columnists. Knud Sønderby, in his novel *Midt i en Jazztid* (1931), also ridiculed young women for similar reasons. See Emil Bønnelycke, *Ny Ungdom* (Copenhagen, 1925), pp. 136–39; Knud Sønderby, *Midt i en Jazztid* (Copenhagen, 1931), pp. 96–97.

56. "Dame-brevkasse," *Søndags B.T.,* no. 41 (October 7, 1928), p. 10.

57. Oral history interview, Roskilde, Denmark, April 13, 1991. That a woman's reputation influenced her job opportunities and that respectability was a requirement for most women's jobs are points also made by Karen Dubinsky in her study of young women's lives in turn-of-the-century Canada. See Dubinsky, *Improper Advances,* p. 26.

58. "Pæne Piger," *Aarhus Stiftstidende,* October 4, 1927, p. 3.

59. "Tidens unge Piger," *Berlingske Tidende,* March 27, 1926, p. 11.

60. "Spørgebrevkassen," *Ugebladet,* vol. 5, no. 3 (January 17, 1925), p. 10.

61. "Spørgebrevkassen," *Ugebladet,* vol. 3, no. 7 (June 7, 1923), 11.

62. Oral history interview, Roskilde, Copenhagen, November 30, 1993.

63. Oral history interview, Copenhagen, Denmark, October 31, 1993.

64. Oral history interview, Køge, Denmark, November 28, 1993.

65. Oral history interview, Aarhus, Denmark, November 29, 1990.

66. Avoiding the risk of seeming "cheap" was clearly easier for some women than for others, but, as Karen Dubinsky noted in her study of Canadian women, class alone was not determinative for a woman's moral standing. Women who were judged too anxious for male companionship came from all social backgrounds. So did those who laughed too loudly, seemed too careless in selecting their company, or were too eager to please. See Dubinsky, *Improper Advances,* p. 127.

67. "Den kvindelige Frugtbarheds Fald i Hovedstaden i det 20. Aarhundrede," *Socialt Tidsskrift,* vol 12, no. 10 (1936), pp. 327–36.

68. For a history of birth control and the sex reform movement in Denmark, see Preben Hertoft, *Det er måske galskab. Om seksualreformbevægelsen i Danmark* (Copenhagen, 1983).

69. "Forholdene paa Langelinie," *Nationaltidende,* July 2, 1919, p. 2.

70. Brian Harrison, *Peaceable Kingdom: Stability and Change in Modern Britain* (New York, 1982), p. 161.

71. For a discussion of the role of class status as a marker of female respectability, see Elizabeth Lunbeck, *The Psychiatric Persuasion: Knowledge, Gender and Power in Modern America* (Princeton, N.J., 1994), p. 190.

72. Oral history interview, Copenhagen, Denmark, October 30, 1993.

73. Oral history interview, Copenhagen, Denmark, December 3, 1990.

74. Oral history interview, Nørresundby, Denmark, December 22, 1990.

75. Oral history interview, Aarhus, Denmark, October 17, 1990.

76. Oral history interview, Copenhagen, Denmark, November 19, 1990. Unfortunately, the saying loses its rhyme and much of its charm in translation. In Danish, the saying is "så længe maven tier, da er vi alle piger."

77. Oral history interview, Aarhus, Denmark, February 19, 1990.

78. Oral history interview, Aarhus, Denmark, February 25, 1990.

79. Oral history interview, Aarhus, Denmark, February 23, 1990.

80. Oral history interview, Aarhus, Denmark, February 27, 1990.

81. Oral history interview, Copenhagen, Denmark, February 19, 1990.

82. Oral history interview, Aarhus, Denmark, April 2, 1994.

83. Oral history interview, Copenhagen, Denmark, February 13, 1990. In her work on notions of female respectability among young Scottish women in the 1980s, Jenny Kitzinger has demonstrated the continued existence of the stereotype of the bad girl as Other. See Jenny Kitzinger, "'I'm Sexually Attractive but I'm Powerful': Young Women Negotiating Sexual Reputation," *Women's Studies International Forum*, vol. 18, no. 2 (1995), pp. 187–96.

84. Oral history interview, Copenhagen, Denmark, November 6, 1990.

85. Oral history interview, Copenhagen, Denmark, December 10, 1991.

86. Oral history interview, Copenhagen, Denmark, February 13, 1990.

87. Oral history interview, Aarhus, Denmark, October 17, 1990.

88. Oral history interview, Aalborg, Denmark, December 22, 1990.

89. I have borrowed this phrase from Walkowitz, *Cities of Dreadful Delight*, p. 63.

CHAPTER 4

1. "Hvad de unge Piger siger on Mænd," 1923. Unidentified newspaper clipping in the Emma Grandsgaard Collection of Newspaper Clippings, the Women's History Archives, the State Library, Aarhus, Denmark.

2. Ibid.

3. "En uheldig Tendens," 1925. Unidentified newspaper clipping in the Emma Grandsgaard Collection of Newspaper Clippings, the Women's History Archives, the State Library, Aarhus, Denmark.

4. See, for example, "Beretning for 1928–1929 om Arbejdet i Dansk Kvindesamfunds Aftenhjem for Unge Piger," Department for Small Print, The Royal Library, Copenhagen, Denmark.

More positive assessments of young women's eagerness to socialize with men were few and far between. On occasion, mood hygienists would praise the "cooperative spirit" that modern girls demonstrated in their relations with male peers, and a handful of male journalists approvingly noted that "the typical young woman of today" seemed surprisingly "good-natured and agreeable," but those were the exceptions in a sea of critical reactions. See "Det gode Humør vinder frem," *Politiken*, March 3, 1926, p. 11; and "Nutidens unge piger," 1924. Unidentified newspaper clipping in the Emma Grandsgaard Collection of Newspaper Clippings, the Women's History Achieves, the State Library, Aarhus, Denmark.

5. "Vort uskønne Badeliv," *Vore Damer*, vol. 6, no. 20 (September 26, 1918).

6. Even as older notions of sexual difference began to break down, the idea that men and women could be friends remained implausible to most contemporaries. When, for example, the weekly magazine *Ugebladet* queried its readers in 1925 whether friendship between two young people of different sexes was a possibility, the vast majority of respondents answered in the negative, arguing that sexual attraction and romance inevitably would undercut cross-gender friendships. Whether they blamed this on women's "inability to feel or inspire pure feelings of friendship" or on men's general lack of interest in women they did not find "at least to some extent sexually attractive," most correspondents seemed to agree that sexuality posed a formidable barrier to frank camaraderie between individual men and women, and male-female friendships were almost always assumed to be romantic in nature. See "Venskab mellem Mænd og Kvinder?" *Ugebladet*, vol. 5, no. 2 (January 10, 1925), p. 17. For similar claims, see also "Venskab mellem Mand og Kvinde," *Vore Herrer*, vol 1, no. 13 (September 21, 1916); "Venskab mellem Mand og Kvinde," *Vore Herrer*, vol. 1, no. 14 (October 5, 1916); "Kammerater," *Vore Herrer*, vol. 8, no. 26 (December 20, 1923); "Typer: Kvinden, som Manden elsker," *Vore Herrer*, vol. 8, no. 10 (May 10, 1923); and "Bag det evigt kvindeliges Kulisser. IV. Kammeraten," *Illustreret Tidende*, vol. 62, no. 32 (August 14, 1921), p. 398.

7. For the development of new forms of male–female interaction and courtship in the United States in the postwar decade, see Paula S. Fass, *The Damned and the Beautiful: American Youth in the 1920s* (New York, 1977); Beth L. Bailey, *From Front Porch to Back Seat: Courtship in Twentieth-Century America* (Baltimore, Md., 1988); and John L. Modell: *Into One's Own: From Youth to Adulthood in the United States, 1920–1975* (New York, 1991).

8. Oral history interview, Copenhagen, Denmark, December 2, 1990.

9. Niels Kayser Nielsen: "Klubliv i hverdag og fest," in Else Trangbæk et al. (eds.), *Dansk idrætsliv. Den moderne idræts gennembrud 1860–1940*, vol. 1 (Copenhagen, 1995), pp. 205–21.

10. For information on political youth groups in Denmark in the 1920s, see "Politiske Ungdomsforeninger," Collection of Minor Publications, the Royal Library, Copenhagen, Denmark.

11. "En Appel til den konservative Ungdom," *Konservativ Ungdom*, no. 18 (December 3, 1920), p. 6.

12. "Vaagn op," *Konservativ Ungdom*, no. 13 (October 1, 1920), p. 97.

13. "Kampen on Ungdommen. Sport og Dans," *Fremad*, vol. 10, no. 17 (January 6, 1917), pp. 2–3.

14. Oral history interview, Copenhagen, Denmark, October 31, 1993.

15. Information gathered from "Ungdomsforeninger og -huse" and "Selskabelige foreninger," Collection of Minor Publications, the Royal Library, Copenhagen.

16. "Om Baller," *Medlemsblad. Selskabelig Forening Gnisten*, vol. 1, no. 3 (January 1924), p. 10. For discussions on enrollment policies, see "Der var en Tid," *Medlemsblad. Selskabelig Forening Gnisten*, vol. 1, no. 2 (December 1923), p. 7; and "Selskabelig Forenings Medlemstal," *Selskabelig Forening af 1918. Medlemsblad*, vol. 2, no. 11–12 (December 1925), pp. 2–3.

17. "Glædeligt Nytår," *Selskabelig Forening af 1918. Medlemsblad*, vol. 3, no. 1 (January 1926), p. 1.

18. Oral history interview, Copenhagen, Denmark, May 27, 1991.

19. Oral history interview, Aalborg, Denmark, December 22, 1990.

20. Oral history interview, Copenhagen, Denmark, October 3, 1993.

21. "Tidens Noder og Unoder," 1927. Unidentified newspaper clipping in the Emma Grandsgaard Collections of Newspaper Clippings, the Women's History Archives, the State Library, Aarhus, Denmark.

22. For just one example of this interpretation, see Erik Nørgaard, *Jazz, guldfeber og farlige damer* (Copenhagen, 1965).

23. "Kampen for Ungdommen. Sport og Dans," p. 2.

24. Klaus Theweleit, *Male Fantasies*, vols. 1–2 (Cambridge, 1987–1989).

25. Sandra Gilbert and Susan Gubar, *No Man's Land: The Place of the Woman Writer in the Twentieth Century*, vols. 1–2 (1989); see also Sandra Gilbert, "Soldier's Heart: Literary Men, Literary Women, and the Great War," *Signs*, vol. 8, no. 3 (1983), pp. 422–50.

26. Brian Harrison, *Separate Spheres: The Opposition to Women's Suffrage in Britain* (London, 1978); and Susan Kingsley Kent, *Making Peace* (Princeton, N.J., 1993).

27. Mary Louise Roberts: *Civilization without Sexes: Reconstructing Gender in Postwar France, 1917–1927* (Chicago, 1994).

28. Françoise Barret-Ducrocq, *Love in the Time of Victoria: Sexuality and Desire among Working-Class Men and Women in Nineteenth-Century London* (New York, 1991), p. 110.

29. "Hvad jeg ikke forstår hos Kvinder," *Eva. Skønhed og Kærlighed*, vol. 1, no. 3 (1928), p. 8; and "Hvad jeg ikke forstår hos Mænd," *Eva. Skønhed og Kærlighed*, nol. 1, no. 4 (1928), p. 6. For other examples, see also "Den stærke Mands Svage Sider," *Vore Herrer*, vol. 7, no. 1 (January 5, 1922); "Den stærke Mands Smaa Svagheder," *Vore Herrer*, vol. 7, no. 3 (February 2, 1922); and "Hattepindepartiet melder sig," *Vore Herrer*, vol. 1, no. 6 (June 15, 1916).

30. See file no. 11316, the Danish Film Museum and Archives, Copenhagen.

31. In Danish, the 1927 cabaret song was called "Vi hader Kvinder." The text was written by Aage Steffensen, and the musical score was by Emil Reesen. Other examples of popular cabaret songs addressing the issue of gender conflict and gender antagonism included "La Garçonne" (1925), "Kvinden er en Gaade!" (1924), "Han har Charme" (1924), "Amanda Skou!" (1924), "Der er ikke den Ting, Kvinden ikke kan" (1927), and "Hvor skal Manden kunne vide, hvad Kvinden allerhelst vil ha-" (1926). Information from the Popular Music Archives, the State Library, Aarhus, Denmark.

32. "Goddag - og Tak for sidst." Text by Alfred Kjerulf, musical score by Edvard Brink, 1925. From the Popular Music Archives, the State Library, Aarhus, Denmark.

33. "Deres Forhold i Privatlivet. Klar Besked om Omgangsformerne mellem unge Kvinder og unge Mænd. Kammeratskabsforholdet. Om at hilse rigtigt. De unges Moral," *København*, August 4, 1924, p. 11.

34. "Deres Forhold i Privatlivet," p. 11.

35. Ibid.

36. *Skik og Brug i Selskabslivet* (Copenhagen, 1919), p. 70.

37. "Flirts Spørgekasse," *Flirt*, vol. 3, no. 48 (March 8, 1923), p. 9.

38. "Hvorfor er de danske Mænd saa ubehøvlede?" *Vore Herrer*, vol. 8, no. 24 (November 21, 1923).

39. *Illustreret Tidende*, vol. 64, no. 19 (February 5, 1922), p. 398.

40. "Den Kvindelige Kvinde," 1923. Unidentified newspaper clipping in the Emma Grandsgaard Collection of Newspaper Clippings, the Women's History Archives, the State Library, Aarhus, Denmark.

41. "Svaret paa et Brev," *Politiken*, July 13, 1919, p. 13.

42. "Aabent Brev til Københavneren," *Politiken*, July 20, 1919, p. 10.

43. "Flirts Spørgekasse," *Flirt*, vol. 2, no. 36 (December 14, 1922), p. 10.

44. "Etikette og Mode-Brevkasse," *Vore Herrer*, vol. 4, no. 2 (January 23, 1919).

45. "Ugebladets Spørgekasse," *Ugebladet*, vol. 3, no. 70 (October 18, 1923), p. 17.

46. Symptomatically, male chivalry was also a central issue in late nineteenth-century feminist discussions in Britain. For an interesting discussion of this phenomenon, see Susan Kingsley Kent, *Sex and Suffrage in Britain, 1860–1914* (Princeton, N. J., 1987), pp. 157–83.

47. See Kevin White, *The First Sexual Revolution: The Emergence of Male Heterosexuality in Modern America* (New York, 1993), p. 54.

48. "Hvorfor er de danske Mænd saa ubehøvlede?"

49. "Ugebladets Spørgekasse," *Ugebladet*, vol. 3, no. 70 (October 18, 1923), p. 17.

50. "Flirts Spørgekasse," *Flirt*, vol 2, no. 36 (December 14, 1922), pp. 10–11.

51. Karen Dubinsky, *Improper Advances: Rape and Heterosexual Conflict in Ontario, 1880–1929* (Chicago, 1993), p. 132.

52. "Den moderne Tid," *Nationaltidende*, June 28, 1921, p. 4.

53. At the turn of the century, many American working-class girls looked to men to pay their way when going out. See Peiss, *Cheap Amusements*, pp. 53–55; and Joanne J. Meyerowitz, *Women Adrift: Independent Wage Earners in Chicago, 1880–1930* (Chicago and London, 1988), pp. 101–104. The early decades of the twentieth century also witnessed the emergence of the dating system among American middle-class youths, which gave young men the right to invite, but also the duty to pay for, a female companion. See, for example, Bailey, *From Front Porch to Back Seat*, pp. 13–24; Ellen K. Rothman, *Hands and Hearts: A History of Courtship in America* (New York, 1984), pp. 203–44.

The custom that men paid for women's leisure activities was not exclusively American. According to Christina Benninghaus, many young people in Weimar

Germany engaged in similar practices. See Christina Benninghaus, " 'But You Need to Give Me a French Kiss': Gender Relations and the Culture of Treating among German Adolescents in the 1920s." Paper presented at the 11th Berkshire Conference on the History of Women, Rochester, New York, 1999. Whether this was the case in other European countries, and why this never became the custom in Denmark, remains unclear.

54. Oral history interview, Randers, Denmark, April 16, 1994.

55. Oral history interview, Copenhagen, Denmark, May 27, 1991.

56. Michael Curtin, *Property and Position: A Study of Victorian Manners* (New York, 1987), p. 273.

57. Oral history interview, Copenhagen, Denmark, December 10, 1993.

58. "Nutidens unge Piger," 1924. Unidentified newspaper clipping in the Emma Grandsgaard Collection of Newspaper Clippings, the Women's History Archives, the State Library, Aarhus.

59. "Kønskampen fortsætter," *Nationaltidende*, April 23, 1924, p. 3.

60. According to Kevin White, a similar breakdown of what he calls the Victorian system of masculine morality took place in the United States in the 1910s and 1920s, leaving men "to their own worst behavior." See White, *The First Sexual Revolution*, p. 148.

61. "Sommerens badende Dametyper," 1922. Unidentified newspaper clipping in the Emma Grandsgaard Collection of Newspaper Clippings, the State Library, Aarhus, Denmark. For other examples, see, for instance, Anders W. Holm, "Den røde Pige," *Flirt*, vol. 2, no. 8 (April 1922), p. 1; and "Jeg har mødt hende tit," *Hvepsen*, vol. 1, no. 4 (1925).

Men's insistence that they were the victims of sexually aggressive women was not an exclusively Danish phenomenon. According to Karen Dubinsky, many Canadian men expressed similar sentiments in the early twentieth century. See Dubinsky, *Improper Advances*, p. 21.

62. "Nutidens unge Piger," *Berlingske Tidende*, March 3, 1926, p. 4.

63. "Den dansende Ungdom og Høfligheden," *B.T.*, September 9, 1928, p. 2.

64. "Kvindemoderne," *Berlingske Tidende*, July 31, 1925, p. 3.

65. Here quoted from *Selskabelig Takt og Tone. Korrekt Optræden i Selskaber og i det daglige Liv* (Copenhagen, 1930), p. 67.

66. "Til Københavnerinden," *Politiken*, July 27, 1919, p. 10. For another example of such admonitions to young women, see "Fra Ham til Hende," *Nationaltidende*, July 20, 1924, p. 15.

67. "Flirts Spørgekasse," *Flirt*, vol. 3, no. 45 (February 15, 1923), p. 9; "Vi har fra en af vore Læserinder modtaget følgende henvendelse til Principalerne," *Vore Herrer*, vol. 7, no. 18 (September 14, 1922); "Danse-spørge-kasse," *Flirt*, vol. 2, no. 18 (August 10, 1922), p. 11; and "Flirts Spørgekasse," *Flirt*, vol. 3, no. 49 (March 15, 1923), p. 9.

68. Whether older feminists did not feel this an issue of relevance to them or were equally at a loss about how to mount a counterattack is unclear. Under all circumstances, they remained conspicuously silent about this topic throughout the 1920s.

69. Copenhagen municipal court, file no. 167/1927, the Regional Archives for Sealand, Copenhagen. Whether this was an exceptional case is difficult to determine since only a handful of records pertaining to rape, sexual assault, and indecent behavior can be located. According to regional archivist Vibeke Philipsen, the overwhelming majority of these records were destroyed in the late 1950s and early 1960s because they were deemed historically "insignificant."

70. Information compiled from *Statistisk Tabelværk*, series V, vol. B 8 (1931), p. 48; and *Statistisk Tabelværk*, series V, vol. B 9 (1939), p. 37.

71. The early twentieth-century shift of courtship from the home (for middle-class youths) and the immediate neighborhood (for working-class youths) to more anonymous public arenas seems to have been a phenomenon characteristic of many Western nations. See, for instance, Rothman, *Hands and Hearts*, pp. 203–44; Peiss, *Cheap Amusements*, pp. 34–114; Bailey, *From Front Porch to Back Seat*, pp. 13–24; and Dubinski, *Improper Advances*, pp. 113–42.

72. Ernst Kaper: "Fornuftige Breve til en ung Pige," unpublished manuscript in the Manuscript Collection, File no. Utilg. 359, "Borgmester Kapers efterladte papirer m.m.," the Royal Library, Copenhagen, Denmark. In his study of twentieth-century American youth culture, John Modell found a similar reaction among older adults. Like their Danish counterparts, they interpreted the rejection of older courtship patterns as a rejection of romance itself. See Modell, *Into One's Own*, p. 86.

73. Oral history interview, Køge, Denmark, November 28, 1993.

74. Oral history interview, Copenhagen, Denmark, December 2, 1990.

75. See, for example, "Miskendt," *Ugebladet*, vol. 3, no. 82 (November 1, 1923), pp. 8–9.

76. "Spørgebrevkassen," *Ugebladet*, vol. 3, no. 4 (May 6, 1923), p. 23.

77. "Flirts Spørgekasse," *Flirt*, vol. 2, no. 32 (November 16, 1922), p. 8.

78. "Dame-brevkasse," *Søndags B.T.*, September 30, 1928, p. 8.

79. "Flirts Spørgekasse," *Flirt*, vol. 2, no. 33 (November 23, 1922), p. 8.

80. "Hvem begynder?" *Ugebladet*, vol. 5, no. 52 (December 30, 1925), pp. 23–24.

81. Oral history interview, Copenhagen, Denmark, December 2, 1990.

82. Oral history interview, Copenhagen, Denmark, October 10, 1993.

83. Oral history interview, Copenhagen, Denmark, October 30, 1993.

84. Oral history interview, Copenhagen, Denmark, October 28, 1993.

85. In her study of courtship patterns among British working-class youths, Judy Giles noted similar patterns of female reticence. See Judy Giles, "Playing Hard to Get: Working Class Women, Sexuality and Respectability in Britain, 1918–1940," *Women's History Review*, vol. 1, no. 2 (1992), pp. 239–55; and Judy Giles: "'You Meet 'Em and That's It': Working Class Women's Refusal of Romance between the Wars in Britain," in Lynne Pierce and Jackie Stacey (eds.), *Romance Revisited* (New York and London, 1995), pp. 279–92.

86. The marriage legislation of 1922 stipulated that if, for instance, a woman had given up a job in anticipation of her impending marriage, she was entitled to financial compensation if her fiancé broke off the engagement.

87. "Spørg Juristen," 1924. Unidentified newspaper clipping in the Emma Grandsgaard Collection of Newspaper Clippings, the Women's History Archives, the State Library, Aarhus.

88. "Spørg Juristen," 1924.

89. "Spørgebrevkassen," *Søndags B.T.*, January 11, 1928, p. 24.

90. "Brevkassen," *Ugebladet*, vol. 5, no. 3 (January 21, 1925), p. 22.

PART III

1. "Frk. Karen Hansen," *Kvindelig Idrætsforenings Medlemsblad*, vol. 8, no. 3 (June 3, 1923), pp. 26–27.

2. For other examples, see "Fru Kaja Rossing," *Telefonen*, vol. 8, no. 12 (December 1, 1916), p. 4; and "Vore Lykønskninger," Magasin du Nord's corporate archives, Copenhagen, Denmark.

3. Hans Chr. Johansen (ed.), *Dansk historisk statistik 1814–1980* (Copenhagen, 1985), pp. 114–15.

4. Søren Mørck *Den ny Danmarkshistorie 1880–1960* (Copenhagen, 1982), p. 28; and Danmarks Statistik: *Vielsestavler for kvinder. VITX.XLS* (Copenhagen, 1990).

5. Oral history interview, Copenhagen, Denmark, December 10, 1991.

CHAPTER 5

1. "Hvad synes De om Ægteskabet? En Forespørgsel til vore kvindelige Læsere," 1921. Unidentified newspaper clipping in the Emma Grandsgaard Collection of Newspaper Clippings, the Women's History Archives, the State Library, Aarhus, Denmark.

2. "Hvad synes De om Ægteskabet? Nogle Svar til vores Enquete," 1921. Unidentified newspaper clipping in the Emma Grandsgaard Collection of Newspaper Clippings, the Women's History Archives, the State Library, Aarhus, Denmark.

3. "Hvad synes De om Ægteskabet?" 1921.

4. Ibid.

5. Ibid.

6. Ibid.

7. Oral history interview, Copenhagen, Denmark, October 30, 1993.

8. "Bliver Kvinder lykkelige som gifte?" *Politiken*, August 1, 1915, p. 10.

9. Examples of such popular literature include Lisa Michaely, *Lykkens Tinde* (Copenhagen, 1915); Ellen Reumert, *Født Pebersvend* (Copenhagen, 1915); Ingeborg Vollquartz, *Lillians Forlovelse* (Copenhagen, 1915); and Ingeborg Vollquarts, *Lillians Ægteskab* (Copenhagen, 1916).

10. For the history of Danish first-wave feminism, see Gyrithe Lemcke, *Dansk Kvindesamfunds Historie gennem 40 Aar* (Copenhagen, 1912); Kirsten Gloerfelt-Tarp, *Kvinden i Samfundet* (Copenhagen, 1937); and Aagot Lading, *Dansk Kvindesamfunds Arbejde gennem 25 Aar* (Copenhagen, 1939).

11. For brief histories of the Danish suffrage campaigns, see Inga Dahlsgaard, "The Struggle for Political Rights," in *Women in Denmark. Yesterday and Today* (Copenhagen, 1980), pp. 126–40; and Drude Dahlerup, "Women's Entry into

Politics: The Experience of the Danish Local and General Elections 1908–1920," *Scandinavian Political Studies*, vol. 1, nos. 2–3 (1978), pp. 139–62.

12. See, for instance, Jutta Bojsen-Møller, "Kvinderne og Ægteskabet," *Berlingske Tidende*, March 11, 1911, p. 3.

13. Viggo Bentzon, *Hvad nyt bringer Ægteskabsloven?* (Copenhagen, 1920), p. 4.

14. Because Norway, Sweden, and Denmark had long sought to maintain comparable family legislation, and because feminists in the other Scandinavian countries placed similar pressures on their governments to reform the existing marriage law, the commission was appointed as a collaborative, cross-national Nordic body.

15. "Bekendtgørelse af 26. juli 1912 angaaende Autorisation af nye Ritualer for Daab, Nadvere og Brudevielse," *Lovtidende A for 1912*, no. 38 (August 29, 1912), pp. 1035–45. Unfortunately, it has not been possible to determine what motivated this decision. According to archivists, the records have either been lost or were never made available. Inquiries at the Ministry for Church Affairs in Copenhagen yielded even less information.

16. Bentzon, *Hvad nyt bringer Ægteskabsloven?* p. 60.

17. Ibid.

18. H. G. Bechman, "Ægteskab," *Tilskueren. Maanedsskrift for Litteratur, Kunst, Samfundsspørgsmaal og almenfattelige videnskabelige Skildringer*, vol. 37, no. 5 (May 1920), p. 178.

19. Vinding Kruse, "Ægteskabsloven," *Gads danske Magasin*, vol. 15 (October 1921), p. 483.

20. "Moderne Ægteskab," *København*, February 16, 1921, pp. 3–4.

21. "Foredrag ved Universitetets social-akademiske Forelæsninger," *Tidens Kvinder*, vol. 1 (April 26, 1923), p. 19.

22. Harald Nielsen, *Moderne Ægteskab* (Copenhagen, 1919), p. 46.

23. "Lov no. 56 af 18. marts 1925 on Ægteskabets Retsvirkninger," *Lovtidende A-B* (Copenhagen, 1925), p. 209.

24. Ibid.

25. C.I.F. Svein, "Den Nye Ægteskabslov." Unidentified newspaper clipping in the Emma Grandsgaard Collection of Newspaper Clippings, the Women's History Archives, the State Library, Aarhus, Denmark.

26. Dahlerup, "Women's Entry into Politics," pp. 139–62.

27. Hans Chr. Johansen (ed.), *Dansk historisk statistik 1814–1980* (Copenhagen, 1985), p. 114.

28. Here quoted from "Ægteskabsloven," *Politiken*, April 12, 1919, pp. 1–3.

29. Here quoted from "Ægteskabsloven. Fortsat," *Tidens Kvinder*, vol. 2, no. 30 (July 24, 1920), p. 5.

30. Here quoted from "Ægteskabsloven. Sluttet," *Tidens Kvinder*, vol. 2, no. 31 (July 31, 1920), p. 5.

31. Oral history interview, Aarhus, Denmark, February 25, 1990.

32. The declining cultural legitimacy of spinsterhood was an international phenomenon in the early twentieth century. See, for instance, Sheila Jeffreys, *The Spinster and Her Enemies: Feminism and Sexuality 1880–1930* (London, 1985); Sheila Jeffreys, "Sex Reform and Antifeminism in the 1920s," in The London

Feminist History Group (eds.), *The Sexual Dynamics of History: Men's Power, Women's Resistance* (London, 1983), pp. 177–202; and Christina Simmons, "Modern Sexuality and the Myth of Victorian Repression," in Cathy Peiss and Christina Simmons (eds.), *Passion and Power: Sexuality in History* (Philadelphia, 1989), pp. 157–77.

33. See, for instance, Merry Wiesner, *Women and Gender in Early Modern Europe* (Cambridge, 1993); Lyndal Roper, *The Holy Household: Women and Morals in Reformation Augsburg* (Oxford, 1989); and Lawrence Stone, *The Family, Sex and Marriage in England, 1500–1800* (London, 1977).

34. "Ægteskabets vanskelige problem. Hvem skal man gifte sig med?" *Socialdemokraten*, March 7, 1920, p. 8.

35. Letter from Erika Christensen to Edna Juul, November 13, 1923. Letter in private ownership of Anne Marie Juul, Aalborg, Denmark.

36. "Kunsten at bevare Kærligheden i Ægteskabet," *Flirt*, vol. 3, no. 43 (February 1, 1923), p. 5.

37. One of the first Danish publications to advocate female sexual pleasure in marriage was Christian Christensen, *Arbejderne og Børneflokken*, which first appeared in 1910. By 1923, when the sixth edition was printed, at least 15,500 copies of the book were in popular circulation. See Preben Hertoft, *Det er måske en galskab. Om seksual reformbevægelsen i Danmark* (Copenhagen, 1983), pp. 21–29.

38. "Ægteskab eller - ?" *Politiken*, March 28, 1920, p. 15.

39. "Hvad danner Grundlaget for et lykkeligt Ægteskab - ?" *Berlingske Tidende*, November 28, 1925, p. 2.

40. "Hvorledes bliver et Ægteskab lykkeligt? Vi offentliggør i Dag de tre præmierede Indlæg," *B.T.*, May 27, 1930, p. 12.

41. "Hendes Ferie. Skal Mand og Kone holde Ferie sammen? - Modstridende Indlæg," *B.T.*, May 29, 1925, p. 11.

42. "Kvinder og Ægteskab," *Politiken*, May 12, 1925, p. 10. For other examples of the emphasis placed on shared interests, see, for instance, "Ægteskabsdiskussionen. Musik i Hjemmet," *Socialdemokraten*, March 16, 1920, p. 7; and "Kvinden, Sporten og Hjemmet. Fru Ulla Ulrich fortæller om, hvor godt det er for Mand og Kone at have fælles Interesser," *B.T.*, May 18, 1930, p. 10.

43. See, for instance, Bonnie Smith, *Changing Lives: Women in European History since 1700* (Lexington, Mass., and Toronto 1989), pp. 410–53; Ute Frevert, *Women in German History: From Bourgeois Emancipation to Sexual Liberation* (New York, 1989), pp. 168–204; and Ellen Holzman, "The Pursuit of Married Love: Women's Attitudes toward Sexuality and Marriage in Great Britain, 1918–1939," *Journal of Social History*, vol. 16 (1982), pp. 39–52.

44. The fact that many popular movies also celebrated this ideal, and that promotional materials about movie stars invariably depicted them as part of such marriages unquestionably served to strengthen young women's enthusiasm even further.

45. I. M. Holten-Nielsen, *Hjemmets Verden. Haandbog og Raadgiver for ethvert Hjem* (Copenhagen, 1923) p. 6.

46. "Flirts Spørgekasse," *Flirt*, vol. 2, no. 24 (September 21, 1922), p. 10.

47. "Flirts Spørgekasse," *Flirt*, vol. 2, no. 33 (November 23, 1922), p. 8.

48. "Typer: Kvinden, som Manden elsker," *Vore Herrer*, vol. 8, no. 10 (May 10, 1923).

49. "Kvindetyper: Den unge Frue," *Vore Herrer*, vol. 8, no. 7 (March 29, 1923).

50. "Hvis er Skylden? Ligger Grunden til de mange Skilsmisser ikke ofte i Kvindernes Mangel paa Evne til at forny sig?" *Vore Damer*, vol. 12, no. 7 (May 1, 1923), p. 19.

51. "Kvindetyper: Den unge Frue," *Vore Herrer*, vol. 8, no. 7 (March 29, 1923).

52. For a striking example of this fusion of categories, see Den moderne Eva, *Vore Damers Skønhedspleje* (Copenhagen, 1920).

53. "Hvordan bevarer man sin Mands Kærlighed?" *Aftenlæsning*, vol. 1, no. 3 (1926), p. 17.

54. "Flirts Spørgekasse," *Flirt*, vol. 2, no. 32 (November 16, 1922), p. 9.

55. In her study of social and sexual mores in postwar America, Dorothy Brown noted a similar trend. Much like their Danish counterparts, American advice givers insisted that marriages failed "not because of slovenly housekeeping or inept childrearing but because of uninteresting wives. The thrifty, industrious 'domestic drudge' was a hindrance" to marital happiness. See Dorothy Brown, *Setting a Course: American Women in the 1920s* (Boston, 1987), p. 105.

56. "Hvordan bevarer man sin Mands Kærlighed?" p. 17.

57. "Smaa Leveregler. Aftenerne i Hjemmet," *Illustreret Familiejournal*, vol. 46, no. 3 (January 18, 1922), p. 34.

58. "Bør en Hustru fortælle sin Mand alt?" *Aftenlæsning*, vol. 1, no. 8 (1926), p. 17.

59. See Karin Lützen, *Hvad hjertet begærer. Kvinders kærlighed til kvinder 1825–1985* (Copenhagen, 1986), pp. 154–76.

60. This shift was clearly part of an international trend. See, for instance, Lesley Hall, "Impotent Ghosts from No Man's Land, Flappers' Boyfriends, or Crypto-Patriarchs? Men, Sex and Social Change in 1920s Britain," *Social History*, vol. 21, no. 1 (1996), pp. 54–70; Michael Gordon, "From an Unfortunate Necessity to a Cult of Mutual Orgasm: Sex in American Marital Education Literature, 1830–1940," in James Hensley (ed.), *Studies in the Sociology of Sex* (New York, 1975), pp. 53–77; Peter Laipson: " 'Kiss without Shame, for She Desires It': Sexual Foreplay in American Marital Advice Literature, 1900–1925," *Journal of Social History*, vol. 29, no. 3 (1996), pp. 507–25. For a fuller discussion of the history of sexual advice literature, see also Roy Porter and Lesley Hall, *The Facts of Life: The Creation of Sexual Knowledge in Britain, 1650–1950* (New Haven, Conn., 1995).

61. Frank Lesser, *Ægtemandens Bog. Hvad enhver gift Mand bør vide om hvordan man skal behandle sin Hustru* (Copenhagen, 1929).

62. "Hvis er Skylden?" p. 19.

63. "Den glade Kvinde," *Aftenlæsning*, vol. 1, no. 50 (April 13, 1927), p. 6.

64. When assessing the impact of changing sexual ideologies on women's lives in the 1920s, some historians have emphasized the positive aspects, noting that the new public discourse increased women's knowledge of their own bodies, alerted husbands to their wives' erotic desires, and provided spouses with a shared lan-

guage in which to discuss sexual matters. See, for instance, Holzman, "The Pursuit of Married Love"; Laipson, " 'Kiss without Shame, for She Desires It"; and Porter and Hall, *The Facts of Life*, pp. 202–23. Others have argued that the new emphasis on sexual fulfillment in marriage was implicitly oppressive to women, turning wives into eroticized sex objects for their husbands. See, for instance, Jeffreys, "Sex Reform and Anti-Feminism in the 1920s"; Jeffreys, *The Spinster and Her Enemies*; Jackson, "Sexual Liberation or Social Control?" pp. 1–17; and Margaret Jackson, *The Real Facts of Life: Feminism and the Politics of Sexuality c. 1850–1940* (London, 1994). The Danish case seems to suggest that the new emphasis on marital eroticism was a mixed bag for women. On the one hand, it encouraged a more positive attitude toward sex within marriage that seemed to appeal to many young women. On the other hand, it placed a new burden on wives from whom less than whole-hearted enthusiasm about sex would no longer be acceptable.

65. "Smaa Leveregler," *Illustreret Familie-Journal*, vol. 46, no. 8 (March 31, 1922), p. 35.

66. Oral history interview, Copenhagen, Denmark, November 19, 1990.

67. Oral history interview, Copenhagen, Denmark, December 3, 1990.

68. Oral history interview, Copenhagen, Denmark, May 31, 1991.

69. See Elaine Tyler May, *Great Expectations: Marriage and Divorce in Post-Victorian America* (Chicago, 1980).

70. "Brevkassen," *Ugebladet*, vol. 5, no. 3 (January 21, 1925), p. 22.

71. "Flirts Spørgekasse," *Flirt*, vol. 2, no. 32 (November 16, 1922), pp. 9–10.

72. "Flirts Spørgekasse," *Flirt*, vol. 3, no. 42 (January 25, 1923), p. 9.

73. "Typer: Ægtemanden," *Vore Herrer*, vol. 7, no. 11 (June 8, 1922).

74. "Dame-Brevkasse," *Søndags B.T.*, no. 41 (October 7, 1928), p. 10.

75. "Ugebladets Spørgekasse," *Ugebladet*, vol. 3, no. 69 (August 2, 1923), p. 17.

76. Commenting on British nineteenth-century marriages, Randolph Trumbach has suggested that "middle class companionship and intimacy was brought into existence by the words that passed between husbands and wives as much as by anything else." See Randolph Trumbach, "Review Essay: Is There a Modern Sexual Culture in the West; or, Did England Never Change between 1500 and 1900?" *Journal of the History of Sexuality*, vol. 1 (1990), pp. 296–309. By the 1920s, conversation and intimacy seemed in Denmark to be expectations held by young women across class lines.

77. "Brevkasse," *Eva. Ungdom og Skønhed*, vol. 1, no. 4 (March 1925), p. 29.

78. "Ugebladets Spørgekasse," *Ugebladet*, vol. 3, no. 78 (October 4, 1923), p. 18.

79. "Redaktionen har modtaget følgende vedr. Artiklerne om den stærke Mands smaa Svagheder," *Vore Herrer*, vol. 7, no. 9 (May 11, 1922).

80. "Hvordan bliver et Ægteskab lykkeligt?" *B.T.*, May 7, 1930, p. 12.

81. "La femme X skriver om Mændenes Skavanker," *Vore Herrer*, vol. 4, no. 21 (October 16, 1919).

82. See, for instance, "La femme X skriver om Mændenes Skavanker"; "La femme X skriver om Mændenes Skavanker," *Vore Herrer*, vol. 4, no. 26 (Decem-

ber 25, 1919); and "Jeg kender en Mand, der elsker sin Kone," *Vore Herrer*, vol. 8, no. 3 (February 1, 1923).

83. "Kammerater," *Ugebladet*, vol. 3, no. 85 (November 21, 1923), pp. 8–9.

84. While conflicts and disappointments over intimacy, conversation, and egalitarian interaction repeatedly surfaced in postwar public discourse on marriage, marital sexuality remained an area surrounded by silence. It is, of course, possible that spouses were satisfied and delighted with this aspect of their marriage and therefore did not seek help and advice. More likely, disappointed spouses did not feel free to ask about such issues, or they were, as Ellen Holzmann has suggested, more willing to accept less than fulfilling experiences in this area of their life. See Holzmann, "The Pursuit of Married Love," pp. 48–49. Nonetheless, other evidence does suggest that marital sexuality was an issue of concern among spouses. In 1921, Marie Stopes's British best-seller, *Married Love*, which discussed marital sexuality with remarkable frankness, was translated into Danish. In the course of the following eight years, it was reissued in nine editions, selling more than 25,000 copies.

85. To determine whether new marital expectations led to more divorces, I randomly sampled 1,150 separation and divorce records from the late 1910s and 1920s. To encompass potential regional variation, my sample includes records from four different counties: Copenhagen county; North Jutland county, in which Aalborg, a large industrial town with a considerable working-class population, is located; Vejle county, which includes the medium-sized town of the same name; and Ringkøbing county, which was almost exclusively rural. In all four counties, requests for legal separation were mixed with divorce requests. Consequently, my sample includes both types of cases. A prerequisite for access to the case records was an agreement concerning confidentiality and the protection of the privacy of the subjects of the case records. To honor this agreement, I have assigned each of the 1,150 cases a number (1–1150). These numbers are not the actual case numbers originally assigned by the record keepers. I have also changed all the names used in this study and have eliminated all pieces of information that might reveal the identity of the involved individuals.

86. Case #749.

87. In almost 15 percent of the cases, a request for separation or divorce was only submitted after the couple's twenty-fifth wedding anniversary. In more than one-fifth of all cases (20.3 percent), the marriage had lasted more than twenty years.

88. Only 4.5 percent of the divorcing couples belonged to the middle, upper-middle, or upper classes. Obviously, the popular images of divorcees as spoiled and pampered young women living comfortably off alimony payments and middle-age businessmen who deserted their wives for younger, more attractive women had little basis in reality.

89. Case #778.

90. Case #843.

91. Case #214.

92. Case #746.

93. Case #555. Questioned by county officials, Mrs. A. denied her husband's accusations, maintaining that she "in all cases [had] acted as she ought to toward

her husband, partly by taking good care of the home, partly by being economical, and partly by working with what she could in order to keep up the home."

94. Case #1014.

95. Case #101.

96. Case #1107.

97. Case #283.

98. Case #997.

99. Case #711.

100. Case #313.

101. Case #98.

102. Case #1006.

103. Case #948.

104. Case #217.

105. Case #242. In 25 percent of all the cases I surveyed the request for separation or divorce was withdrawn at least once. Often, however, the request was resubmitted within a short time span, if promises were broken. One husband managed to convince his wife to withdraw her request for separation because of his alcoholism and physical abuse no fewer than six times in the course of five years. Her seventh application laconically stated: "He's at it again. Please go ahead with the separation." The couple was finally separated in 1928 (Case #187).

106. Case #147.

107. Case #88.

108. Case #294.

109. Case #777.

110. Oral history interview, Aarhus, Denmark, February 23, 1990.

111. Oral history interview, Copenhagen, Denmark, November 18, 1990.

112. *Politiken*, January 1, 1915, p. 8.

113. *Nationaltidende*, March 11, 1915, p. 9.

114. *Politiken*, May 2, 1915, p. 11.

115. *Socialdemokraten*, July 8, 1915, p. 8.

116. *Politiken*, February 13, 1915, p. 14.

117. *Politiken*, March 3, 1928, p. 13.

118. *Dagens Nyheder*, January 2, 1929, p. 16.

119. *Socialdemokraten*, October 19, 1928, p. 9.

120. *Politiken*, July 25, 1928, p. 10.

CHAPTER 6

1. Svend Aage Hansen and Ingrid Henriksen: *Dansk socialhistorie 1914–1939. Sociale brydninger* (Copenhagen, 1980), p. 345. For additional information about married women's labor market participation, see also Jens Warming, *Danske Samfundsproblemer i statistisk Belysning* (Copenhagen, 1934); Kirsten Gloerfeldt-Tarp (ed.), *Kvinden i Samfundet* (Copenhagen, 1937); Kirsten Geertsen, *Arbejderkvinder i Danmark 1914–24* (Greenå, 1977); and Søren Mørck, *Den ny Danmarkshistorie 1880–1960* (Copenhagen, 1982), p. 315.

2. Kirsten Gloerfelt-Tarp, "Den gifte Kvinde i Erhvervslivet," in Kirsten Gloerfelt-Tarp (ed.), *Kvinden i Samfundet*, p. 229.

3. Geertsen, *Arbejderkvinder i Danmark 1914–24*, pp. 45–46.

4. Oral history interview, Copenhagen, Denmark, November 5, 1993.

5. Oral history interview, Nørresundby, Denmark, December 21, 1993.

6. See P. C. Matthiessen, *Some Aspects of the Demographic Transition in Denmark* (Copenhagen, 1970); id., *Befolkningens vækst* (Copenhagen, 1976); and Jørgen Wedebye, *Befolkningsforhold* (Copenhagen, 1978).

7. Mørck, *Den ny Danmarkshistorie*, pp. 31–33.

8. On the decline of domestic service in Denmark in the decades around the turn of the century, see Tinne Vammen, *Rent og urent: Hovedstadens piger og fruer 1880–1920* (Copenhagen, 1986); and Ingeborg Bach et al., "Fra tjenestepige til lønarbejder 1900–1925," in Anne Margrete Berg et al. (eds.), *Kvindfolk. En danmarkshistorie fra 1600 til 1980*, vol. 2 (Copenhagen, 1984), pp. 25–40.

9. See Mørck, *Den ny Danmarkshistorie*, pp. 27–33.

10. According to Bente Rosenbeck, the work of Danish farm wives did not begin to change significantly until after World War II. See Bente Rosenbeck: *Kvindekøn. Den moderne kvindeligheds historie 1880–1980* (Copenhagen, 1987), pp. 230–52.

11. I have borrowed this characterization from Victoria de Grazia and Ellen Furlough, who define "the modern consumer household" as "one dependent on market exchange for most of its supplies and services." See Victoria de Grazia, with Ellen Furlough (eds.), *The Sex of Things: Gender and Consumption in Historical Perspective* (Berkeley, Calif. 1996), p. 151.

12. See, for instance, Ruth Cowan, *More Work for Mother: The Ironies of Household Technology from the Open Hearth to the Microwave* (New York, 1983); Glenna Matthews, *"Just a Housewife": The Rise and Fall of Domesticity in America* (New York, 1987); Caroline Davidson, *A Woman's Work Is Never Done: A History of Housework in the British Isles, 1650–1950* (London, 1982); and Graham Thomas and Christine Zmroczek, "Household Technology: The Liberation of Women from the Home?" in Paul Close and Rosemary Collins (eds.), *Family and Economy in Modern Society* (Houndsmills, England, 1985), pp. 104–5.

13. See Matthews, *"Just a Housewife"*; and Nancy Folbre, "The Unproductive Housewife: The Evolution in Nineteenth-Century Economic Thought," *Signs*, vol. 16, no. 3 (1991), pp. 463–84.

14. "Kunst og Huslighed," *Nationaltidende*, August 19, 1923, p. 13.

15. Ibid.

16. Frieda Buehl, "Den kvindelige Værnepligt," *Louiseforeningens Blad*, vol. 5, no. 11 (November 15, 1920), pp. 54–55.

17. Danish women's eagerness to desert domestic service is documented in Rigmor Skade and Kirsten Gloerfelt-Tarp, "Kvindens Beskæftigelse i Husholdning og Erhverv," in Gloerfelt-Tarp (ed.), *Kvinden i Samfundet*, pp. 54–92; and in Vammen, *Rent og urent*, pp. 49–112.

18. "Den moderne Kvinde," *Berlingske Tidende* (1921). Unidentified newspaper clipping in the Emma Grandsgaard Collection of Newspaper Clippings, the Women's History Archives, the State Library, Aarhus, Denmark.

19. "Den moderne Husmoders Besværligheder," *Socialdemokraten*, June 29, 1922, p. 3.

20. Ibid.

21. "Det evige Problem," *Politiken*, April 18, 1915, p. 11.

22. "Vore Husmødre," *København*, October 3, 1921, p. 6.

23. In the early years of the twentieth century, such organizing of homemakers was not a uniquely Danish phenomenon. In the other Scandinavian countries, similar organizations were formed in the late 1910s, leading to the formation of the Nordic Association of Housewives in 1920. See Kari Melby, "The Housewife Ideology in Norway between the Two World Wars," *Scandinavian Journal of History*, vol. 14, no. 2 (1989), pp. 181–93.

Outside Scandinavia, housewives' organizations also sprang up in the early years of the twentieth century. In Germany, the National Union of German Housewives Associations was formed in 1915. See Ute Frevert: *Women in German History: From Bourgeois Emancipation to Sexual Liberation* (New York, 1989), p. 199; and Renate Bridenthal, " 'Professional' Housewives: Stepsisters of the Women's Movement," in Benate Bridenthal et al. (eds.), *When Biology Became Destiny* (New York, 1984), pp. 153–73. By 1921, the British Women's Co-operative Guild represented the interests of more than 50,000 working-class wives. See Gillian Scott: "A 'Trade Union for Married Women': The Women's Co-operative Guild 1914–1920," in Sybil Oldfield (ed.), *This Working-Day World: Women's Lives and Culture(s) in Britain 1914–1945* (London, 1994), pp. 18–28.

24. The Copenhagen Housewives' Association was preceded by a number of housekeeping associations for farmwives founded in the early years of the twentieth century. The latter were typically connected with agricultural schools or agricultural societies, and they saw housework as an integrated part of agricultural production. Throughout the 1920s, their concerns remained different from those of urban housewives' organizations, and only rarely did the two kinds of organizations collaborate. See Gerda Petri and Minna Kragelund, *Mor Magda - og alle de andre. Husholdning som fag fra 1900 til i dag* (Copenhagen, n.d.).

25. Even though the leadership of housewives' organizations was dominated by middle-aged, middle-class women, the rank-and-file membership was much more diverse. In contrast to most other women's organizations in the 1920s, housewives' organizations never seemed to have any problems recruiting members of the postwar generation, and the national federation included such working-class groups as the Workers' Housewives Society. See *De danske Husmoderforeninger 1920–1945. Festskrift* (Copenhagen, 1945); Aagot Lading, "Husmoderbevægelsen," in Vita Aller (ed.), *Dansk Kvinde i Dag* (Copenhagen, 1942); Marianne Groth Bruun, " 'Enighed gør stærk!' En analyse af husmødrene og deres arbejde i mellemkrigstidens Danmark," *Historievidenskab*, vol. 21 (1980), pp. 10–23; Marianne Groth Bruun, "Da husmødrene organiserede sig," in Berg et al. (eds.), *Kvindfolk*, vol. 2, pp. 290–304; and Inga Dahlsgård, *Women in Denmark Yesterday and Today* (Copenhagen, 1980), pp. 150–76.

26. "De danske Husmoderforeningers Program," *Husmoderen*, vol. 8, no. 3 (March, 1925), p. 51.

27. Carla Meyer: "Nytaar 1922," *Husmoderen*, vol. 5, no. 1 (January 1922), p. 1.

28. "Husmoderfaget som Erhverv," *Husmoderen*, vol. 3, no. 6 (June 1920).

29. "Arbejdet i Hjemmet - det betydningsfuldeste i Verden," *Aftenlæsning*, vol. 1, no. 13 (1926), p. 17; Mathilde Einar Lundsgaard, "Den nygifte Husmoder

før og nu," 1927. Unidentified newspaper clipping in the Emma Grandsgaard Collection of Newspaper Clippings, the Women's History Collection, the State Library, Aarhus, Denmark.

30. "Hjemmets Kvinder," *Illustreret Familie-Journal*, vol. 42, no. 1 (January 3, 1918), pp. 35–36.

31. Karen Braae, "Fremtidens Husmoder," *Politiken*, April 24, 1922, pp. 1–2.

To illustrate her point, she explained that "once when I was explaining my ideas to a well-known Copenhagen personality, he answered me: 'Well, my wife never had to go to the university in order to learn to mend stockings; in my time women used to be born with that kind of skills.' —'Do you have any sons?' I asked him, purposefully ignoring his irony. He looked at me somewhat disoriented, but finally said yes. 'In that case I should like to know whether you also would find it completely unnecessary to give your son a thorough business education just because he has demonstrated natural talents for business,' I asked. I seem to remember that he could not think of an answer" (Braae, pp. 1–2).

32. In 1923, the remark of a prospective female university student who claimed in a newspaper interview that "[i]f I fail my examination, I can always become a housewife—anybody can do that," so infuriated housewife Elisabeth Olrik from Aarhus that she felt compelled to write a letter to the editor of the national newspaper *Nationaltidende*. "A housewife's vocation is a complicated science that [demands] great knowledge," she insisted. "Therefore, it is far from all women who are suitable for domestic labor. . . . It is about time that we give up the belief that it is only stupid [women] who work in the home." See "Striden om Kunst og Huslighed," *Nationaltidende*, July 8, 1923, p. 11.

33. Dida Dederding, "Husmoderens Arbejde," *Husmoderen*, vol. 3, no. 3 (March 1920).

34. In 1895, Eline Eriksen and Magdalene Lauridsen had founded the Sorø School of Home Economics. In 1901, Ingeborg Suhr-Mailand opened the Suhrske Housewifery School and Teacher-Training College, and a few years later Birgitte Berg Nielsen, a feminist and longtime advocate of formal education for women who worked in the home opened a similar school. See Dahlsgård, *Women in Denmark Yesterday and Today*, pp. 150–53.

For histories of the early efforts to promote home economics, see Petri and Kragelund, *Mor Magda - og alle de andre*; Ninna Kiessling, "Kampen for en videnskabelig husholdningsuddannelse," in Hanne Rimmen Nielsen and Eva Lous (eds.), *Kvinder Undervejs. Dansk Kvindesamfund i Aarhus 1886–1986* (Aarhus, 1986), pp. 124–36; Bruun, " 'Enighed gør Stærk!' "; and Bruun, "Da husmødrene organiserede sig."

35. The fact that 85 percent of all Danish women would at some point in their lives marry was a piece of statistical information that organized housewives frequently used to promote their cause. See, for instance, "Hvor bærer Udviklingen hen?" *Husmoderen*, vol. 9, no. 10 (May 24, 1926), p. 1; and "Husmoderbevægelsens første Tiaar og dens Fremtidsmaal," *Berlingske Tidende*, May 25, 1930, p. 7.

36. Nina Bang, "Den huslige Uddannelse," *Husmoderen*, vol. 9, no. 9 (May 10, 1926), p. 136.

37. By the 1920s, domestic science courses had at least theoretically been a part of the primary school curriculum for girls for some time. They were formally introduced with the Education Act of 1899, but already prior to that Copenhagen schools had decided to offer girls such courses, and kitchen facilities were under construction in many public schools. However, because it was not obligatory, because of the costs involved, and because of a shortage of qualified teachers, domestic science remained a rarity in urban schools in the early decades of the twentieth century. In rural schools it was almost nonexistent. See Bang, "Den huslige Uddannelse," p. 136.

38. As Judy Giles has noted, the new styles of femininity that incorporated energy, enthusiasm, and cheerfulness contributed in significant ways to the creation of the "modern" housewife. See Judy Giles, "A Home of One's Own: Women and Domesticity in England, 1918–1950," *Women's Studies International Forum*, vol. 16, no. 3 (1993), p. 244.

39. "Den praktiske Husmoder," *Aftenlæsning*, vol. 1, no. 4 (1926), p. 8.

40. In 1926, for example, housewives' organizations arranged an impressive 112 demonstrations, 153 courses, and 114 lectures for their members. More than 31,000 housewives attended the events. See "Det store husmodermøde," *Berlingske Tidende*, September 8, 1927, p. 9.

41. "Kvindeligt Erhverv," *Husmoderen*, vol. 10. no. 13 (July 10, 1927), pp. 239–40.

42. "Den moderne Husmoder," 1924. Unidentified newspaper clipping in the Emma Grandsgaard Collection of Newspaper Clippings, the Women's History Archives, the State Library, Aarhus, Denmark.

43. "Nutidens Husmoder," 1929. Unidentified newspaper clipping in the Emma Grandsgaard Collection of Newspaper Clippings, the Women's History Archives, the State Library, Aarhus, Denmark.

44. I. M. Holten-Nielsen, *Hjemmets Verden. Haandbog og Raadgiver for ethvert Hjem* (Copenhagen, 1923), p. 55.

45. As Mary Nolan has pointed out, the adoption of the language of production and the efforts to introduce rational housekeeping practices was an international phenomenon in the 1920s. See Mary Nolan, *Visions of Modernity: American Business and the Modernization of Germany* (New York and Oxford, 1994), p. 212. Danish housekeeping experts were clearly informed about these developments, even though only few of them actually partook in international conferences.

46. "Nogle Raad til den moderne Husmoder," *B.T.*, September 7, 1921, p. 6.

47. Karen Braae, "Fremtidens Husmoder," *Politiken*, April 24, 1922, pp. 1–2.

48. Carla Meyer, "System i Arbejdet," in *Husmoderforeningens Program*. Published by De danske Husmoderforeninger, 1925.

49. "Er Husarbejdet kedeligt?" *Husmoderen*, vol. 12, no. 2 (January 24, 1929), p. 1.

50. See Sue Bowden and Avner Offer, "The Technological Revolution That Never Was: Gender, Class, and the Diffusion of Household Appliances in Interwar England," in de Grazia, with Furlough (eds.), *The Sex of Things*, pp. 244–74; Christine Zmroczek, "The Weekly Wash," in Sybil Oldfield (ed.), *This Working-Day World*, pp. 7–17; Nolan, *Visions of Modernity*, pp. 206–26; and Anna Jorunn

Audem and Kari Melby, *Oppe først og sist i seng. Husarbeid i Narge fra 1850 til i dag* (Oslo, 1985), pp. 127–33.

51. Kirsten Geertsen, *Arbejderkvinder i Danmark. Vilkår og kamp 1924–1939* (Copenhagen, 1982), p. 222.

52. Hansen and Henriksen, *Dansk socialhistorie 1914–1939*, p. 228; see also Mørck, *Den ny Danmarkshistorie*, pp. 331–32; and Rosenbeck, *Kvindekøn*, pp. 285–308.

53. According to Mary Nolan, the same was the case in Germany in the 1920s. As she argues, "Consumption and household technology played a distinctly subordinate role in the German vision of rationalization." See Nolan, *Visions of Modernity*, p. 216. For a similar argument, see also Nancy Reagin, "How to Fill a Market Basket: The Politics of Women's Consumption in Weimar and Nazi Germany," paper presented at the Tenth Berkshire Conference on the History of Women, North Carolina, 1996.

54. "Hvor bærer Udviklingen hen?" *Husmoderen*, vol. 9, no. 10 (May 24, 1926), p. 1.

55. Oral history interview, Aarhus, Denmark, February 19, 1990.

56. Oral history interview, Roskilde, Denmark, February 11, 1990. That many men also felt that the money they earned was in fact theirs is apparent in many of the letters they wrote to popular magazines and advice columnists. See, for instance, "Redaktionen har modtaget endnu et Brev fra 'Den gamle Adam' til 'Den moderne Eva,' " *Vore Herrer*, vol. 7, no. 11 (June 8, 1922).

57. Elisa Møller Andersen, "Kvinders Arbejde i vor Tid," *Politiken*, January 24, 1925, p. 11.

58. "Kvinder og Penge," *Politiken*, March 3, 1927, p. 4.

59. Ibid.

60. "Vore Møder. Den nye Ægteskabslov," *Husmoderen*, vol. 8, no. 5 (May 1925), p. 108.

61. "Kunsten at skabe et lykkeligt Ægteskab," *København*, December 7, 1923, p. 6, emphasis added.

62. "Den moderne Husmoders Besværligheder," *Socialdemokraten*, June 29, 1922, p. 3, emphasis added.

63. "Mere om Husmødrene og Pengene," *Husmoderen*, vol. 2, no. 11 (November 1919), p. 3.

64. "Skal Manden gøre sin Kone Regnskab?" *B.T.*, July 16, 1925, p. 11.

65. "Skal Manden gøre sin Hustru Regnskab? Nogle Svar fra Læserne," *B.T.*, July 28, 1925, p. 11.

66. Elisabeth Johansen, "Brev til Husmødrene," *Politiken*, May 1, 1921, p. 9.

67. See, for instance, Karen Braae, *Hvordan afpasser jeg bedst mit Budget efter min Indtægt?* (Copenhagen, 1922); Agnes Elgstrøm, *Hvorfor og hvordan skal vi lægge Budget for vor Husholdning?* (Copenhagen, 1928); Holten-Nielsen, *Hjemmets Verden. Haandbog og Raadgiver for ethvert Hjem*; Eva Ander Nørgaard, "Regnskaber," *Husmoderen*, vol. 6, no. 11 (November 1923), pp. 227–28; and "Økonomi," *Illustreret Tidende*, vol. 62, no. 18 (May 8, 1921), p. 217.

68. "Husholdningspengene," *Politiken*, February 1, 1925, p. 10; see also Braae, *Hvordan afpasser jeg bedst mit Budget efter min Indtægt*, p. 4.

69. See, for instance, "Den moderne Husholdning," *Ugebladet*, vol. 3, no. 73 (August 30, 1923).

70. "Kvinderne og Husholdningspengene," *Illustreret Familie-Journal*, vol. 46, no. 45 (November 15, 1922), p. 6.

71. Ibid.

72. "Bør en Hustru være sin Mands økonomiske Raadgiver?" *Nationaltidende*, January 29, 1920, p. 6.

73. Although it is difficult to estimate how many women kept account books, the available evidence suggests that it was a sizable proportion. Housewives certainly flocked to lectures on how to create a budget or keep an account book, and night classes on similar topics drew large and inquisitive crowds. Simultaneously, women's magazines were bombarded with letters in which housewives requested instructions on how best to keep their records. Booklets on the art of budgeting and accounting sold in large numbers, and when the Federation of Housewives' Societies published its own account book in 1923, members stood in line to obtain copies. It is also suggestive that all but seven of the women interviewed for this project recalled having kept account books for at least a period of time during the early years of their marriage.

74. "Husmødrene og Husholdningspengene," *Ekstrabladet*, May 2, 1923, p. 7.

75. Ibid.

76. See, for instance, "Ugebladets Spørgekasse," *Ugebladet*, vol. 3, no. 70 (August 9, 1923), p. 15.

77. See, for instance, "Flirts Spørgekasse," *Flirt*, vol. 2, no. 33 (November 23, 1922), p. 12.

78. See, for instance, "Spørgebrevkassen," *Ugebladet*, vol. 8, no. 24 (June 19, 1928), p. 24.

79. "Vore Dages Ægteskaber," *Socialdemokraten*, December 16, 1922, p. 4.

80. "Skal Konen have Regnskab? Meningerne er delte!" *B.T.*, July 20, 1925, p. 14.

81. "Vore Husmødre," *Berlingske Tidende*, May 28, 1927, p. 11.

82. "Husmødrenes store Aftenmøde," 1928. Unidentified newspaper clipping in the Emma Grandsgaard Collection of Newspaper Clippings, the Women's History Archives, the State Library, Aarhus, Denmark.

83. Folbre, "The Unproductive Housewife." Although Folbre bases her conclusions on Anglo-American cases, her findings seem to apply to continental Europe as well.

84. "En Tak til de danske Husmødre," *Berlingske Tidende*, January 1, 1918, p. 3.

85. K. K. Steincke, "En Ros til de danske Husmødre," *Politiken*, July 4, 1917, p. 2.

86. Jens Warming, "Bør der oprettes en Husmoderforening?" *Gads danske Magasin*, vol. 11 (October 1916), pp. 10–23; and Jens Warming, "Bør der oprettes en Husmoderforening? II," *Gads danske Magasin*, vol. 11 (November 1916), pp. 76–85.

In her history of the Federation of Danish Housewives' Associations published in 1945, Johanne Appel argued that Jens Warming's articles had been of absolutely crucial importance for establishing a new self-confidence among housewives and that they had provided much of the incentive for the formation of housewives' organizations in the late 1910s. See Johanne Appel: "De danske Husmoderforeninger 1920–1931," in *De danske Husmoderforeninger 1920–1945. Festskrift* (Copenhagen, 1945), pp. 1–16.

87. Warming, "Bør der oprettes en Husmoderforening?" p. 10.

88. "Husmødrenes Situation i disse vanskelige Krigsaar," *Vore Damer*, vol. 5, no. 2 (January 11, 1917), p. 2.

89. "Vort Ansvar," *Kvinden og Samfundet*, vol. 33, no. 7 (March 3, 1917), p. 68.

90. In the first issue of *Husmoderen*, the monthly periodical initially published by the Copenhagen Housewives' Organization and later by the Federation of Danish Housewives' Organizations, the editor Karen Braae reminded homemaking women that they constituted "a state within the state" and that collectively they possessed a power that would allow them "to reach almost any goal." See Karen Braae, "Hvad *er* Husmoderforeningen og hvad *vil* Husmoderforeningen?" *Husmoderen*, vol. 1, no. 1 (November 1918), p. 1.

91. Braae, "Hvad *er* Husmoderforeningen og hvad *vil* Husmoderforeningen?" p. 3.

92. "Breve fra Medlemmerne," *Husmoderen*, vol. 1, no. 1 (November 1918), p. 5.

93. "Husmødrenes Ansvar for vort Lands Økonomi," *Politiken*, November 10, 1917, p. 9.

94. Case #602.

95. "Husmoderstanden og vort Lands Økonomi. Et Interview med Carla Meyer," *Nationaltidende*, May 3, 1918, p. 3.

96. "Til Københavns Byraad. Andragende fra Københavns Husmoderforening," 1917. Petition in the Women's History Archives, the State Library, Aarhus, Denmark.

97. In 1920, for example, a broad coalition of women's organizations including the feminist Danish Women's Society, the national Federation of Danish Housewives' Associations, and the Organization of Domestic Science Teachers thus petitioned the government for the right of housewives to be represented on "all relevant commissions, committees and boards whose assignments affect the conditions of our homes." See "Danske Kvindeforeningers Andragende til Regering og Rigsdag." Here quoted from *Kvinden og Samfundet*, vol. 36, no. 18 (1920), p. 159.

98. Karl-Gustav Hildebrand, "Economic policy in Scandinavia during the inter-war period," *Scandinavian Economic History Review*, vol. 23, no. 2 (1975), pp. 99–115.

99. See, for instance, Harald Tandrup, "Kronens Fald," *Politiken*, March 31, 1922, p. 3; and Erik Hovmann Hansen, "Kronen paa Skraaplanet," *Aarhus Stiftstidende*, June 3, 1921, pp. 7–8.

100. "Aarsberetning for De danske Husmoderforeninger 1923–24." Membership publication in the Collection of Minor Publications, the Royal Library, Copenhagen, Denmark.

101. Elna Asby, "Lad os Sætte Nøjsomheden i System," *Kvinden og Samfundet*, vol. 36, no. 12 (June 30, 1920), pp. 120–21.

102. "Hjemmenes Arbejde," *Kvinden og Samfundet*, vol. 36, no. 21 (December 15, 1920), pp. 179–80.

103. Case #209.

104. "Mænds Luksus-forbrug," *Berlingske Tidende*, July 30, 1922, p. 3.

105. "Vor Tids Kvindesag," *Berlingske Tidende*, January 20, 1928, p. 4.

106. In his provocative article "The Flapper, the Housewife and the Making of Modernity," Martin Pumphrey has argued that the juxtaposition of the flapper and the modern housewife as two very different female figures in the 1920s ignores the fundamental similarities in their lives that stemmed from partaking in the emerging consumer economy. While his attempt to break down the artificial boundary between "flappers" and housewives is important, this argument overlooks the crucial difference between consumption for individual pleasure and consumption for the well-being of a household. See Martin Pumphrey: "The Flapper, the Housewife and the Making of Modernity," *Cultural Studies*, vol. 1, no. 2 (1987), pp. 179–94.

107. See, for instance, Melby, "The Housewife Ideology in Norway," pp. 181–93; and Bridenthal, " 'Professional' Housewives," pp. 153–73.

CONCLUSION

1. "Tanker ved Aarsskiftet," 1929. Unidentified newspaper clipping in the Emma Grandsgaard Collection of Newspaper Clippings, the Women's History Archives, the State Library, Aarhus, Denmark.

2. "Tanker ved Aarsskiftet," 1929.

3. Oral history interview, Copenhagen, Denmark, October 31, 1993.

4. Oral history interview, Copenhagen, Denmark, October 28, 1993.

5. Ironically, the entry into consumer culture was both facilitated and impeded by the fact that most young Danish women continued to live with their parents until marriage. Given the low wages that most young women earned, living independently would have allowed them even less disposable income. But as long as daughters continued to live at home, they were of course subject to their parents' authority to a much greater extent than if they had been on their own.

6. "Kønnenes Kamp," *Berlingske Tidende*, January 21, 1923, p. 7.

7. "Clara Raphaels Hus," *Tidens Kvinder*, vol. 2, no. 20 (May 15, 1920), p. 4.

8. "De unge Piger og Kvindesagen," *Politiken*, March 11, 1925, p. 9.

9. "Manden og Kvinden," 1928. Unidentified newspaper clipping in the Emma Grandsgaard Collection of Newspaper Clippings, the Women's History Archives, the State Library, Aarhus, Denmark.

10. "Nutidens unge Piger," 1931. Unidentified newspaper clipping from the Emma Grandsgaard Collection of Newspaper Clippings, the Women's History Archives, the State Library, Aarhus, Denmark.

11. Ibid.

12. Ibid.

13. "Moden og de unge Piger," 1926. Unidentified newspaper clipping in the Emma Grandsgaard Collection of Newspaper Clippings, the Women's History Archives, the State Library, Aarhus, Denmark.

14. "Den unge Kvinde af Idag," *Aarhus Stiftstidende*, June 13, 1927, p. 4.

15. "Hvad mener de unge Piger om Mændene?" *B.T.*, October 23, 1928, pp. 4–5.

16. Oral history interview, Copenhagen, Denmark, October 10, 1993.

17. Oral history interview, Roskilde, Denmark, April 13, 1991.

Select Bibliography

PRIMARY SOURCES

Archival Records and Manuscript Collections

The Copenhagen Municipal Archives (Copenhagen)
   Copenhagen Municipal Council records; Archives of municipal officials and politicians; Personal papers of Elizabeth Kaper, Memoir Collection
The Danish Film Museum's Archives and Library (Copenhagen)
   Subject files; Newspaper clipping files
The Labor Movement Archives and Library (Copenhagen)
   Union Records; Union and labor movement publications; Memoir Collection
The Local Historical Archives for Aalborg Municipality (Aalborg)
   Memoir Collection; Records of women's organizations; Theater and restaurant records
Magasin du Nord (Copenhagen)
   Corporate archives
The National Archives (Copenhagen)
   Parliamentary papers
The Regional Archives for Northern Jutland (Viborg)
   Separation and divorce proceedings and case records from Northern Jutland County, Vejle County, and Ringkøbing County
The Regional Archives for Sealand (Copenhagen)
   Separation and divorce proceedings and case records from Copenhagen County
The Royal Library (Copenhagen)
   Manuscript collections; Personal papers of Ernst Kaper; Personal papers of Gyrithe Lemcke; Records of Virgilia Christian Reform Society; Collection of Minor Publications
The State Library (Aarhus)
   The Popular Music Archives; The Women's History Collection; The Emma Grandsgaard Collection of Newspaper Clippings; Oral History Collection

Interviews

Andersen, Agnete (Copenhagen), December 10, 1991
Appelgaard, Magda (Aarhus), February 23, 1990
Bak, Emma Spangsgaard (Copenhagen), November 13, 1990
Bang-Petersen, Mathilde (Copenhagen), November 18, 1990
Berg, Helene (Copenhagen), November 5, 1993
Berthelsen, Julie (Silkeborg), March 13, 1994
Blom, Johanne (Copenhagen), December 7, 1993
Bruun, Anne (Aarhus), March 15, 1994
Buhl, Emilie (Nørresundby), December 21, 1993
Christensen, Amanda (Copenhagen), October 28, 1993

228 ≋ Bibliography

Ege, Louise (Copenhagen), December 14, 1993
Enevold, Lily (Helsingør), November 20, 1993
Eriksen, Anna (Copenhagen), February 10, 1990
Eriksen, Gerda (Copenhagen), November 6, 1990
Gregersen, Emma (Copenhagen), October 30, 1993
Hansen, Charlotte (Copenhagen), October 10, 1993
Hansen, Henny (Copenhagen), November 1, 1993
Hansen, Meta (Roskilde), February 11, 1990
Hedegaard, Marie (Aalborg), December 22, 1993
Højberg, Martine (Silkeborg), April 12, 1994
Ingvardsen, Dora (Copenhagen), October 31, 1993
Jensen, Edith (Copenhagen), October 12, 1993
Jensen, Magda Gammelgaard (Aarhus), February 27, 1990
Jensen, Margrethe (Helsingør), November 30, 1993
Jensen, Rosa (Copenhagen), February 13, 1990
Johansen, Emilie (Nørresundby), December 22, 1990
Kortsen, Petra (Aarhus), May 15, 1991
Kristensen, Ingrid (Slagelse), November 26, 1993
Lundgaard, Agnes (Aarhus), November 29, 1990
Madsen, Mary Ellen (Copenhagen), October 28, 1993
Mangart, Inger (Copenhagen), February 6, 1990
Markfeldt, Henriette Marie (Copenhagen), November 3, 1993
Munk, Anne Kirstine (Copenhagen), December 2, 1990
Nedergaard, Henny (Aarhus), February 19, 1990
Nielsen, Netta (Copenhagen), May 27, 1991
Nielsen, Regitze (Aalborg), December 22, 1990
Nørgaard, Johanne (Copenhagen), October 3, 1993
Nørlev, Viola (Copenhagen), November 19, 1990
Nybrandt, Gerda (Aarhus), February 23, 1990
Nyrop, Agnes (Aarhus), February 28, 1990
Okkels, Jenny (Aalborg), May 14, 1991
Øst, Gertrud (Copenhagen), December 1, 1993
Petersen, Stine (Randers), April 16, 1994
Petersen, Thora (Aarhus), March 31, 1994
Poulsen, Ernestine P. (Aarhus), April 2, 1994
Rasmussen, Inger-Marie (Roskilde), April 13, 1991
Rerup, Ingeborg (Aarhus), February 26, 1994
Sejr, Agnes (Køge), November 28, 1993
Skovgaard, Karla (Aarhus), October 17, 1990
Smed, Thora (Copenhagen), October 10, 1993
Sommersted, Hedvig (Copenhagen), December 3, 1990
Sørensen, Gudrun Skall (Aalborg), February 26, 1990
Sørensen, Nikoline (Copenhagen), December 10, 1993
Spang-Bak, Emilie (Copenhagen), December 3, 1993
Suhr, Inga (Copenhagen), May 31, 1991
Thorsen, Vera (Copenhagen), December 19, 1993

Thorup, Elna (Roskilde), December 2, 1993
Vestergaard, Jutta (Aarhus), February 25, 1990
Winther, Esther (Aarhus), February 28, 1994

Periodicals, Serials, and Newspapers

Aalborg Stiftstidende (1914–30)
Aarhus: Hver 14. Dag (1926)
Aarhus Stiftstidende (1914–30)
Aarhusianerinden: Damernes Blad (1929)
Adam (1925)
Aftenlæsning (1926–27)
Arbejdernes Almanak (1914–30)
B.T. (1916–30)
Berlingske Tidende (1914–30)
Blæksprutten (1910–30)
Bog og Naal: Nordisk Tidsskrift for kvindelig Undervisning og Opdragelse (1918–30)
Boksning: Illustreret Ugeblad for al Sport samt Film og Teater (1923)
City: Maanedsjournal (1927–28)
Charme (1927)
Dagens Nyheder (1914–20)
Damernes Magasin (1928–30)
Danmarks Barber- og Frisør-Tidende (1914–30)
Dansk Barber-, Frisør- og Parykmager-Tidende (1914–18)
Dansk Handels- og Kontormedhjælper Tidende (1918–19)
Dansk Husmoderblad (1918–20)
Dansk Kvindeblad: Konservativt politisk Organ (1913–19)
Dansk Reklame (1927–30)
Ekstrabladet (1914–30)
Eva (1916–21)
Eva (1928)
Eva: Ungdom og Skønhed (1925–28)
Eva: Skønhed og Kærlighed (1928)
Fagblad for danske Damefrisører (1915–21)
Flirt (1921–23)
Fremad: Organ for socialdemokratisk Ungdom i Danmark (1914–22)
Gads danske Magasin (1914–25)
Hjemmet: Illustreret Ugeblad (1914–30)
Hus og Hjem: Husmoderens Blad (1914–30)
Husmoderen (1918–30)
Hvepsen (1925)
Hver 8. Dag (1914–28)
Illustreret Fagblad for danske Damefrisører (1921–30)
Illustreret Familie-Journal (1914–30)
Illustreret Tidende (1914–22)
Klodshans: Magasin for Humor og Satire (1914–30)

Klokken 5: Socialdemokratisk Aftenblad (1918–25)
København (1919–30)
Københavnerinden og Femina (1929)
Konservativ Ungdom (1914–30)
Kristeligt Dagblad (1914–30)
Kvindelig Idrætsforenings Medlemsblad (1923–30)
Kvinden og Samfundet: Organ for Dansk Kvindesamfund (1914–30)
Kvindernes Oplysningsblad (1925–29)
Louiseforeningens Blad (1916–21)
Pensionat-Bladet (1916–17)
Politiken (1914–30)
Nationaløkonomisk Tidsskrift (1914–40)
Nationaltidende (1914–30)
Socialdemokraten (1914–30)
Søndags B.T. (1921–30)
Statistisk Aarbog for Danmark (1914–30)
Statistisk Aarbog for København og Frederiksberg (1914–30)
Statistisk Tabelværk (1914–30)
Strøget: Illustreret Ugeblad (1916–20)
Strøget: Det pikante Boulevardblad (1927)
Strøgets Klange (1925)
Tidens Kvinder (1923–30)
Tidens Kvinder: Organ for Danske Kvinders Nationalraad (1919–20)
Tilskueren: Maanedsskrift for Litteratur, Kunst, Samfundsspørgsmaal og almen-fattelige videnskabelige Skildringer (1914–20)
Ugebladet (1923–30)
Ugebladet Det nye Strøg (1925)
Ugebladet for Husmoderen og Hjemmet (1913)
Ugens Roman (1926–27)
Ugens Spejl: Organ for Lønarbejdere i Barber-, Frisør- og Parykmagerfaget (1919–30)
Ugens Tilskuer: Tidsskrift for Politik, Litteratur og Samfundsspørgsmaal (1914–20)
Verden og Vi (1914–30)
Vore Damer (1913–30)
Vore Herrer (1916–24)

Books

Andersen, Karen M. *Hvad er Dannelse? Foredrag ved det kvindelige Gymnasi-astmøde i Skibelund 1919* (Aarhus, 1919).
———. *At højne Moralen blandt de Unge. Et Foredrag* (Copenhagen, 1920).
———. *Den unge Kvindes Synd* (Copenhagen, 1920).
———. *Den unge Pige i Overgangsalderen* (Odense, 1922).
Bahnsen, Poul, and Knud Secher. *Kvinde og Mand: Forskel og Lighed i legemlig og sjælelig Henseende* (Copenhagen, 1927).
Barn af Aalborg (Aalborg, 1959).
Barn af Aalborg 2 (Aalborg, 1984).

Bentzon, Viggo. *Hvad nyt bringer Ægteskabsloven?* (Copenhagen, 1920).

Bergstrøm, Vilhelm. *Magasinpigen* (Copenhagen, 1922).

———. *Under Byens Himmel* (Copenhagen, 1923).

Bjerre, Poul. *Ægteskabets Omdannelse* (Copenhagen, 1929).

Blom, Ida, and Anna Tranberg (eds.). *Nordisk Lovoversikt. Viktige lover for kvinner ca. 1810–1980* (Oslo, n.d.).

Bønnelycke, Emil. *Ny Ungdom* (Copenhagen, 1925).

Borgberg, Svend. *Krig og Køn. Bidrag til en erotisk nyorientering* (Copenhagen, 1918).

Borup, Anne Marie Lind. *De mange Aar. Erindringer* (Odense, 1970).

Braa, Karen. *Hvordan afpasser jeg bedst mit Budget efter min Indtægt?* (Copenhagen, 1922).

Burchardi, Adolf. *Hvordan jeg bærer mig ad med at være glad* (Ølgod, 1923).

Buthler, I. W. *Skønhed-Kønsliv-Livsglæde eller Den intime Raadgiver. Anvisninger og Raad angaaende Skønhedshygiejnen* (Copenhagen, 1918).

———. *Vejen til Skønhed. Anvisninger og Raad angaaende Skønhedshygiejne* (Copenhagen, 1918).

Christensen, Agnes Nyrop, and J. C. Gottlieb. *Hvad alle bør vide om moderne Dans* (Copenhagen, 1919).

Dalmark, Charlotte. *Humørhygiejne. En Vejledning for ung og gammel* (Copenhagen, 1922).

Damernes Bog (Copenhagen, 1924).

De unges Idræt gennem 20 Aar, 1905–1925 (Copenhagen, 1925).

Den sande Kærlighed eller Kunsten at vælge den rette (Copenhagen, 1920).

Dybdahl, Vagn (ed.). *Ung i Aarhus* (Aarhus, 1964).

———. *Ung i Aarhus. Ny samling* (Aarhus, 1965).

Elgstrøm, Agnes. *Hvorfor og hvordan skal vi lægge Budget for vor Husholdning* (Copenhagen, 1928).

Engelbreth, Christoffer. *Ansigtets Kosmetik. Populær Vejledning i Hudens Behandling og Skønhedspleje* (Copenhagen, 1909).

———. *Kvindens Hygiejne* (Copenhagen, 1918).

Forelskelse og Forlovelse. Raadgiver for Unge (Copenhagen, 1916).

Gad, Emma. *Takt og Tone. Hvordan vi omgaas* (Copenhagen, 1919).

Hansen, Aase. *Ebba Berings Studentertid* (Copenhagen, 1930).

Harris, F. *Kammeratægteskab* (Copenhagen, 1928).

Hansen, Frede. *Dagsøvelser i Gymnastik for Kvinder* (Horsens, 1928).

Haugan, Kamma et al. (eds). *Tolv kvinder fra århundredskiftet* (Copenhagen, 1979).

Hegar, Alfred. *Den seksuelle Drift eller sundt Kønsliv. En social-medicinsk studie* (Copenhagen, 1919).

Hegar, Alfred et al. *Forholdet mellem Kvinde og Mand* (Copenhagen, 1919).

Herskind, Grete. *Den moderne Kvindegymnastik* (Copenhagen, 1929).

Høflighed: Stejftog inden for Dagliglivets smaa Problemer (Copenhagen, 1928).

Holten-Nielsen, I. M. *Hjemmets Verden. Haandbog og Raadgiver for ethvert Hjem* (Copenhagen, 1923).

Hvorledes man kysser: Raadgiver for alle forelskede, forlovede og nygifte (Copenhagen, 1922).

Jensen, Thit. *Gerd. Det 20. Aarhundredes Kvinde* (Copenhagen, 1918).

Kaarsberg, Hans. *Feminismens Agitation in Danmark. Dens Sejr og Sejrens Pris* (Copenhagen, 1922).

Knudsen, Else. *Ungt Ægteskab* (Copenhagen, 1917).

Knudsen, Thora. *Tvungen eller frivillig Undervisning for enhver Kvinde i Husmoderens og Moderens Gerning. Foredrag paa Dansk Kvindesamfunds Fællesmøde i Kolding, Juni 1912* (Copenhagen, 1912).

———. *Vore Hjem. Paa hvilken maade støtter vi dem bedst: Et foredrag* (Copenhagen, 1916).

København ved Nat (Copenhagen, 1923).

Koefoed, Clara. *Vor Tid og Vor Ungdom: Et Forsvar og et Angreb* (Copenhagen, n.d.).

Kohl, Aage von. *Vore Døtres Moral* (Copenhagen, 1923).

Kræmer, Vera von. *Os betroet. Vi og vore Døtre* (Copenhagen, 1932).

Kunsten at være gift - og dog lykkelig (Copenhagen, 1929).

Kvindelig Idrætsforening. Festskrift 1906–1931 (Copenhagen, 1931).

Kvinden i den moderne Karikatur (Copenhagen, 1928).

Kvindens Kønsmoral. For den modne Alder. Kønslivets Hemmeligheder og Love (Copenhagen, 1919).

Lesser, Frank. *Ægteskabsbogen. Hvordan man begrænser Børnefødslerne* (Copenhagen, 1927).

———. *Hvad enhver ung Kvinde bør vide inden Ægteskab—om Ægteskab* (Copenhagen, 1928).

———. *Ægtemandens Bog. Hvad enhver gift Mand bør vide om hvordan man skal behandle sin Hustru* (Copenhagen, 1929).

———. *Hvad enhver Mand bør vide om det seksuelle Spørgsmaal* (Copenhagen, 1929).

Leunbach, J. H. *Kvinden og forplantningen. Hvad alle kvinder bør vide* (Copenhagen, 1925).

———. *Kønslivets problemer i nutiden* (Copenhagen and Oslo, 1926).

Lindsey, Ben B. *Moderne Ungdoms Oprør*. With an introduction by K. K. Steincke (Copenhagen, 1927).

———. *Kammeratægteskabet*. With an introduction by K. K. Steincke (Copenhagen, 1928).

Marden, Orison Swett. *Vær glad! Livsglæde er en Livsmagt* (Copenhagen, 1916).

Meyer, Johanne. *Ny Kønsmoral og friere Form for Ægteskabet* (Copenhagen, 1910).

Michaelis, Karin. *Hemmeligheden* (Copenhagen and Oslo, 1927).

Mikaely, Lisa. *Lykkens Tinde* (Copenhagen, 1915).

Møller, Louis. *Hvordan man kysser. Raadgiver for alle Forelskede* (Copenhagen, 1922).

Nielsen, Birgitte Berg. *Kvindesag og Husgerning. Foredrag holdt ved Dansk Kvindesamfunds Fællesmøde juli 1920* (Copenhagen, 1920).

Nielsen, Harald. *Moderne Ægteskab* (Copenhagen, 1919).

Nielsen, Kaj. *Kærlighed og Erotik. Fragment til Belysning af Kærlighedens Mysterium* (Copenhagen, 1926).

Raske Fjed. 10 arbejdende Kvinders Livshistorie (Copenhagen, 1932).

Rasmussen, Marie. *Hjemmene og Ungdommen og det private Liv og Sædelighe-den* (Copenhagen, 1922).

———. *Nogle Tanker om vort Ansvar for de Unges Moral* (Copenhagen, 1924).

Reumert, Ellen. *Født Pebersvend* (Copenhagen, 1915).

———. *Jonna: Nutidsfortælling* (Copenhagen, 1921).

Sådan var Aarhus. Lette Vidnesbyrd om Aarhus i 1920'erne og 1930'erne (Aarhus, 1973).

Samboende familier i København, Frederiksberg og Gentofte Kommune d. 1/2–1921 (Copenhagen, 1921).

Selskabelig Takt og Tone. Korrekt Optræden i Selskaber og i det daglige Liv (Copenhagen, 1930).

Skønhed er Magt og Kvindens Største Rigdom. Gode Raad til daglig Sundheds-og Skønhedspleje desuden Haarfarvning og et Kapitel om den gode Tone (Copenhagen, 1929).

Sønderby, Knud. *Midt i en Jazztid* (Copenhagen, 1931).

Stopes, Marie Carmichael. *Ægteskabelig Lykke. Et nyt Bidrag til Løsningen af de seksuelle Spørgsmaal i Ægteskabet* (Copenhagen, 1921).

Strømstad, Poul (ed.). *Københavnere fortæller. Erindringer fra det gamle København* (Copenhagen, 1972).

Svendstorp, Aage et al. (eds.). *Ung i Aalborg. Kendte aalborgensere skriver on storbyen i lillebyens perspektiv* (Aalborg, 1976).

Sygeplejersker fortæller. Glimt af sygeplejens historie (Copenhagen, 1987).

Tesch, C. A. *Nutidens kvindelige Ungdom* (Copenhagen, 1930).

Thor, Rigmor. *Jeg har levet og elsket. Erindringer* (Copenhagen, 1990).

Vera, Fru. *Amors Central. Hvorledes man gør Lykke hos Herrerne. Bliver elsket, attraaet, beundret, hurtig forlovet og gift. Uundværlig Vejledning for unge Piger* (Copenhagen, 1918).

Vollquartz, Ingeborg. *Lillians Forlovelse* (Copenhagen, 1915).

———. *Lillians Ægteskab* (Copenhagen, 1916).

———. *Lillians Datter* (Copenhagen, 1917).

Vore Damers Skønhedspleje (Copenhagen, 1921).

Warming, Jens. *Danmarks erhvervs- og samfundsliv. En Lærebog i Danmarks Statistik* (Copenhagen, 1930).

———. *Danske samfundsproblemer i statistisk Belysning* (Copenhagen, 1934).

Watt, Leonhard. *Bogen imod Ægteskabet. Ægteskabsloven og Alimentationslo-vens Faldgruber for Mænd* (Copenhagen, 1929).

———. *Bogen imod Kvinderne. En Advarsel til unge Mænd, der tænker paa at gifte sig* (Copenhagen, 1929).

SECONDARY SOURCES

Aakerman, Sune. "Internal Migration, Industrialisation and Urbanisation," *Scandinavian Economic History Review*, vol. 23, no. 2 (1975), pp. 149–58.

Aller, Vita (ed.). *Dansk Kvinde i Dag* (Copenhagen, 1942).

Andersen, Ellen. *Fra Bommesi til Nylon. Af Undertøjets historie gennem 200 Aar* (Copenhagen, 1952).

Andersen, Jens. *Thit - den sidste valkyrie* (Copenhagen, 1990).

Ash, Juliet, and Lee Wright (eds.). *Components of Dress: Design, Manufacturing, and Image-Making in the Fashion Industry* (London and New York, 1988).

Avdem, Anna Jorunn, and Kari Melby. *Oppe først og sist i seng. Husarbeid i Norge fra 1850 til idag* (Oslo, 1985).

Bach, Ingeborg et al. "Fra tjenestepige til lønarbejder 1900–1925," in Anne Margrethe Berg et al. (eds.), *Kvindfolk. En danmarkshistorie fra 1600 til 1980*, vol. 2 (Copenhagen, 1987), pp. 230–52.

Bailey, Beth. *From Front Porch to Back Seat: Courtship in Twentieth Century America* (Baltimore, 1988).

Banner, Lois W. *American Beauty* (Chicago and London, 1983).

Banta, Martha. *Imaging American Women: Idea and Ideals in Cultural History* (New York, 1987).

Barret-Ducrocq, Françoise. *Love in the Time of Victoria: Sexuality and Desire among Working-Class Men and Women in Nineteenth-Century London* (New York, 1991).

Barrett, Michele. *Ideology and the Cultural Production of Gender* (New York, 1985).

Bell, Quintin. *On Human Finery* (New York, 1976).

Bendtsen, Lone et al. "Det uendeligt smaa og det uendeligt store - i arbejderklassens hverdagsliv i mellemkrigstiden." Unpublished M.A. thesis, Department of History, Roskilde University, Denmark, 1980.

Benninghaus, Christina. "'But You Need to Give Me a French Kiss': Gender Relations and the Culture of Treating among German Adolescents in the 1920s." Paper presented at the 11th Berkshire Conference on the History of Women, Rochester, New York, 1999.

Berg, Anne Margrethe, et al. (eds.). *Kvindfolk. En danmarkshistorie fra 1600 til 1980*, vols. 1–2 (Copenhagen, 1984).

Bergsøe, Flemming. *Dyrehavsbakken* (Copenhagen, 1952).

Besse, Susan K. *Restructuring Patriarchy: The Modernization of Gender Inequality in Brazil, 1914–1940* (Chapel Hill, N.C., and London, 1996).

Biografteaterforeningerne 1910–1960 (Copenhagen, 1960).

Blüdnikow, Bent. "Denmark during the First World War," *Journal of Contemporary History*, vol. 24 (1989), pp. 683–703.

Bonde, Hans. *Mandighed og sport* (Odense, 1991).

———. "Køn, klasser og kropskultur," *Idrætshistorisk Årbog 1985* (Copenhagen, 1985).

———. "Masculine Movements. Sport and Masculinity in Denmark at the Turn of the Century," *Scandinavian Journal of History*, vol. 21, no. 2 (1996), pp. 63–89.

Bordo, Susan. "Reading the Slender Body," in Mary Jacobus et al. (eds.), *Body/Politics: Women and the Discources of Science* (New York and London, 1990), pp. 82–98.

———. "Postmodern Subjects, Postmodern Bodies," *Feminist Studies*, vol. 18, no. 1 (Spring 1992), pp. 159–75.

Bourke, Joanna. *Dismembering the Male: Men's Bodies, Britain and the Great War* (Chicago, 1996).

Bowden, Sue, and Avner Offer. "The Technological Revolution That Never Was: Gender, Class, and the Diffusion of Household Appliances in Interwar England," in Victoria de Grazia, with Ellen Furlough (eds.), *The Sex of Things* (Berkeley, Calif., 1996), pp. 244–74.

Brandon, Ruth. *The New Women and the Old Men: Love, Sex and the New Woman Question* (New York and London, 1990).

Braybon, Gail. *Women Workers in the First World War: The British Experience* (London, 1981).

Braybon, Gail, and Penny Summerfield. *Out of the Cage: Women's Experiences in Two World Wars* (New York and London, 1987).

Breidahl, Axel, and Axel Kjerulf. *Københavnerliv 1912–1937* (Copenhagen, 1938).

———. *Københavnerliv gennem et halvt Aarhundrede. Gemt og glemt i Alvor og Skæmt, 1912–1937*, vols. 1–2 (Copenhagen, 1938).

Bridenthal, Renate. "Beyond 'Kinder, Küche, Kirche': Weimar Women at Work," *Central European History*, vol. 6, no. 2 (1973), pp. 148–66.

———. "'Professional' Housewives: Stepsisters of the Women's Movement," in Renate Bridenthal et al. (eds.), *When Biology Became Destiny* (New York, 1984), pp. 153–73.

———. "Something Old, Something New: Women between the Two World Wars," in Renate Bridenthal et al. (eds.), *Becoming Visible. Women in European History*, 2nd ed. (Boston, 1987), pp. 473–98.

Bridenthal, Renate et al. (eds.). *When Biology Became Destiny: Women in Weimar and Nazi Germany* (New York, 1984).

Broadberry, S. N. "The North European Depression of the 1920s," *Scandinavian Economic History Review*, vol. 32 (1984), pp. 159–67.

Broby-Johansen, R. *Omrids af Modens Historie. Set fra et københavnsk Modehus 1847–1947* (Copenhagen, 1947).

Brown, Dorothy. *Setting a Course: American Women in the 1920s* (Boston, 1987).

Brumberg, Joan Jacobs. *The Body Project: An Intimate History of American Girls* (New York, 1997).

Bruun, Marianne Groth. "'Enighed gør Stærk!' En analyse af husmødrene og deres arbejde i mellemkrigstidens Danmark," *Historievidenskab*, vol. 21 (1980), pp. 10–23.

———. "Da husmødrene organiserede sig," in Anne Margrethe Berg et al. (eds.), *Kvindfolk. En danmarkshistorie fra 1600 til 1980*, vol. 2 (Copenhagen, 1984), pp. 65–92.

Bryld, Mette et al. (eds.). *Overgangskvinden. Kvindeligheden som historisk kategori - kvindeligheden 1880–1920* (Odense, 1982).

Butsch, Richard (ed.). *For Fun and Profit: The Transformation of Leisure into Consumption* (Philadelphia, 1990).

Cahn, Susan K. *Coming On Strong: Gender and Sexuality in Twentieth-Century Women's Sport* (New York, 1994).

Callaghan, Karen (ed.). *Ideals of Feminine Beauty: Philosophical, Social and Cultural Dimensions* (Westport, Conn., 1994).

Caulfield, Sueann. "Getting into Trouble: Dishonest Women, Modern Girls, and Women-Men in the Conceptual Langauge of *Vida Policial*, 1925–1927," *Signs*, vol. 19, no. 1 (1993), pp. 146–76.

Chapkis, Wendy. *Beauty Secrets: Women and the Politics of Appearance* (Boston, 1986).

Charles-Roux, Edmonde. *Chanel: Her Life, Her World—and the Woman behind the Legend She Herself Created* (New York, 1975).

Chernin, Kim. *The Obsession: Reflections on the Tyranny of Slenderness* (New York, 1981).

Christensen, Hilda Rømer, and Hanne Rimmen Nielsen (eds.). *Tidens Kvinder. Om kvinder i mellemkrigstiden* (Aarhus, 1985).

Clair, Jean (ed.). *The 1920s. Age of the Metropolis* (Montreal, 1991).

Cohn, Einar. *Danmark under den store Krig. En økonomisk Oversigt* (Copenhagen, 1928).

Cott, Nancy F. *The Grounding of Modern Feminism* (New Haven, Conn., and London, 1987).

Cowan, R. S. *More Work for Mother: The Ironies of Household Technology from the Open Hearth to the Microwave* (New York, 1983).

———. "The 'Industrial Revolution' in the Home: Household Technology and Social Change in the 20th Century," *Technology and Culture*, vol. 17 (1976), pp. 1–23.

Cruickshank, C. G. *Variations on a Catastrophe: Some French Responses to the Great War* (New York, 1982).

Curtin, Michael. *Property and Position: A Study of Victorian Manners* (New York, 1987).

Dahlerup, Drude. "Women's Entry into Politics: The Experience of the Danish Local and General Elections 1908–1920," *Scandinavian Political Studies*, vol. 1, nos. 2–3 (1978), pp. 139–62.

Dahlsgaard, Inga. *Women in Denmark Yesterday and Today* (Copenhagen, 1980).

Daniel, Robert. *American Women in the 20th Century: The Festival of Life* (San Diego, Calif., 1987).

Dansk Idræt gennem 50 Aar (Copenhagen, 1946).

Danstrup, John. *A History of Denmark* (Copenhagen, 1947).

Davidoff, Leonore, and Belinda Westover. "From Queen Victoria to the Jazz Age: Women's World in England, 1880–1939," in Leonore Davidoff et al. (eds.), *Our Work, Our Lives, Our Words* (London, 1986), pp. 1–35.

Davidson, Caroline. *A Woman's Work Is Never Done: A History of Housework in the British Isles, 1650–1950* (London, 1982).

De danske Husmoderforeninger 1920–1945. Festskrift (Copenhagen, 1945).

Dinnesen, Niels Jørgen, and Edvin Kau. *Filmen i Danmark* (Copenhagen, 1983).

Drotner, Kirsten. "The Modern Girl and Mass Culture," *Ethnologia Scandinavica* (1988), pp. 95–101.

Dubinsky, Karen. *Improper Advances: Rape and Heterosexual Conflict in Ontario, 1880–1929* (Chicago, 1993).

Due-Nielsen, Carsten. "Denmark and the First World War," *Scandinavian Journal of History*, vol. 10 (1985), pp. 1–18.

Eksteins, Modrus. *The Rites of Spring: The Great War and the Birth of the Modern Age* (Boston, 1989).

Engel, Barbara Alpern. *Between the Field and the City: Women, Work and Family in Russia* (Cambridge, Mass., 1994).

Erenberg, Lewis A. *Steppin' Out: New York Nightlife and the Transformation of American Culture, 1890–1930* (Westport, Conn., 1981).

Evans, Caroline, and Minna Thornton. "Fashion, Representation, Femininity," *Feminist Review*, no. 38 (1991), pp. 48–66.

Fass, Paula S. *The Damned and the Beautiful: American Youth in the 1920s* (Oxford and New York, 1977).

Finkelstein, Joanne. *The Fashioned Self* (Philadelphia, 1991).

Folbre, Nancy. "The Unproductive Housewife: The Evolution in Nineteenth-Century Economic Thought," *Signs*, vol. 16, no. 3 (1991), pp. 463–84.

Freedman, Estelle B. "The New Woman: Changing Views of Women in the 1920s," *Journal of American History* (1973), pp. 372–93.

Frevert, Ute. *Women in German History: From Bourgeois Emancipation to Sexual Liberation* (New York, 1989).

Fussell, Paul. *The Great War and Modern Memory* (Cambridge, Mass., 1979).

Gaines, Jane, and Charlotte Herzog (eds.). *Fabrications: Costume and the Female Body* (New York and London, 1990).

Gantzel, Gunhild (ed.). *Scala-Minder* (Copenhagen, 1941).

Garber, Marjorie. *Vested Interests: Cross-Dressing and Cultural Anxiety* (New York and London, 1992).

Gay, Peter. *Weimar Culture: The Outsider as Insider* (New York, 1968).

Geertsen, Kirsten. *Arbejderkvinder i Danmark 1914–24* (Greenå, 1977).

———. *Arbejderkvinder i Danmark. Vilkår og kamp 1924–1939* (Copenhagen, 1982).

———. *Dannet ung Pige søges. Kvinder på Kontor 1900–1940* (Holme Olstrup, 1990).

Gersdorff, Ute von. *Frauen im Kriegsdienst 1914–1945* (Stuttgart, 1969).

Gilbert, Sandra M. "Soldier's Heart: Literary Men, Literary Women, and the Great War," in Marilyn J. Boxer and Jean H. Quataert (eds.), *Connecting Spheres: Women in the Western World, 1500 to the Present* (New York and Oxford, 1987), pp. 232–45.

Gilbert, Sandra M., and Susan Gubar. *No Man's Land: The Place of the Woman Writer in the Twentieth Century*, vols. 1–2 (New Haven, Conn., 1988).

Giles, Judy. *Women, Identity and Private Life in Britain, 1900–1950* (New York, 1995).

———. " 'Playing Hard to Get': Working-Class Women, Sexuality and Respectability in Britain, 1918–1940," *Women's History Review*, vol. 1, no. 2 (1992), pp. 1–17.

———. "A Home of One's Own: Women and Domesticity in England, 1918–1950," *Women's Studies International Forum*, vol. 16, no. 3 (1993), pp. 239–53.

———. " 'You Meet 'Em and That's It': Working Class Women's Refusal of Romance Between the Wars in Britain," in Lynne Pierce and Jackie Stacey (eds.), *Romance Revisited* (New York and London, 1995), pp. 279–92.

Gloerfelt-Tarp, Kirsten (ed.). *Kvinden i samfundet* (Copenhagen, 1937).

Gluck, Sherna Berger, and Daphne Patai (eds.). *Women's Words: The Feminist Practice of Oral History* (New York and London, 1991).

Glucksmann, Miriam. *Women Assemble: Women Workers and the New Industries in Inter-War Britain* (London, 1990).

Gordon, Linda. *Heroes of Their Own Lives: The Politics and History of Family Violence* (New York, 1988).

Gordon, Michael. "From an Unfortunate Necessity to a Cult of Mutual Orgasm: Sex in American Marital Education Literature, 1830–1940," in James Hensley (ed.), *Studies in the Sociology of Sex* (New York, 1975), pp. 53–77.

Grazia, Victoria de. "Puritan Mind, Pagan Bodies: American Mass Culture in the Making of Europe's 'New Woman', 1920–1945." Paper presented at the Sixth Berkshire Conference on the History of Women, 1984.

Grazia, Victoria de, with Ellen Furlough (eds.). *The Sex of Things: Gender and Consumption in Historical Perspective* (Berkeley, Calif., 1996).

Grossman, Atina. "The New Woman and the Rationalization of Sexuality in Weimar Germany," in Ann Snitow et al. (eds.), *Powers of Desire* (New York, 1983), pp. 153–71.

Grossman, Atina. " 'Satisfaction Is Domestic Happiness": Mass Working-Class Sex Reform Organizations in the Weimar Republic," in Michael N. Dobkowski and Isidor Wallimann (eds.), *Towards the Holocaust: The Social and Economic Collapse of the Weimar Republic* (Westport, Conn., 1983), pp. 265–93.

———. " 'Girlkultur' or Thoroughly Rationalized Female: A New Woman in Weimar Germany," in Judith Friedlander et al. (eds.), *Women in Culture and Politics: A Century of Change* (Bloomington, Ind., 1986), pp. 62–80.

Grover, Kathryn. *Fitness in American Culture: Images of Health, Sport and the Body 1830–1940* (Amherst, Mass., 1989).

Haine, W. Scott. "The Development of Leisure and the Transformation of Working-Class Adolescence, Paris 1830–1940," *Journal of Family History*, vol. 17, no. 4 (1992), pp. 451–76.

Hall, Lesley. "Impotent Ghosts from No Man's Land, Flappers' Boyfriends, or Crypto-Patriarchs? Men, Sex and Social Change in 1920s Britain," *Social History*, vol. 21, no. 1, (1996), pp. 54–70.

Hall, Linda. "Fashion and Style in the Twenties: The Change," *The Historian* (1972), pp. 485–97.

Hansen, Miriam. "Adventures of Goldilocks: Spectatorship, Consumerism and Public Life," *camera obscura*, vol. 22 (1990), pp. 51–71.

Hansen, Svend Aage. *Early Industrialisation in Denmark* (Copenhagen, 1970).

———. *Økonomisk vækst i Danmark 1720–1914* (Copenhagen, 1972).

———. *Økonomisk vækst i Danmark 1914–1975* (Copenhagen, 1975).

———. *Økonomisk vækst i Danmark 1720–1983* (Copenhagen, 1984).

Hansen, Svend Aage, and Ingrid Henriksen. *Dansk socialhistorie 1914–1939. Sociale brydninger* (Copenhagen, 1980).

Harrison, Brian. *Separate Spheres: The Opposition to Women's Suffrage in Britain* (London, 1978).

———. *Peaceable Kingdom: Stability and Change in Modern Britain* (New York, 1982).

Hausen, Karin. "Unemployment Also Hits Women: The New and the Old Woman on the Dark Side of the Golden Twenties in Germany," in Peter Stachura (ed.), *Unemployment and the Great Depression in Weimar Germany* (New York, 1986), pp. 78–120.

Hending, Arnold. "Det københavnske Hollywood," *Historiske Meddelelser om København*, series, 4, vol. 4 (1954–57), pp. 641–88.

Hertoft, Preben. *Det er måske en galskab. Om seksualreformbevægelsen i Danmark* (Copenhagen, 1983).

Higonnet, Margaret Randolph et al. (eds.). *Behind the Lines: Gender and the Two World Wars* (New Haven, Conn., and London, 1987).

Hildebrand, Karl-Gustav. "Economic Policy in Scandinavia during the Interwar Period," *Scandinavian Economic History Review*, vol. 23 (1975), pp. 99–115.

Hollander, Anne. *Seeing through Clothes* (New York, 1978).

Holm, Axel. "Den kvindelige Frugtbarheds Fald i Hovedstaden i det 20. Aarhundrede," *Socialt Tidsskrift*, vol. 12, no. 10 (October 1936), pp. 327–36.

Holzman, Ellen M. "The Pursuit of Married Love: Women's Attitudes toward Sexuality and Marriage in Great Britain, 1918–1939," *Journal of Social History*, vol. 16 (1982), pp. 39–51.

Hyldtoft, Ole. *Københavns Industrialisering 1840–1914* (Copenhagen, 1984).

Hynes, Samuel. *A War Imagined: The First World War and English Culture* (New York, 1991).

Jackson, Margaret. *The Real Facts of Life: Feminism and the Politics of Sexuality c. 1850–1940* (London, 1994).

———. "Sexual Liberation or Social Control? Some Aspects of the Relationship between Feminism and the Social Construction of Sexual Knowledge in the Early Twentieth Century," *Women's Studies International Forum*, vol. 6, no. 1 (1983), pp. 1–17.

Jacobus, Mary et al. (eds.). *Body/Politics: Women and the Discourses of Science* (New York and London, 1990).

Jeffreys, Sheila. *The Spinster and Her Enemies: Feminism and Sexuality 1880–1930* (London, 1985).

———. "Sex Reform and Antifeminism in the 1920s," in The London Feminist History Group (eds.), *The Sexual Dynamics of History: Men's Power, Women's Resistance* (London, 1983), pp. 177–202.

Jensen, Bernhardt. *Som Aarhus morede sig. Folkelige forlystelser fra 1890'erne til 2. verdenskrig* (Aarhus, 1966).

Jensen, Birthe Skov. "Den tidlige kvindegymnastik," in Per Jørgensen et al. (eds.), *Idrætshistorisk Årbog 1985* (Copenhagen, 1985), pp. 83–107.

Johansen, Hans, Chr. (ed.). *Dansk historisk statistik 1814–1980* (Copenhagen, 1985).

Jones, W. Glyn. *Denmark: A Modern History* (London, 1986).

Kent, Susan Kingsley. *Sex and Suffrage in Britain, 1860–1914* (Princeton, N.J., 1987).

———. *Making Peace: The Reconstruction of Gender in Interwar Britain* (Princeton, N.J., 1994).

Kidwell, Claudia. *Suiting Everyone: The Democratization of Clothing in America* (Washington, D.C., 1974).

Kidwell, Claudia, and Valerie Steele (eds.). *Men and Women: Dressing the Part* (Washington, D.C., 1989).

Kiessling, Ninna. "Kampen for en videnskabelig husholdningsuddannelse," in Hanne Rimmen Nielsen and Eva Lous (eds.), *Kvinder undervejs. Dansk Kvindesamfund i Aarhus 1886–1986* (Aarhus, 1986), pp. 124–36.

Kitzinger, Jenny. "'I'm Sexually Attractive but I'm Powerful': Young Women Negotiating Sexual Reputation," *Women's Studies International Forum*, vol. 18, no. 2 (1995), pp. 187–96.

Kjerrumgaard-Jørgensen, Else Margrethe. "Københavnsk cyklisme i det 19. århundredes slutning," *Historiske Meddelelser om København*, series 4, no. 1 (1947–49).

Kjersgaard, Erik. *A History of Denmark* (Copenhagen, 1974).

Kocha, Jürgen. *Facing Total War: German Society 1914–1918* (Cambridge, Mass., 1984).

Københavns Kvindelige Idrætsforening 1886–1936 (Copenhagen, 1936).

Lading, Aagot. *Dansk Kvindesamfunds Arbejde gennem 25 Aar* (Copenhagen, 1939).

———. *Kvindens Stilling i det danske Samfund* (Copenhagen, 1943).

Laipson, Peter. "'Kiss without Shame, for She Desires It': Sexual Foreplay in American Marital Advice Literature, 1900–1925," *Journal of Social History*, vol. 29, no. 3 (1996), pp. 507–25.

Laqueur, Thomas. *Making Sex: Body and Gender from the Greeks to Freud* (Cambridge, Mass., 1990).

Larsen, Hans Kryger, and Carl-Axel Nilsson. "Consumption and Production of Bicycles in Denmark 1890–1980," *Scandinavian Economic History Review*, vol. 32 (1984), pp. 143–58.

Leach, William R. "Transformations in a Culture of Consumption: Women and Department Stores, 1890–1925," *Journal of American History*, vol. 71, no. 2 (1984), pp. 319–42.

Lemcke, Gyrithe. *Dansk Kvindesamfunds Historie gennem 40 Aar* (Copenhagen, 1912).

Leuchtenburg, William E. *The Perils of Prosperity: 1914–1932* (Chicago, 1958).

Lewis, Jane. *Women in England, 1870–1950: Sexual Divisions and Social Change* (Bloomington, Ind., 1984).

Lindeberg, Lars. *De så det ske. Danmark under 1. verdenskrig* (Copenhagen, 1966).

Light, Alison. *Forever England: Femininity, Literature and Conservatism between the Wars* (London and New York, 1991).

Lindsay, Irina. *Dressing and Undressing for the Seaside* (Essex, 1983).

Linvald, Steffen. *København har moret sig* (Copenhagen, 1966).

Lummis, Trevor. *Listening to History: The Authenticity of Oral Evidence* (London, 1987).

Lunbeck, Elizabeth. *The Psychiatric Persuasion: Knowledge, Gender and Power in Modern America* (Princeton, N.J., 1994).

Lützen, Karin. *Hvad hjertet begærer. Kvinders kærlighed til kvinder 1825–1985* (Copenhagen, 1986).

Maltby, Richard (ed.). *Passing Parade: A History of Popular Culture in the Twentieth Century* (Oxford, 1989).

Marchand, Roland. *Advertising the American Dream: Making Way for Modernity, 1920–1940* (Berkeley, Calif., 1986).

Markussen, Ole. "Danish Industry, 1920–1939: Technology, Rationalization and Modernization," *Scandinavian Journal of History*, vol. 13 (1988), pp. 233–56.

Marwick, Arthur. *Women at War 1914–1918* (London, 1977).

Mason, Tim. "Women in Germany, 1925–1940: Family, Welfare and Work," parts I and II, *History Workshop Journal* (Spring 1976 and Autumn 1976), pp. 74–113, 5–32.

Matthews, Glenna. *"Just a Housewife": The Rise and Fall of Domesticity in America* (New York, 1987).

Matthews, Jill. "'They Had Such a Lot of Fun': The Women's League of Health and Beauty," *History Workshop Journal*, issue no. 30 (1990), pp. 22–54.

Matthiessen, P. C. *Some Aspects of the Demographic Transition in Denmark* (Copenhagen, 1970).

———. *Befolkningens vækst* (Copenhagen, 1976).

May, Elaine Tyler. *Great Expectations: Marriage and Divorce in Post-Victorian America* (Chicago and London, 1980).

Maynes, Mary Jo. *Schooling in Western Europe: A Social History* (Albany, N.Y., 1985).

———. *Taking the Hard Road: Life Course in French and German Workers' Autobiographies in the Era of Industrialization* (Chapel Hill, N.C., 1995).

McGovern, James R. "The American Woman's Pre–World War I Freedom in Manners and Morals," *Journal of American History*, vol. 55 (1968), pp. 315–33.

McRobbie, Angela, and Mica Nava (eds.). *Gender and Generation* (London, 1984).

McMillan, James F. *Housewife or Harlot: The Place of Women in French Society 1879–1940* (New York, 1981).

Melby, Kari. "The Housewife Ideology in Norway between the Two World Wars," *Scandinavian Journal of History*, vol. 14, no. 2 (1989), pp. 181–93.

Melman, Billie. *Women and the Popular Imagination in the Twenties: Flappers and Nymphs* (New York, 1987).

——— (ed.). *Borderlines: Genders and Identities in War and Peace, 1870–1930* (New York and London, 1998).

Meyerowitz, Joanne J. *Women Adrift: Independent Wage Earners in Chicago, 1880–1930* (Chicago and London, 1988).

Miller, Kenneth E. *Government and Politics in Denmark* (Boston, 1968).

Mitchell, B. R. (ed.). *European Historical Statistics, 1750–1970* (New York, 1975).

Mizejewski, Linda. *Ziegfeld Girl: Image and Icon in Culture and Cinema* (Durham, N.C., and London, 1999).

Modell, John. *Into One's Own: From Youth to Adulthood in The United States 1920–1975* (Berkeley, Calif., and Oxford, 1989).

Mørch, Søren. *Den ny Danmarkshistorie 1880–1960* (Copenhagen, 1982).

Ng, Vivian. "The Reconstruction of Gender in China, 1897–1911: The New Woman." Lecture presented at the Department of History, University of Minnesota, October 16, 1989.

Nielsen, Hanne Rimmen, and Eva Lous (eds.). *Kvinder undervejs. Dansk Kvindesamfund i Aarhus 1886–1986* (Aarhus, 1986).

Nielsen, Niels Kayser. "Klubliv i hverdag og fest," in Else Trangbæk et al. (eds.), *Dansk Idrætsliv. Den moderne idræts gennembrud 1860–1940*, vol. 1 (Copenhagen, 1995), pp. 205–21.

Nolan, Mary. *Visions of Modernity: American Business and the Modernization of Germany* (New York and Oxford, 1994).

Nørgaard, Erik. *Jazz, guldfeber og farlige damer* (Copenhagen, 1965).

———. *Levende billeder i Danmark. Fra "Den gamle Biograf" til moderne tider* (Copenhagen, 1971).

———. *Dansk reklames barndom eller Røde næser bortfjernes med overraskende resultat* (Copenhagen, 1973).

Oakley, Steward. *A Short History of Denmark* (New York, 1972).

Olesen, Thorsten Borring, and Nils Arne Sørensen. "Da Chaperonen forsvandt. Kærlighed, seksualitet og engelske middelklassekvinder i 1. verdenskrig," *Den jyske historiker*, no. 41 (1987), pp. 96–116.

Park, Roberta J. "Sports, Gender and Society in a Transatlantic Perspective," in J. A. Mangan and Roberta J. Park (eds.), *From "Fair Sex" to Feminism: Sport and the Socialization of Women in the Industrial and Post-Industrial Eras* (London, 1987), pp. 58–93.

Peiss, Kathy. *Cheap Amusements: Working Women and Leisure in Turn-of-the-Century New York* (Philadelphia, 1986).

———. *Hope in a Jar: The Making of America's Beauty Industry* (New York, 1997).

———. "Making Faces: The Cosmetics Industry and the Cultural Construction of Gender, 1890–1930," *Genders*, no. 7 (Spring 1990), pp. 143–69.

Perrot, Michelle. "The New Eve and the Old Adam: Changes in French Women's Condition at the Turn of the Century," in Margaret Randolph Higonnet et al. (eds.), *Behind the Lines: Gender and the Two World Wars* (New Haven, Conn., and London, 1987), pp. 51–60.

Personal Narratives Group (eds.). *Interpreting Women's Lives: Feminist Theory and Personal Narratives* (Bloomington, Ind., 1989).

Persson, Karl Gunnar (ed.). *The Economic Development of Denmark and Norway since 1870* (Hants, England, 1993).

Petri, Gerda, and Minna Kragelund. *Mor Magda - og alle de andre. Husholdning som fag fra 1900 til i dag* (Copenhagen, n.d.).

Porter, Roy, and Lesley Hall. *The Facts of Life: The Creation of Sexual Knowledge in Britain, 1650–1950* (New Haven, Conn., 1995).

Pumphery, Martin. "The Flapper, the Housewife and the Making of Modernity," *Cultural Studies*, vol. 1, no. 2 (1987), pp. 179–94.

Quataert, Jean H. "Women's Work and Worth: The Persistence of Stereotype Attitudes in the German Free Trade Unions, 1890–1929," in Norbert C. Soldon (ed.), *The World of Women's Trade Unionism: Comparative Historical Essays* (Westport, Conn., 1985), pp. 93–124.

Rigler, Edith. *Frauenleitbild und Frauenarbeit in Österreich* (Vienna, 1976).

Rabinovitz, Lauren. "Temptations of Pleasure: Nickelodeons, Amusement Parks, and the Sights of Female Sexuality," *camera obscura*, vol. 23 (May 1990), pp. 71–90.

Rapp, Rayna, and Ellen Ross. "The 1920s: Feminism, Consumerism, and Political Backlash in the United States," in Judith Friedlandet et al. (eds.), *Women in Culture and Politics: A Century of Change* (Bloomington, Ind., 1986), pp. 52–61.

Reagin, Nancy. "How to Fill a Market Basket: The Politics of Women's Consumption in Weimar and Nazi Germany." Paper presented at the 10th Berkshire Conference on the History of Women, Chapel Hill, North Carolina, 1996.

Roberts, Mary Louise. *Civilization without Sexes: Reconstructing Gender in Postwar France, 1917–1927* (Chicago and London, 1994).

———. " 'This Civilization No Longer Has Sexes': La Garçonne and Cultural Crisis in France After World War I," *Gender and History*, vol. 4, no. 1 (1992), pp. 49–69.

Rosenbeck, Bente. *Kvindekøn. Den moderne kvindeligheds historie 1880–1980* (Copenhagen, 1987).

———. *Kroppens Politik: Om køn, kultur og videnskab* (Copenhagen, 1992).

Rothman, Ellen K. *Hands and Hearts: A History of Courtship in America* (New York, 1984).

Rupp, Leila J. "Feminism and the Sexual Revolution in the Early Twentieth Century: The Case of Doris Stevens," *Feminist Studies*, vol. 15 (1989), pp. 289–309.

Russett, Cynthia Eagle. *Sexual Science: The Victorian Construction of Womanhood* (Cambridge, Mass., 1989).

Ryan, Mary P. *Women in Public: Between Banners and Ballots, 1825–1880* (Baltimore, 1990).

———. "The Projection of a New Womanhood: The Movie Moderns in the 1920's," in Jean E. Friedman and William G. Slade (eds.), *Our American Sisters: Women in American Life and Thought* (Boston, 1982), pp. 175–95.

Saa gik 75 aar. 1868 - Magasin du Nord - 1943 (Copenhagen, 1943).

Sandfeldt, Gunnar. *Den stumme scene. Dansk biografteater indtil lydfilmens gennembrud* (Copenhagen, 1966).

Sato, Barbara Hamill. "The *Moga* Sensation: Perceptions of the *Modan Garu* in Japanese Intellectual Circles During the 1920s," *Gender and History*, vol. 5, no. 3 (1993), pp. 363–81.

Scott, Gillian. "A 'Trade Union for Married Women': The Women's Co-operative Guild 1914–1920," in Sybil Oldfield (ed.), *This Working-Day World: Women's Lives and Culture(s) in Britain 1914–1945* (London, 1994), pp. 18–28.

Scott, Joan W. "Gender: A Useful Category of Historical Analysis," *American Historical Review*, vol. 91, no. 5 (1986), pp. 1053–75.

Scott, Joan, and Louise Tilly. *Women, Work and Family* (New York, 1978).

Sekula, Allan. "The Body and the Archive," *October*, no. 39 (1986), pp. 3–64.

Silverberg, Miriam. "The Modern Girl as Militant," in Gail Lee Bernstein (ed.), *Recreating Japanese Women 1600–1935* (Berkeley, 1991), pp. 239–66.

Silverberg, Miriam. "Constructing the Japanese Ethnography of Modernity," *Journal of Asian Studies*, vol. 51, no. 1 (1992), pp. 30–54.

Simmons, Christina. "Companionate Marriage and the Lesbian Threat," *Frontiers*, vol. 4, no. 3 (1979), pp. 54–59.

———. "Modern Sexuality and the Myth of Victorian Repression," in Kathy Peiss and Christina Simmons (eds.), *Passion and Power. Sexuality in History* (Philadelphia, 1989), pp. 157–77.

Smith, Bonnie G. *Changing Lives: Women in European History Since 1700* (Lexington, Mass., and Toronto, 1989).

Smith-Rosenberg, Carroll. "The New Woman as Androgyne: Social Disorder and Gender Crisis, 1870–1936," in Carroll Smith-Rosenberg, *Disorderly Conduct: Visions of Gender in Victorian America* (New York, 1985), pp. 245–96.

Spies, Margrethe (ed.). *De svandt, de svandt. Danske hjem i 1920'erne og 1930'erne* (Copenhagen, 1980).

Statistisk Aarbog 1920 (Copenhagen, 1921).

Stearns, Peter N. *American Cool: Constructing a Twentieth-Century Emotional Style* (New York and London, 1994).

Steedman, Carolyn. *Past Tenses: Essays on Writing, Autobiography and History* (London, 1992).

Steele, Valerie. *Fashion and Eroticism: Ideals of Feminine Beauty from the Victorian Era to the Jazz Age* (Oxford, 1985).

———. *Paris Fashion: A Cultural History* (New York and Oxford, 1988).

Stone, Lawrence. *The Family, Sex and Marriage in England, 1500–1800* (London, 1977).

———. *Road to Divorce: England 1530–1987* (Oxford, 1990).

Susman, Warren I. " 'Personality' and the Making of Twentieth-Century Culture," in Warren I. Susman. *Culture as History: The Transformation of American Society in the Twentieth Century* (New York, 1973), pp. 271–85.

Theweleit, Klaus. *Male Fantasies*, vols. 1–2 (Cambridge, Mass., 1987–89).

Thom, Deborah. *Nice Girls and Rude Girls: Women Workers in World War I* (London and New York, 1998).

Thomas, Graham, and Christine Zmroczek. "Household Technology: The Liberation of Women from the Home?" in Paul Close and Rosemary Collins (eds.), *Family and Economy in Modern Society* (Houndsmills, England, 1985), pp. 101–28.

Trangbæk, Else. *Mellem leg og disciplin. Gymnastikken i Danmark i 1800-tallet* (Copenhagen, 1987).

———. *Dansk idrætsliv*, vols. 1–2 (Copenhagen, 1995).

———. "Discipline and Emancipation through Sports: The Pioneers of Women's Sport in Denmark," *Scandinavian Journal of History*, vol. 21, no. 2 (1996).

Trumbach, Randolph. "Review Essay: Is There a Modern Sexual Culture in the West; or, Did England Never Change between 1500 and 1900?" *Journal of the History of Sexuality*, vol. 1 (1990), pp. 296–309.

Turim, Maureen. "Seduction and Elegance: The New Woman of Fashion in Silent Cinema," in Shari Benstock and Suzanne Ferriss (eds.), *On Fashion* (New Brunswick, N.J., 1994), pp. 140–58.

Vammen, Tinne. *Rent og urent. Hovedstadens piger og fruer 1880–1920* (Copenhagen, 1986).

Vertinsky, Patricia. *The Eternally Wounded Woman: Women, Exercise and Doctors in the Late Nineteenth Century* (Manchester, 1990).

———. "Exercise, Physical Capability, and the Eternally Wounded Woman in Late Nineteenth-Century North America," *Journal of Sport History*, vol. 14 (1987), pp. 7–27.

———. "Body Shape: The Role of the Medical Establishment in Informing Female Exercise and Physical Education in Nineteenth-Century America," in J. A. Mangan and Roberta J. Park (eds.), *From "Fair Sex" til Feminism: Sport and the Socialization of Women in the Industrial and Post-Industrial Eras* (London, 1987), pp. 256–81.

Vicinus, Martha. *Independent Women: Work and Community for Single Women 1850–1920* (Chicago and London, 1985).

Walkowitz, Judith R. *City of Dreadful Delight: Narratives of Sexual Danger in Late-Victorian England* (Chicago, 1992).

Wall, Richard and Jay Winter (eds.). *The Upheaval of War: Family, Work and Welfare in Europe, 1914–1918* (Cambridge, 1988).

Wedeby, Jørgen. *Befolkningsforhold* (Copenhagen, 1978).

White, Kevin. *The First Sexual Revolution: The Emergence of Male Heterosexuality in Modern America* (New York, 1993).

Willett, C., and P. Cunnington. *The History of Underclothes* (London and Boston, 1981).

Williams, Rosalind H. *Dream Worlds: Mass Consumption in Late 19th Century France* (Berkeley, 1982).

Williamson, Judith. *Consuming Passions: The Dynamics of Popular Culture* (London, 1986).

Wilson, Elizabeth. *Adorned in Dreams: Fashion and Modernity* (London, 1985).

———. *The Sphinx in the City: Urban Life, the Control of Disorder, and Women* (Berkeley, 1991).

Woollacott, Angela. *On Her Their Lives Depend: Munitions Workers in the Great War* (Berkeley, 1994).

Yellis, Kenneth A. "Prosperity's Child: Some Thoughts on the Flapper," *American Quarterly*, vol. 21 (1969), pp. 44–64.

Zmroczek, Christine. "The Weekly Wash," in Sybil Oldfield (ed.), *This Working-Day World* (London, 1994), pp. 7–17.

Index